THE EVERYTHING
VAMPIRE
BOOK

Dear Reader,

As the three of us can attest, there's nothing better than settling into a well-worn couch on a dark, stormy night eating popcorn and watching Christopher Lee sink his teeth into the jugular of his mesmerized conquest. No matter how much one chooses to deny it, the fact remains that vampires are among the most erotic and exotic creatures on the planet. Not only do they entice our inner sensuality, they also prey on our fears and the intense debate of what you would do if you could live forever. Now if that isn't a subject worth sinking your teeth into, then we don't know what is.

If you're a vampire aficionado, then you'll no doubt appreciate their decadent history, from the revenants of ancient folklore to their amazing evolution through literature and cinema. Our study took us back to, well, the dawn of man, in search of legends, blood symbolism, undead creatures, mythological deities, and a seemingly never-ending crypt bulging at the seams with historical vampiric accounts, literature, and an astonishing body of cinematic works. What we learned is that vampires aren't just another Saturday afternoon creature feature. Indeed not. Vampires are an amalgam of dreams and nightmares, of life and death, and of emotion and philosophy, punctuated by raw predatory capacity. For our parts, like any vampire worth its fangs, we stalked, we obsessed, we attacked, and we hope to leave a lasting impression.

Barb Karg, Arjean Spaite, & Rick Sutherland

Welcome to the EVERYTHING® Series!

These handy, accessible books give you all you need to tackle a difficult project, gain a new hobby, comprehend a fascinating topic, prepare for an exam, or even brush up on something you learned back in school but have since forgotten.

You can choose to read an *Everything*® book from cover to cover or just pick out the information you want from our three useful boxes: Fangtastic Folklore, Vampire Bites, and Screen Screams. We give you everything you need to know on the subject, but throw in a lot of fun stuff along the way, too.

We now have more than 400 *Everything*® books in print, spanning such wide-ranging categories as weddings, pregnancy, cooking, music instruction, foreign language, crafts, pets, New Age, and so much more. When you're done reading them all, you can finally say you know *Everything*®!

Vampire legends, lore, and literature

Vampire terminology

Vampires in film and television

PUBLISHER Karen Cooper

DIRECTOR OF ACQUISITIONS AND INNOVATION Paula Munier

MANAGING EDITOR, EVERYTHING SERIES Lisa Laing

COPY CHIEF Casey Ebert

ACQUISITIONS EDITOR Lisa Laing

EDITORIAL ASSISTANT Hillary Thompson

Visit the entire Everything® series at *www.everything.com*

THE
EVERYTHING®
VAMPIRE BOOK

From Vlad the Impaler
to the vampire Lestat—a history of
vampires in literature, film, and legend

Barb Karg, Arjean Spaite, and Rick Sutherland

Aadamsmedia
Avon, Massachusetts

For Piper Maru. Our life. Our love. Our eternal light.

And for Anne Rice. For her eloquence, her incredible life's work, and her belief that in the darkness and light of life there remain shadows that call to us, beckoning that we may better understand that within the preternatural unknown there is much worth knowing.

An Everything® Series Book.
Everything® and everything.com® are registered trademarks of F+W Media, Inc.

Published by Adams Media, a division of F+W Media, Inc.
57 Littlefield Street, Avon, MA 02322 U.S.A.
www.adamsmedia.com

ISBN 10: 1-60550-631-1
ISBN 13: 978-1-60550-631-9

Printed in the United States of America.

J I H G F E D C B A

Library of Congress Cataloging-in-Publication Data
available from the publisher.

This publication is designed to provide accurate and authoritative information with regard to the subject matter covered. It is sold with the understanding that the publisher is not engaged in rendering legal, accounting, or other professional advice. If legal advice or other expert assistance is required, the services of a competent professional person should be sought.

—From a *Declaration of Principles* jointly adopted by a Committee of the American Bar Association and a Committee of Publishers and Associations

Many of the designations used by manufacturers and sellers to distinguish their products are claimed as trademarks. Where those designations appear in this book and Adams Media was aware of a trademark claim, the designations have been printed with initial capital letters.

Interior illustration credits: Movie camera © iStockphoto / Mümin Durmaz, Gothic Background © iStockphoto / Danny Chung, Gothic cross © iStockphoto / Danny Chung

This book is available at quantity discounts for bulk purchases.
For information, please call 1-800-289-0963.

Contents

Acknowledgments

Let it be said, that with all publications that require intense historical study and research, it is most definitely not a singular pursuit. When the subject is one that requires delving into a creature built more of legend than in reality, that pursuit becomes that much trickier. To that end, there are many individuals we'd like to thank for their gracious aid in pursuing a bitingly dark subject with a light-heartedness for which we are eternally grateful.

For starters, we'd like to thank Adams Media for their support and encouragement, especially editor extraordinaire Lisa Laing, whose wit and exceptional professionalism we've greatly admired for all the years we've worked together, and director of innovation and epitome of class, Paula Munier, whom we love more than Cabernet and chocolate. We'd also like to thank copy chief Casey Ebert, layout artist and designer Denise Wallace, and proofer Jeffrey Litton, for their swift and smart handling of *The Everything® Vampire Book*.

Above all, we're indebted to our friends and families. George and Trudi Karg, Chris, Glen, Ethan and Brady, Dale Sutherland, Kathy, Anne Terry, Jim Spaite, Dan, Matt, and Adam Spaite, Jean Collins, and guardian angels Rebecca Sutherland, Arnold Collins, and Rosalia Fisch. We also send our love to Ellen and Jim, Jim V., the Scribe Tribe, Becca, J.R., Gorgeous Sue, Doc Bauman, Mary, Jamie, Michele and the gang for taking such great care of us and our kids, Richard Fox and his merry gang, and the Blonde Bombshell. A special shout goes out to Antje Harrod for the amazing and diligent research she did for the book. Heart and soul, medear, you're the absolute best! And lest we forget, the lights of our lives, Sasha, Harley, Mog, Jinks, Maya, Scout, Bug, and especially Jazz and Piper. We thank you all. We adore you all. We love you with all our hearts. We thank you all. We adore you all. We love you with all our hearts.

Top Ten Things
You'll Learn about Vampires

I. The evolution of the literary vampire from Bram Stoker to Anne Rice to Stephenie Meyer, and all the famous and infamous dark devils authors have conjured up.

2. The terrifying and tumultuous history of Vlad the Impaler and whether Bram Stoker based Dracula on the notorious Romanian ruler.

3. How vampires are created, how they survive, and all the characteristics of the traditional and avant-garde types.

4. How you can ascertain if your neighbor is a nosferatu and all you need to know to make an informed decision about whether or not to become a vampire.

5. A complete history of silver screen bloodsuckers from the Silent Era to the present, including the cinematic vampire Hall of Fame.

6. Renowned television bloodsuckers in made-for-tv movies, kiddie nosferatu, and everything from *The Munsters* to *Buffy the Vampire Slayer*.

7. All the tools you need to protect yourself against a pesky vampire, and the secrets of how to detect and destroy it.

8. Famous historical accounts of alleged vampires, vampire epidemics, and the most evil, real-life, bloodthirsty, vampiric criminals.

9. Modern-day vampiric practices by those who believe in vampires or purport to be them.

10. The legends and lore surrounding Transylvania and the story behind the real Castle Dracula.

Introduction

O ver the centuries, there have been many incarnations of vampires throughout the world as documented in legend, folklore, historical accounts, fiction and nonfiction writings, cinema, and alleged firsthand accounts of sightings and interactions. These range from the Greek *lamia*, to Bram Stoker to Christopher Lee's Hammer films to the notorious case of London's alleged Highgate Vampire and even a host of intriguing modern-day blood barhoppers and individuals who practice blood fetish rituals.

For just as long, historians, scholars, authors, filmmakers, and various vampire experts have written about and portrayed vampires and forms of vampirism in all measure of creative caricatures, many of which have proven legendary, and some downright comedic. As with all discussions of bloodsuckers, there exists a wide range of opinions and accounts that in some cases have, over the decades and centuries, taken on a life of their own. As with all things dubbed "paranormal," this is a natural anomaly. For the purposes of this book, we cover a wide variety of vampires and vampirism in their various incarnations, from the traditional "I vant to suck your blood" ghoul, to the romantic drawing room bloodsucker, to accounts of "real" vampires to current cult vampiric practices. We also include a trio of different tips to flesh out our fiendish findings: Fangtastic Folklore covers vampiric facts, legends, and lore, as well as vampire literature; Screen Screams highlight all measure of vampiric cinema; and Vampire Bites focus on vampire terminology.

By and large, the vampire, perhaps more so than any other legendary character, has been fictionalized and romanticized to the extent that it's almost overwhelming. But along the way, many diligent researchers, writers of fiction and nonfiction, historians, scholars, scientists, vampirologists, and folklorists have tackled the subject with the most tenacious and thorough aplomb one can employ when writing about a character rife with history, mystery, romance, and violence. That said, it must be stated that for the majority of folks, vampires and vampirism is nothing more than a legend. However, for some individuals, the practices and existence of vampires is very real, and their opinions, as well as those of scholars, historians, and experts must be acknowledged as well. As with legendary mysterious figures such as Bigfoot and the Loch Ness Monster, there remains the possibility that if something hasn't been clearly disproven, there *is* the possibility that it can indeed exist. Where vampires are concerned for the world's majority, however, it's unlikely that most folks would believe of their existence unless a bona fide, scientifically proven bloodsucker appeared on *Larry King Live*. Such is the course of modern-day human nature.

Regardless, there are many, many aspects of the vampire that remain a current fascination, from its traditional origins, literature, film, and folklore to other intriguing and complex conceptual aspects involving the psychological, spiritual, physical, and emotional realms and even the subjects of magnetic, astral, and psychic vampirism to name a few. To say that a vampire or the subject of vampirism is one-dimensional is a gross misstatement, as there exists an exceptional kaleidoscope of history, lore, and societal underpinnings that play into the seemingly eternal subtext of the vampire legend. All of that is what we seek to expose and introduce to you. We hope to provide a well-rounded initiation into a world filled with light and dark and a huge gray area whereby you alone can decide if creatures of the night do indeed walk among us, watching and waiting and perhaps even hoping that we gain a new understanding of why they hunt, how they live, and how they survive—whether in real life or purely in our minds—under the greatest measure of adversity. They are, and shall forever be known, as Vampyr. They shock. They seduce. They frighten. And on occasion they even make us laugh. But be warned. If one thing holds true when it comes to all things vampire related—their bite *is* worse than their bark.

CHAPTER 1

MASTERS OF
IMMORTALITY

As one of the most famous creatures in horror history, the vampire has seen an evolution that few creatures built of lore, legend, fiction, and film have enjoyed. Do they really exist, or are they just a figment of our imaginations? From dusk till cock's crow, the dark belongs to the vampire. But as you'll come to learn, they see much more than their preternatural vision allows and endure a palpable remnant of humanity that belies their bloodlust. Here now, we begin our journey into the wildly exotic, erotic world of the vampire.

"CHILDREN OF THE NIGHT . . . WHAT MUSIC THEY MAKE"

It's after one, and in the dead of night, you're suddenly awakened. In the haziness of what you think must be a dream state, you venture to return to slumber, but something doesn't feel right. Unmoving, you let your eyes wander around the room, the darkness mingled with shadows emanating from the streetlight outside your window. Nothing appears amiss. You listen carefully. Aside from a passing car, it *sounds* like your room. But still, something seems off. The fine hairs on the back of your neck suddenly stand on end and you feel a sudden chill. Your gaze lingers on the far corner of the room—the darkest corner. Like a fog upon the moors, the kaleidoscope of your imagination takes control. Is someone or some *thing* there? There's no movement, and all remains still, save for the increasingly loud ticking of your clock. As your fear begins to dissipate, your body relaxes and your mind's eye starts to see the frivolity of the situation.

Taking a final glance at the dark corner, relieved by the knowledge that all is well, you roll over and close your eyes, enveloping yourself in warmth, and comfortable in the temptation of sweet dreams to come. As your breathing settles into its regular gait, you fall into sleep. Only then is there motion in the dark corner. A faint rustle, and then a shadow that emerges from the blackness like a whisper. With a fleetness beyond reckoning to the human eye, the shadow is now hovering over you, lithe and cloaked. There's little other recognizable shape, save for a quick flash of alabaster skin as a deft finger pushes aside the hair that covers your neck. You hear a deep inhalation, as the vein in your neck throbs.

You've just had your first encounter with a vampire.

"I AM DRACULA . . . I BID YOU WELCOME"

When you hear the word "vampire," it's likely that the first image that comes to mind is that of a tall, dark, handsome man with luminous eyes, clothed in a fine black tuxedo enveloped by an exquisite opera cloak. Indeed, that image put into our respective heads courtesy Bela Lugosi in the 1931 classic film *Dracula* is the perfect representation of the traditional *drawing room vampire*, one so deceptively aristocratic that he melds perfectly into respectable society. By definition, as conceived in folklore—particularly in Europe—a *vampire* is a reanimated corpse, or *revenant*, who rises from the grave to partake of the blood or flesh of the living through the use of elongated canine teeth. These vampiric creatures of lore are decidedly *not* the debonair likes of Christopher Lee nor the lavish and exquisite vampires of Anne Rice's imaginings. No, these are hideous corpses more in keeping with *Night of the Living Dead* than *Love at First Bite*. Take heed of that warning, as in Chapter 2 we introduce you to the first "vampires," transporting you back through the ages and legends surrounding vampires and vampiric revenants the world over.

VAMPIRE BITE

Throughout the entirety of vampiric folklore, the actual term "vampire" is rarely used in historical lore. Instead, most creatures, vampiric or otherwise, are commonly thought of as revenants, which defines an individual who has returned from the dead and who is further termed "undead."

"I Never Drink . . . Wine"

To truly understand vampires it's necessary to examine the quintessential triad of the realm: folklore, Bram Stoker and his precursors, and film. It is from that trio that all of the vampires as we know them today have spawned. The vampire legend truly is immortal, and as you'll learn within the pages of this tome, there's no ending to the ultimate tale of nefarious neckaholics. In Chapters 3 and 4 we explore the earliest literary malfeasants: Lord Ruthven, Sir Francis Varney, the seductive Carmilla, and the father of all vampires, Dracula. Bram Stoker's seminal 1897 masterpiece, *Dracula*, set into stone the very depth, depravity, seduction, and classic societal, political, emotional, sexual, and spiritual subtext that lives on to the present day. Dracula, Abraham Van Helsing, and the entire cast of characters are arguably the most mimicked literary ensemble in history.

Along those lines, in Chapters 5 and 6, we also go in depth into the infamous Romanian Prince Vlad the Impaler. Is he truly the basis for Count Dracula, or is there more to the story than meets the eye? And where the heck *is* Transylvania?

"Evil Is a Point of View"

Human fears perfectly meld into a vampire's repertoire like ice on a hot tin roof. Inherent fear coupled with a vampire's powers renders us ripe for the picking, and as we all know, save for a few trifle practices, vampires have very little to fear, assuming they are well versed in their own inception, history, boundaries, and have studied their prey. And make no mistake . . . aside from the purpose of overcoming loneliness with a select few individuals, the majority of humanity is, from the vampire's standpoint, looked upon as prey. Or at the very least . . . a tempting morsel. That said, it's best you delve into Chapters 7–12 to examine the symbolism of vampirism, learn how to detect and protect yourself against pesky nightcrawlers, and follow the adventures of a score of historic and real-life slayers.

Fangtastic Folklore

For superstitious communities and entire populations, especially those whose social behaviors are dictated by all measure of religious virtue and/or traditions or any number of reasons, vampires are often associated with the devil, a concept that in many ways was born with Stoker's *Dracula*. In that understanding, a vampire is a creature to be reviled and ultimately destroyed lest they cause entire populations to lose their mortal souls.

"To Die . . . That Must Be Glorious"

As previously mentioned, one crucial element of the vampiric triad is cinema. The vampire and vampirism in general has been represented in film in myriad ways, and those ways need to be recognized so that a complete discussion of vampires is more than just a coffin klatch. In Chapters 14 and 15, we enter the overflowing mausoleum of vampire cinema beginning with its origins and influences, paying homage to the greatest silver screen blood-suckers in history. What you'll find in Chapters 16 and 17 is a comprehensive vampire filmography that's sure to get your jugular pumping, as is our examination in Chapter 18 of small-screen bloodsuckers.

"YOU KNOW TOO MUCH TO LIVE"

Of course, as with all lore, literature, and film, there are many offshoots of the traditional biting rituals as represented by Stoker's *Dracula*, including vampiric plagues and outer space soul suckers, or conversely, the withholding of predatory violence due to true romantic love between human and preternatural being. Vampires are complex creatures, and that the very definition of vampirism has been stretched to accommodate even deeper levels of physical, emotional, spiritual, and psychic turmoil is evidence of their evolution as you'll see in Chapter 13, where we highlight popular writers of modern-day fiction, and Chapter 19, where we examine vampires in the modern era.

VAMPIRE BITE

Oddly enough, there doesn't seem to be an expert consensus as to what a group of vampires is called. Throughout film and both fiction and nonfiction they're variously referred to as a *clutch*, a *brood*, or a *coven*. In folklore, they're often referred to as a *pack*, while in some arenas they are also known as a *clan* or divided into *bloodlines*.

Whether vampires truly exist or not is up to you. We, like so many other chroniclers of history and lore, can do no more than explore the vampiric realm and limn its depths—however sane or supernatural they may be. To quote Sir Anthony Hopkins's eccentric and affable Van Helsing in *Bram Stoker's Dracula*: "We've all become God's madmen . . . all of us." With that in mind, it's time for us to play Van Helsing and let you in on the secrets of the most seductive, exotic, erotic, hypnotic, and dangerous creatures on the planet.

CHAPTER 2

Vampires in Lore

Throughout the centuries and amid dozens of cultures, vampires remain a centerpiece of the darker sides of lore and mythology, and our current passion for night terrors provided by legend, modern film, and literature indicates there's no sign of impending boredom in all things bloodthirsty. Part of that fascination may be attributed to our fervent multicultural and multireligious views that there is—with little doubt and even less scientific evidence—life after death. And if there is ongoing life in the spiritual world, is it really a leap of faith to believe that there may well be life after death that exists in the underbelly of our own world?

LIVE LONG AND PROSPER

Any research of vampires or vampirism throughout history inevitably leads to what's considered to be the genesis of the bloodsucker as we know it today—Bram Stoker's seminal 1897 novel, *Dracula* (see Chapters 3 and 4). While much of the hoopla born of *Dracula* is deserved in its conception and the brilliance in which the vampiric genre has evolved, it must be noted that there exists a much richer history surrounding the legends of what are commonly referred to as *revenants*—individuals who return from the dead. Like the revered Greek and Egyptian gods of mythology, there are numerous legends, superstitions, and beliefs highlighting a dark contingent of vampiric creatures that tour the underworld and play to our most basic fears. What brings the beasts of folklore to the forefront—aside from the telling of their terrifying escapades—is the fact that it's precisely *their* legacy that humans have followed in real life to expunge themselves of alleged vampires by digging up and defacing corpses (see Chapter 11). Given that most vampiric folklore rarely uses the word "vampire," does the traditional vampire evolve from these auspicious actions fueled by stories of the undead? You bet they do.

VAMPIRE BITE

The *incubus* of ancient folklore was believed to be a male demon who forced unwanted sexual relations with a sleeping woman. In female form, the demon is known as a *succubus*. Both apparitions are often linked to early European vampiric entities, including the German *alp* and the Hungarian *lidéric*. Even Brazil has its own form of incubus with the *boto*, who seduces women and leads them to the river. Of course, the incubus made for a handy—and plausible—excuse for unwanted pregnancies.

Tales of vampiric revenants vary greatly depending on their country of origin, their subsequent incarnation, and which folklorist or historian is telling of their exploits. After all, the very aspect of folklore is that it's based on scant documented writings and loads of stories handed down throughout the centuries from one generation to the next. The majority of creatures now cited as vampires or vampiric in nature are typically human and/or animal hybrids, zombielike beasts, and birth demons. That said, it's time to delve into the origins of the folkloric vampire by focusing on some of the more popular bloodsuckers in mythological and folkloric history.

European Bloodsuckers

There's little question that the vampire we've come to revere in entertainment and fear in reality wouldn't exist without the lurid tales of life-sucking demons throughout Europe. Although independence from world powers and influence was a cornerstone of the birth of America as an international power, as a people we are still inextricably linked to European cultures through history and heritage, and the vampire of Europe is the forefather of the vampiric mythologies we embrace and the basis for virtually all film and fictional forays into the world of the undead.

Fangtastic Folklore

Although they weren't representative of the classic vampire, many of the gods and goddesses of ancient lore are associated with blood sacrifice and consumption. In Egyptian mythology, the supreme god, Ra, sent the goddess Sekhmet to earth to punish mankind for mocking him. Drunk on the blood of mortals, Sekhmet began a frenzied slaughter of every human. Ra subdued her by tricking her into drinking beer dyed with crimson potions, the alcoholic effect finally calming her rage.

Unlike seductive and dashingly debonair bloodsuckers, or the sultry, vixenish vamps of popular culture, the blood drinker of European lore was invariably hideously ugly and foul smelling, and absolutely the *last* creature on earth you'd want passionately nibbling your neck in the middle of the night. While legends of horrific nightcrawlers permeated nearly all of Europe, it was eastern Europe that gave birth to the lore that has evolved into the mythology of modern society.

With a history that predates even ancient Rome, the people of eastern Europe survived political and cultural upheavals over many centuries, and there's evidence that the commingling of Christianity with traditional religions helped foster the lore of the undead, partially through the belief that life truly existed after one's passing. The righteous were rewarded with a warm welcome into the arms of the angels, while sinners and malcontents were condemned to spend eternity in servitude to the devil—and nowhere was the devil's work more predominant than on this very planet.

To a largely ignorant and illiterate population bedeviled by bouts of inexplicable plague and other disease epidemics, the source of their misery was often attributed not to the vagaries of nature but to the recently deceased who'd somehow led an unholy life or fallen prey to demons. (See Chapter 7.) Rather than moving on to a life of sanctity in the hereafter, the less than virtuous clung to their feeble existence and simply crawled out of their graves to spitefully harass the living.

GREEK ORIGINS

While most of us are familiar with the mythological gods of ancient Greece, it's less well known that according to legend, it was those same all-powerful deities who bred the creatures who would become the ancestors of vampires throughout the folklore of European history. The origination of vampiric demons in ancient Greece began in the world of the supernatural and remained there for centuries. Not surprising to vampire aficionados, it was Zeus, the supreme god of Greek mythology, who would become responsible for the creation of one of the earliest life-sucking demons in history—and he did it with an all-too-mortal dalliance of fooling around with another woman.

The *Lamia*

The writings and legends of ancient Greeks, including references from Aristophanes and Aristotle, tell the tale of an illicit love affair between the all-powerful Zeus and the Libyan princess *Lamia*, who's variously described as the daughter of the sea god Poseidon or a daughter of Poseidon's son, Belus. The downside of this celestial fling is that it attracted the wrath of

Hera, Zeus's jealous wife, who took vengeance upon the unfortunate Lamia by kidnapping and killing all of her God-spawned children and driving the bereft woman into exile.

Grief-stricken and unable to retaliate against the power of the gods who'd brought her such misery, Lamia began a campaign of exacting revenge upon humankind by stealing and sucking the life from the babies of mortal mothers. In later legendary incarnations, *lamia* evolved into a legion of unearthly beings with the upper bodies of women and the lower shapes of serpents. These creatures are called *lamiai*, and they suck the blood of children and can also alter their horrific appearances at will to seduce young men and lead them to ruin or death.

Fangtastic Folklore

When we discuss the gods, demons, and religion of Greek mythology, it's helpful to remember that to the ancient Greeks these "legends" had nothing to do with fiction or fantasy. We have the benefit of science, education, and a healthy dose of skepticism, but the Greeks, like the ancient Egyptians, believed in the existence of their gods and their supernatural designs for humankind with as much conviction as modern believers do in their own choice of religion and deity.

The *Vrykolakas*

In Greece, the most ancient of the demons with vampiric tendencies are directly tied to the supernatural world of spirits sired by the gods, but soon after Greece's conversion to Christianity, there grew the cultural suspicion that demons and the recently deceased were often one and the same. In modern terms, the dead who return to life are revenants, and in Greece, they're known as *vrykolakas*. Although there are various spellings of the term and variations of the word itself throughout regions of Greece, the vrykolakas are generally considered to be the most virulent demons of the undead, who return to life to cause misery to the living.

The belief in vrykolakas was, in fact, so prevalent that the Greek Orthodox Church was compelled to address the issue in the first century to help allay the fears of the populace and offer solutions to the suspected mischief of the wandering undead. It's no great surprise that the Church offered the opinion that those most likely to return from the dead had perished before receiving proper clerical rites. This included stillborn children, those who'd led sinful lives or were excommunicated, and, in a bizarre twist, those born on a holy day were particularly at risk—no doubt because of the blasphemy of competing with days devoted to the saints.

The long litany of possible reasons for the creation of vrykolakas was, in many ways, a stern admonition from the Church for its followers to toe the lines of religious devotion or suffer the hideous consequences. The Church's common sense solution to the pesky vrykolakas was to simply dig up the body of the suspected troublemaker and burn the remains to ash; a remedy that would mollify a nervous population for centuries.

VAMPIRE BITE

The word *vrykolakas* trickled into common Greek usage from the southern Slavic people of the Balkans. The term originally developed from descriptions of wearers of wolf pelts and gradually evolved into a depiction of demons with wolflike characteristics. Although the Greek interpretation of vrykolakas was essentially vampiric in nature, variations of the same term were used by the Slavs to describe the equally frightful *lycanthropes* or *lycans*, otherwise known as *werewolves*.

SLAVIC VAMPIRES

The importance of the earliest Greek references to vampiric creatures is often understated, but the Greeks gave us much of the first written reports of such unholy beings, with accounts dating back as far as the first century. As with the vrykolakas, the Slavic influence is crucial to the development of Greek vampire legends, and although the early Slavs weren't known for creating a rich written history, they would certainly become the bearers of lore that would eventually creep into western Europe, and eventually into our worst nightmares. The Slavic people were instrumental in the development of the Slavic countries, including Slovakia, the Czech Republic, Belarus, Russia, Ukraine, Bosnia, Bulgaria, Croatia, Montenegro, and Serbia, and from there, vampiric legends would multiply.

The *Upir* and *Nelapsi*

The mainstays of rural Slovakian and Czech vampire folklore are known as *upir* or the parallel *nelapsi*, both of which are the revived and rotting corpses of the recently deceased. The *upir* is believed to be particularly troublesome because it's thought to have two hearts and two souls, and will suck the blood from its victims, often suffocating them with a crushing embrace. What's worse, the *upir* not only spreads deadly disease, but it can kill with a glance from its evil eye. According to one report in the early 1700s, the people in a Bohemian village of what is now the Czech Republic drove a stake into the corpse of a suspected *upir*. The hideous creature merely laughed and thanked them for giving him a stick to fight off pesky dogs. The startled villagers quickly solved their vampiric dilemma by burning the corpse.

Fangtastic Folklore

A unique addition to Bulgarian vampire lore is the *ustrel*, which is created from the souls of children born on Saturday but who pass away before being baptized. It's believed that the *ustrel*, in the invisible form of a spirit, can claw its way out of the grave to drain the blood from livestock and hide behind the horns or hind legs of its prey. The *ustrel* myth provides a seemingly logical explanation for a sudden loss of sheep and cattle to indeterminate causes and helps foster widespread belief in a variety of vampiric beings.

The Bulgarian *Vampir*

Among the most common legends of Bulgarian folklore are tales of the *vampir*, a deceased human who returns to life from the grave, maintaining every physical evidence of its former existence as a perfectly healthy human. So convincing is this rejuvenation that *vampirs* can safely move to areas where they aren't known and live a seemingly anonymous but normal existence by day, and create havoc with the living by night. An unusual aspect of the Bulgarian myth is the orthodox religious perspective that the dead are believed to spend forty days after their passing with their guardian angel traveling to the places they'd known in life before moving on to the spiritual world. If proper burial procedures burial weren't followed to the letter, the dead would be unable to find their way to the next life and would remain on earth as vampires. Other reasons for a probable vampiric rebirth are a life of sinful behavior or drunkenness, or even a sudden and violent death.

The Bosnian *Lampir*

The incarnation of the vampire in Bosnia is the *lampir*, which is thought primarily to be the harbinger of epidemics. With no scientific understanding of the reasons or cures for deadly contagious diseases, the first to fall ill and perish is assumed to be at fault. The *lampir* crawls from its grave as a hideously rotting and disease-ridden corpse for the sole purpose of infecting and bringing grief to those who subsequently succumb and die of disease. It was reported that after the Austrians gained control of Bosnia from the Ottoman Empire in 1878 that the practice of exhuming and burning the corpses of suspected *lampirs* was widespread in the region—a practice the new regime took a decidedly dim view of.

The Russian *Uppyr*

As with many demonic legends throughout Europe, the Russian vampire, known as the *uppyr*, is closely linked to behavior that runs counter to religious piousness, and anyone branded a heretic or who strays outside the teachings of the Russian Orthodox Church is viewed as a prime candidate for vampirism. As with virtually all of the vampires of European lore, the *uppyr* is the decaying, reanimated remains of a corpse who refused to stay buried. The first written report of vampiric behavior was directed toward a wayward priest in 1078, about a century after Russia adopted Christianity, and became the documented genesis of religious connotations that remained entrenched in vampire lore for centuries. It's interesting to note that practitioners of witchcraft or sorcery—in themselves highly suspect activities—could also become vampires. The implications were clear in the documentations that any activity outside the auspices of the Church would set one up for a ghastly vampiric fate.

THE ROMANIAN INFLUENCE

Although Slavic folklore can be generally credited with the initial development of vampires as the source of virtually every natural calamity that could fall upon a society in the first millennia in eastern Europe, the Slavs also greatly influenced the legends of their non-Slavic neighbors. Of these, Romania is unquestionably the most well known and is inextricably linked to the lore of vampirism in Europe, primarily as a result of Bram Stoker's *Dracula* and the light his novel cast on the often horrific activities of Dracula's alleged real-life inspirational genesis, Romania's Vlad the Impaler (see Chapters 5 and 6). Although Romania has throughout the centuries been bordered by the Slavic regions of what are now Bulgaria, Serbia, and the Ukraine, many of Romania's earliest political and social ties were with its Hungarian neighbors to the west. Despite this amalgam of political and cultural sway, Romania has historically maintained its association with the ancient Roman Empire—which is the very namesake of Romania.

Fangtastic Folklore

Perhaps the long and deeply rooted sense of history that permeates the cultural folklore of Romania is best exemplified by the "Cave with Bones," discovered by a team of cave specialists in the Carpathian Mountains of southwestern Romania in 2002. Radiocarbon dating revealed that human remains recovered from the cave system were over 40,000 years old, making them the oldest ever found in Europe.

The region of eastern Europe of what is now Romania was conquered by the Roman emperor Trajan in A.D. 106 and remained a province of Rome, known as *Roman Dacia*, for nearly two centuries. Geographically isolated from direct Roman influence, the people of Roman Dacia, a commingling of the native population and Roman colonists, developed a powerful independent sensibility. After the fall of Roman power in the third century, the people of Romania survived invasions of Goths, Huns, and Ottoman Turks, and the rule of Austro-Hungary. Through centuries of cultural and political incursions, the Romanians have continued to retain their fierce independence and national identity. They also retain their vampiric legends.

SCREEN SCREAM

In Francis Ford Coppola's 1992 blockbuster *Bram Stoker's Dracula*, Gary Oldman as Prince Vlad in his youthful incarnation pays homage to Romanian lore in his first encounter with Mina Murray (Winona Ryder) in London. At a viewing of the Cinematograph, a white wolf wreaks havoc and gets loose. Cornering Mina, Vlad subdues the wolf by yelling "Strigoi!"

The *Strigoi*

Despite the influences of Slavic vampire legend, the lore of vampires in Romania has maintained its own distinction in terminology and practice. In the Romanian principality of Transylvania—homeland of the legendary Vlad Dracula—vampirism actually pulled double duty as the indistinguishable living vampire, *strigoi vii*, and as the dead vampire, the *strigoi mort*, which is thought to leave its tomb and take the form of an animal to haunt and harass the living. The term *strigoi* (also spelled *strigoii*) is taken from the word *striga,* or witch, entities who are doomed to become vampires after death. In legend, the association between witches and vampires is clear, with the *strigoi vii* and *strigoi mort* believed to gather at night to plot against the living. The *strigoi mort* are the deadliest of the Romanian vampires and will return from the grave to suck the lifeblood of their families and livestock before eventually moving on to attack neighbors in their village.

As is common throughout eastern European lore, candidates for a Romanian vampiric rebirth are those who lead sinful lives or commit suicide. It's also believed that a pregnant woman who permits a vampire to look at her will subsequently give birth to another vampire, but there's little evidence as to exactly how a woman would know that she's indeed fallen under a vampiric gaze. In Romania, the prime revenant contenders are children born out of wedlock, those born with a *caul* (the amniotic membrane of birth that often clings stubbornly to a baby's head), and children who die before baptism. Other legends have it that the seventh son of a seventh son, or the seventh child of the same sex, can also be born as vampires.

The Albanian *Shtriga*

Just as legends of Romanian vampirism take many of their cues from Slavic folklore, the southeastern European nation of Albania has also adopted a similar approach to the undead. As with Romania, the Albanian *shtriga* possesses witchlike characteristics. The term *shtriga*, which evolves from the Latin *strix*, or screech owl, describes a demonic flying creature of the night. The *shtriga* is believed to be a witch who behaves normally during daylight hours, but who at night will transform into an airborne insect, such as a fly or moth, and attack victims to drink their blood.

According to legend, a *shtriga* can be identified by a communal gathering inside a church, where crosses of pig bones are attached to the doorways. The *shtriga* will be unable to exit past the makeshift crucifixes and is thus recognized. Another dead giveaway is to follow a suspected *shtriga* after sunset until she vomits the blood of her victims. A coin can then be soaked in the regurgitated blood, creating an effective charm against further attacks.

GERMANIC VAMPIRES

The vampires of Germany owe their heritage to the Slavic vampires of eastern Europe largely because of Slavic incursions into eastern Germany in the tenth century. The best-known incarnation of vampires in northern Germany are the *nachtzeherer*, or *night waster*, who return from the dead after gnawing on their own extremities and clothing, presenting a hideous *Night of the Living Dead* image of partially eaten hands and arms to the living who happen across them. The *nachtzeherers* are often accompanied by the corpses of women who've died during childbirth, and who help the ghastly vampires attack and devour their living victims.

Although the *nachtzeherer* are believed to be the reanimated result of suicide victims or those who've suffered sudden, inexplicable deaths, the more unusual cause is thought to be the recently deceased who've been buried with their names attached to their clothing. The southern Germanic equivalent of the nachtzeherer is the *blutsauger*, which translates into the creepy, self-descriptive term *bloodsucker*.

Fangtastic Folklore

A variation of the Germanic *alp* is the *schrattl*, a vicious vampire born of a human corpse that has eaten away at its funerary shroud and risen from the grave. *Schrattl* attack their families and livestock first, and then move on to harass the rest of the community, often driving their victims to insanity. The *schrattl* are also similar to vampires in eastern Europe in that they are held responsible for the spread of disease (see Chapter 7).

The *Alp*

One of the most insidious and inconsistent night creatures in Germanic folklore is the *alp*, which takes on a variety of ghoulish characteristics depending on the region of Germany in which it appears. In some areas, the *alp* is a sorcerer capable of assuming the form of a bird or cat in order to work its mischief. In other areas, it's a sexual predator in human form who attacks women and girls in their beds as they sleep. *Alps* are also closely associated with witchcraft and are suspected of being cats or rodents who do the nighttime bidding of witches. One of the more common abilities of *alps* is their power to enter the thoughts of sleeping victims and create horrific nightmares, often resulting in convulsions and fits of hysteria. A common sign of a midnight alp attack is awakening with a sudden, crushing pressure on one's chest and an intense feeling of being suffocated. That same sensation is often described by those attacked by vampiric revenants. To destroy *alps*, individuals who are thought to have risen from the dead are removed from their graves and ceremoniously burned to ashes. If the mischievous *alp* is deemed a living witch, she's sought out and "blooded" with a ritual cut above the right eye to destroy her evil powers.

Woodwives

Generally thought to be protectors of their forested habitats, *woodwives* have the characteristics of benign fairies in many historic German legends,and are said to be elegantly dressed in flowing robes. On a more gruesome note, they are also perfectly capable of attacking hunters and woodcutters who venture deep into the woods and ripping out their throats. The ravaged bodies of forest wanderers who were sometimes found near trails leading into the deep woods were generally assumed to be victims of woodwives who'd taken offence at their incursions.

CREATURES OF THE UNITED KINGDOM

Although tales of vampirism in the United Kingdom in modern times concentrate primarily on the interest in eastern European bloodsuckers, during the eleventh and twelfth centuries the British Isles developed their own ghoulish mythologies. The *baobban sith*, for example, are thought to be seductive maidens who can take on the appearance of crows and ravens to move freely about. In their maiden form, the *baobban sith* lure travelers and hunters into singing and dancing with them, and during the course of the merriment, slay their unsuspecting victims. The Scottish *redcap* is thought to be an evil spirit who inhabits abandoned castles and fortifications, and it attempts to dip its hat into the blood of sleeping wanderers in order to dye its headwear crimson. A fashionable fiend to be certain, but not particularly friendly. Fortunately, religious words and artifacts are enough to drive the redcap to seek other, less-pious victims.

The Welsh *Hag*

The *hag* in Welsh folklore is a female demon who can take several forms, including that of a young maiden, a mature matron, or an ugly old crone. The old crone is the most feared because she signifies impending death and ruin and is generally seen as the symbol of a washerwoman who rinses blood-soaked clothing in streams. Those who run across her are doomed to a brutal fate.

The *Gwrach y Rhibyn*

The *gwrach y rhibyn* is another form of hideously aged woman who can be seen at crossroads threatening travelers, or who's seen only in brief glimpses beside streams and ponds. The wail of the *gwach y rhibyn* is believed to signal impending death, and she's sometimes known to attack sleeping children or the defenseless bedridden to drain their blood, weakening her victims until they perish. Evidence of her visitations is seen in the dried blood that clings to her mouth. It's believed that healthy folks can drive off the *gwach y rhibyn* with brute force.

LATIN AMERICAN VAMPIRES

Independent of the Slavic vampire traditions, the countries of what are now Latin America have developed their own distinctive vampire legends. The Aztec and Mayan civilizations, who ruled much of what is now Central America and Mexico, have a history of bloodthirsty deities that predate the first Spanish explorers, and their influence is still felt in modern lore, particularly in rural areas. In Mayan lore, the *Camazotz* is a monstrous mix of a human male body with the head of a bat that may have developed its origins from the vampire bats of South America. The *Camazotz* personifies death and sacrifice, and people greatly fear the caves that are thought to be his lair.

Cihuateteo

The deities of the *cihuateteo* are thought to be the souls of women who die in childbirth, which gives them the status of warriors. Although the spirit of the *cihuateteo* gives strength to warriors in battle, their physical remains wander the earth to attack children and spread disease and madness. Food offerings are often left at crossroads where the creatures are thought to gather and from where they launch their nighttime assaults on the living. Crossroads are commonplace in vampire legend, also serving as places where vampires can be destroyed.

VAMPIRE BITE The *chupacabra*, which is Spanish for "goat sucker," is one of the most recent vampirish creatures to enter modern legend. Since the 1990s, bloody attacks on livestock in Puerto Rico, Mexico, Texas, and as far north as Maine have been attributed to the elusive *chupacabra*. The few alleged *chupacabras* killed by wary ranchers have turned out to be ill, emaciated, and mange-ridden coyotes.

Tlahuelpuchi

In most of Latin America, the term *bruja*, or witch, is common and often used to describe the ferocious *tlahuelpuchi*, a bloodsucking witch who can transform into a variety of animals in order to roam about freely. These creatures are particularly mean-spirited, sucking the blood and life from innocent infants, while also possessing hypnotic powers that can cause adults to commit suicide. Garlic, onions, and metal can be placed in or around a baby's crib for protection from this fiendish vampire witch, but unexplained infant deaths to this day are still often attributed to the *tlahuelpuchi*, particularly in remote areas of Mexico. The child's unfortunate parents suffer scorn and blame for a lack of vigilant protection.

FANGS IN THE FAR EAST

Although vampires as we've come to love and loathe them in western culture, literature, and film are invariably of European descent, the power, fear, and fascination of vampiric fright knows no borders. The Chinese *jiang shi*, variously spelled as *chiang shih*, is sometimes referred to as the *hopping ghost* and is the reanimated corpse of a victim of drowning, hanging, suicide, or smothering. The *jiang shi* are thought to be particularly vicious, ripping the limbs and heads from their victims. The universally vampiric garlic remedy is effective against these nasty creatures, as are salt and metal filings. And curiously, the sound of thunder is a natural killer of the beasts.

The *Kappa*

The Japanese *kappa* is a creepy critter resembling a hairless monkey with large round eyes and webbed fingers and toes. The *kappa* springs from its hiding places in waterways and ponds and has the distasteful habit of sucking blood from its victims through their intestines. In Malaysia, a pair of these vampirish villains can spring from the bodies of a mother who dies in childbirth, as well as her stillborn baby. The mother then becomes a *langsuyar* and the poor child reappears as a *pontianak*, and both reanimate to seek jealous revenge on living victims, showcasing the unnerving habit of ripping open their bellies to suck out blood.

Penanggala

Another unsettling creature of Indonesian lore is the *penanggala,* which is often described as a midwife who's made a pact with the devil. While she behaves normally during the day, by night she becomes a gruesome detached head with a tail of entrails and intestines dangling from her severed neck. This hideous apparition is capable of flight and goes on the hunt for women in labor. The *penanggala* perches on rooftops to wail during a victim's childbirth and attempts to lap the blood of a mother and newborn with a long, thin tongue sliding down through the rafters.

THE INDIAN EFFECT

To many vampire researchers, India may well have been an original source of some vampire mystique. Throughout the millennia, Indian culture and religion has generated an enormous variety of deities, demons, and superstitious beliefs and legends, and many of the ancient vampirelike Indian entities are still alive and well in modern lore. It's possible that tales of these legendary, and often bloodthirsty demonic entities, made their way into European myth by caravan, conquest, or immigration to commingle and evolve with the lore of other regions many centuries ago.

Rakshasas and *Hatu-dhana*

In ancient Hinduism, the universe was divided into areas of existence, with the subterranean region serving as home to demons and evil spirits. From here were born the frightening *rakshasas*, fanged ogres in human form who inhabit cemeteries, from where they wander into the night to loathsomely slaughter infants and pregnant women. The *hatu-dhana*, sometimes spelled *yatu-dhana*, are an evolutionary step below the *rakshasas* and are believed to ghoulishly feed on the human remains left by a *rakshasa*.

Fangtastic Folklore The goddess Kali is intrinsically linked to blood drinking in Indian lore. A famous legend of Kali describes her battle against the demon god Raktabija in which every drop of blood spilled from his body created a duplicate of him, and the battlefield soon became filled with reproductions. Kali finally destroyed the demon by sucking every last drop of blood from his body (see Chapter 7).

Bhutas and *Vetalas*

Still more demonic deities exist in Indian lore that display horrific vampire characteristics. The *bhuta* represents the spirits of the those who are insane, who were killed by sudden, accidental death, or who suffer physical defects. The *bhuta* inhabit ruins and cremation sites and can enter the bodies of victims to feed on corpses and even the living. They're also held responsible for droughts, crop failures, illness, and insanity—or for that matter, virtually any calamity.

The *vetala*, or *betail*, is another demonic creature that co-opts the bodies of living victims and, like many of the Indian night stalkers, delights in killing children, causing miscarriages, and driving people mad. The sheer range and number of demonic Indian deities and spirits and the countless incarnations of them from region to region is enough to fill several books. There's no question that they've caused many hundreds of thousands of innocents in India to bolt their doors, shutter their windows, and keep candles burning well into the night.

VAMPIRE LORE IN AMERICA

Although the United States has never been known as a hotbed of vampire fright and frenzy, the concept of vampirism did make its way to America and raise its bloody head in New England as early as the Revolutionary War era of the mid-1700s. In the light of modern sensibilities, the apparent commonality with most vampiric dealings in the fledgling country is the link between tuberculosis (called "consumption" in early years) and suspicions of vampire mischief.

Getting Snuffed

One of the earliest American legends involves the family of a prosperous Rhode Island farmer named "Snuffy" Stukeley, who'd fathered fourteen children. Not long after his eldest daughter, Sarah, had taken ill and passed away, several of his brood also became sick and complained of nightmares during which Sarah returned to press upon their chests. After a number of the children had succumbed to illness in rapid succession and another was in the throes of sickness, Snuffy's neighbors suggested he dig up Sarah's body for clues to the seemingly mysterious contagion. Poor Sarah's heart was said to have contained fresh blood—a sure sign of vampirism—and it was quickly extricated and burned. According to the story, only one more child died; the rest remained healthy, thus confirming the sordid vampiric diagnosis.

No Mercy

The Stukeley legend undoubtedly influenced the actions of several families who suffered similar afflictions over the next hundred years in New England. The last of the "vampires" was another Rhode Islander, Mercy Brown, who died in 1892. In the early 1880s, Mercy's mother and sister, Olive, had taken ill and died, and several years later, Mercy's brother, Edwin, began suffering the same apparent ailment. After the lad took a sudden downturn after Mercy's passing, the community surmised that Mercy was the cause of his escalated misery. The bodies of Mrs. Brown, Olive, and Mercy were exhumed and of the three, Mercy's organs were still horrifyingly intact.

Ignoring the obvious fact that her mother and sister were long dead and decomposed, Mercy's heart and liver were placed on a rock, burned to ashes, and the result was fed to Edwin as a remedy on the advice of a physician. In an anticlimatic unhappy ending, Edwin soon passed away himself, and the whole tawdry affair became a media sensation. The only benefit to come of Mercy Brown's ignominious fate was that it put the final nail in the coffin of vampiric witch hunts in early America.

VAMPIRES INTERNATIONAL

The incredible variety of vampiric beings from around the world and the various interpretations of each creature would be enough to sustain *Ripley's Believe It or Not* for centuries. What follows are but a few additional folkloric revenants worth mentioning:

- **Afrit:** An Arabian vampire spirit that rises in smoke from the body of a murder victim to avenge its own death. A spike driven into the ground where the victim was killed is thought to prevent the transformation of an *afrit*.
- **Ekimmu:** The Babylonian spirit of a deceased individual who didn't received proper funerary rites, the *ekimmu* is held responsible for any misfortune or accident that befalls a household.
- **Loogaroo:** In Caribbean lore, the *loogaroo* is an old woman who's made a pact with the devil. After leaving her body at night and shape shifting into a ball of blue light, she must provide the devil with blood from other creatures. Once the devil has been sated, she can return to her human form, only to repeat the nightly process.
- **Obayifo:** In West African lore, the *obayifo* are witchlike creatures who maintain human form by day and prowl at night to suck the blood from children, causing them sickness and death. The *obayifo* are also held responsible for poor crops and the deaths of livestock.

✝ **Phi:** In Thailand the *phi* encompasses an incredible variety of spiritual demons similar to ghosts, elves, and goblins. Every household has their own spirit inhabitants, or *phi*, who become malevolent if their presence isn't ceremoniously acknowledged and respected.

FROM HERE TO ETERNITY

The introduction of vampiric lore and legend is paramount to the understanding of how vampires and vampirism in its widely differing incarnations came to be. As a superstition, scientific or psychological study, and even as a scapegoat, vampires continue to be feared throughout the world, whether in our imaginations or in real life. To answer that preternatural call, we begin by examining the earliest vampire literature and the man whose dramatic characters would forever change the vampire as we know it today—Bram Stoker.

CHAPTER 3

STOKING THE FLAMES

The basis for vampiric legend is in many instances derived from the revenants of folklore. With that rich history, no doubt writers of the day were inspired to create mesmerizing bloodsuckers who would capture public imagination with zealous enchantment. In this chapter, we explore the most famous of those early tales and the authors who helped establish the vampire as we know it today. Like any species, there's much to be learned about its evolution, which in this case, is furthered by several individuals who ventured deep into the dark side of the human psyche.

EARLY WRITINGS OF THE UNDEAD

Of all the prominent authors of celebrated fiction, Bram Stoker is probably the least well-known writer of one of the most famous stories in history. Stoker's frightening depiction of the quintessential vampire in his innovatively constructed 1897 masterpiece *Dracula* brought the world of the undead to life, and his concept of the eternal battle of good versus evil has evolved and flourished into the foundation of literary and cinematic pursuits that have left us breathless, drained, and dying for more. What you may find particularly intriguing is that while Stoker and his characters are unquestionably the most famous, his vampiric tale wasn't the first to come to prominence. He was preceded by John Polidori's story *The Vampyre*, James Malcolm Rymer's penny dreadful *Varney the Vampyre*, and Joseph Sheridan Le Fanu's erotic *Carmilla*. What remains of utmost importance to the genre is that with each written tome and every storyline, saga, and superstition, there's yet another dimension added to a creature that has the unique ability to scare the hell out of us while also tending to our erotic, spiritual, philosophical, and metaphorical natures.

THE VAMPYRE

There's a famous true-life story in literary history that's commonly attached to the inception of Mary Shelley's 1818 masterpiece *Frankenstein*, but it bears repeating in that most folks might not realize its significance to the world of vampire literature. In May of 1816, a quartet was gathered on the shores of Switzerland's Lake Geneva at the Villa Diodati. En route to Italy, but stalled by bad weather, were the English poet Lord Byron, his traveling companion and personal physician John Polidori, poet Percy Bysshe Shelley, and his future wife, Mary Wollstonecraft Godwin. The story goes that as part of a competition or simply in an effort to entertain one another, each individual was to concoct a ghost story to share with the others. It must be said that Polidori's acquaintance with his Lordship was imperfect, with Polidori at first enamored but later despising Byron for his alleged cruelty. What came of that challenge was Byron producing a partial tale about a vampire, Polidori concocting a story hinged on a "skull-headed lady," and eighteen-year-old Mary beginning the basis of *Frankenstein*, which, along with *Dracula*, would become one of the most famous horror novels of all time.

The Finest Form of Flattery

In 1819, *The Vampyre: A Tale*, which Polidori penned using the framework of Byron's story as told at the Villa Diodati, was published in England's *The New Monthly Magazine*. The short story focuses on the sinister bloodsucker Lord Ruthven, who by no small coincidence bears a striking resemblance to Lord Byron. This fact alone created what would come to be known as *Byronic vampires*, meaning those who possess characteristics typical of characters in Byron's body of work or his physical appearance. Some scholars speculate that Polidori's swiping of Byron's original idea was fueled in part by revenge. To make matters worse, *The Vampyre* was initially published under Byron's name, the weight of his reputation quickly leading to many foreign language versions of the tale as well as numerous theatrical productions. Polidori naturally fought for credit in writing the tale, and a massive and seemingly eternal controversy ensued that is debated to this day. Byron eventually denied authoring *The Vampyre*, and Polidori—admitting to Byron having initially conceived the tale—was finally named the author. Tragically, Polidori would gain little from his triumph as he died in 1821, allegedly by his own hand.

How Byronic!

What's highly significant about *The Vampyre* is not only its being recognized as the first true work of vampire fiction, but the character of Lord Ruthven, who as a precursor to Dracula, set into motion the sinister effects of vampirism and the predatory capacities of a creature who, unlike the typical folkloric vampire, is a handsome, self-possessed, evil aristocrat whose love of manipulation is rivaled only by his lust to kill. Ruthven is by all accounts a monster—a charming drawing room noble whose irresistibility and utter ruthlessness has been channeled throughout literature and film ever since. *The Vampyre's* protagonist is a young, wealthy innocent named Aubrey who becomes enamored by the aristocratic Ruthven, slowly learning and accepting what an evil demon his Lordship is. Sadly, it is too late for

Aubrey to save his sister from forced marriage and death at Ruthven's hands. Ruthven's so-called Byronic features, the pallor of his skin, his bloodlust, his eroticism, arrogance, and all his preternatural manipulations immediately incited mimicry in the vampiric literary realm, those inspired likely being James Malcolm Rymer, Sheridan Le Fanu, and Bram Stoker.

Fangtastic Folklore

Frankenstein, The Modern Prometheus was published anonymously in 1818. It wasn't until 1831 that Mary Shelley's name would appear on the cover with a revised addition. It's said that *Frankenstein* was conceived as a result of a dream. Intensely metaphorical, it drew largely upon the scientific, philosophical, and sociopolitical practices of the era. Shelley never actually named her reanimated corpse "Frankenstein," primarily referring to it as "the creature" among other descriptions. Scholars argue that Shelley conceived of the name having actually visited the real Burg (Castle) Frankenstein in Germany.

VARNEY THE VAMPYRE

Though there were many representations of literary vampires spun off Polidori's Lord Ruthven, it wasn't until the mid-1840s that the public was introduced to a different kind of vampire, one whose appearance and ferocity harkens back to the monstrous revenants of folklore. Sir Francis Varney is the star of the penny dreadful turned novel *Varney the Vampyre* or *the Feast of Blood* thought initially to be written by Thomas Preskett Prest, with the general consensus now being that its author is James Malcolm Rymer. Hideous in its conception, Sir Francis Varney (ambiguously cited as the reanimated corpse of 1640 suicide victim Marmaduke Bannerworth) is the epitome of cruelty and banality, his corpselike form stalking young girls in a disjointed epic that ran as 109 separate publications and later as a novel with 220 chapters amounting to over 860 pages.

One of Varney's victims dramatically describes him by saying: "There was a tall, gaunt form—there was the faded ancient apparel—the lustrous metallic-looking eyes—its half-opened mouth, exhibiting tusk-like teeth! It was—yes, it was—the vampyre!"

What Varney represents to vampire literature is yet another stage of evolution that, unlike Lord Ruthven, draws from the dark side of folklore while also retaining the traditional characteristics that have become synonymous with the drawing room vampire in general. Perhaps Varney's most spectacular presentation, aside from the still unknown illustrator who gave brilliant life to the series, is ultimately Varney's demise, which is not by the hands of a vampire slayer but of his own volition. Rather dramatically, Varney leaps into the mouth of Italy's Mt. Vesuvius.

VAMPIRE BITE By definition, the term *reanimation* refers to the restoration of life or consciousness. Commonly used in the horror realm, with everything from Frankenstein to zombies to doppelgangers to killer bunnies, it serves to reinforce revenant folklore, as the majority of so-called vampires were reanimated corpses.

"CARMILLA"

In 1872, another fold of the cloak that would envelope the beginnings of vampire literature and cinema was revealed in the form of Irishman Joseph Sheridan Le Fanu's "Carmilla," a novella published as part of his novel *In a Glass Darkly*. What Le Fanu (often cited as J. Sheridan or simply Sheridan Le Fanu) pulled out of the vampiric crypt is no less critical than Polidori's contributions—some would argue even more so—as he not only brought the erotic vampire to the forefront, he made his antagonistic bloodsucker a woman. Debated with equal fervor by experts of vampire literature, Le Fanu's "Carmilla" also reinforced or established many of the vampiric traits used throughout fiction and scores of films, the most prominent being Carl Theodor Dreyer's 1932 *Vampyr*, Roger Vadim's *Blood and Roses* (aka *Et mourir de plasir*), a trio of Hammer films in 1970 and 1971—*Lust for a Vampire*, *The Vampire Lovers*, and *Twins of Evil*—and the 1974 offering *Terror in the Crypt* to name a few (see Chapters 16 and 17). To understand Le Fanu's brilliance is to delve into the haunting and erotic tale itself.

Perchance to Dream

The protagonist and narrator of "Carmilla" is Laura, who lives with her aged father and servants in a castle in Styria, Austria, near the deserted village of Karnstein. Her first encounter with the demon is at age six, when during one night a pretty young woman appears by her bedside. After calming her to sleep, Laura feels "a sensation as if two needles ran into my breast very deep." With the absence of wounds on her chest, she believes the visitor to be an apparition. At age nineteen, Laura hopes to meet the niece and ward of General Spielsdorf, Mademoiselle Bertha Rheinfeldt, only to learn that she has died. Immediately after receiving word of Bertha's death, Laura and her father witness a strange carriage accident in which a woman and her daughter are involved. Hindered by a life-or-death situation in another town, the mother leaves her daughter in the care of Laura's father, and when Laura and the girl first meet, it becomes evident that they've met before— she's the woman from Laura's "dreams" and claims that Laura is from hers. Her name is Carmilla.

The Cat's Meow

By Laura's own description Carmilla is a stunning beauty, slender and graceful, though languid, and possessing a rich complexion, large eyes, and dark, lustrous hair. Though oddly warned by Carmilla's mother that she's of sound mind, the young woman refuses to speak of her family, where she's from, and reveals absolutely nothing of her personal history or future plans. All that is known is that she's of noble blood from an ancient family. From there, the tale grows dark, especially when Laura realizes that a recently arrived family portrait depicting the Countess Mircalla Karnstein—painted more than a century earlier in 1698—looks *exactly* like Carmilla. At the same time, Laura grows continuously ill, her nights tormented by "a sooty-black animal that resembled a monstrous cat" and a "stinging pain as if two large needles darted, an inch or two apart, deep into my breast." After the biting, the animal would then transform into the figure of a woman.

Of course, during a chance meeting with General Spielsdorf, it's learned that his niece, Bertha, grew ill during the time they had a visitor named Mircalla, who was left in his charge while her mother was away on urgent business. Bertha described to him the same encounters as Laura is experiencing. Acting on a physician's outrageous diagnosis of vampirism, Spielsdorf hid in Bertha's closet and lay in wait seeing for himself a black creature attacking her neck and transforming into Mircalla. Attacking her with a sword, Mircalla fled, and he vowed to find and destroy her.

At the ruins of Karnstein chapel, Spielsdorf and Laura encounter Carmilla, who the General recognizes as Mircalla. He then notes that in her deception, she made an anagram of her given name to form "Carmilla." The following day, with legal authority, the tomb of Countess Mircalla Karnstein is opened. As is often described in folklore, she's perfectly preserved, exudes no smell, and her body is immersed in seven inches of blood. A stake is then driven through her heart and she shrieks, after which she's decapitated and the whole of her burnt to ashes and scattered upon the river.

Fangtastic Folklore

There's little doubt that Sheridan Le Fanu studied the vampires of folklore when writing "Carmilla." When General Spielsdorf asks a woodsman at the chapel why the village of Karnstein lies deserted, the woodsman replies that: "It was troubled by revenants, sir; several were tracked to their graves, there detected by the usual tests, and extinguished in the usual way, by decapitation, by the stake, and by burning; but not until many of the villagers were killed." As you'll learn this is a situation very typical of accounts telling how vampires and other revenants were disposed of.

Girl Power

In the telling of "Carmilla," one can clearly see where Le Fanu was influenced by folkloric tales, in particular the process of staking, beheading, and burning the vampire, the condition of the fiend in its grave, and its transformation into a cat. At one point, Laura even mentions the "Appalling superstition that prevails in Upper and Lower Styria, in Moravia, Silesia, in Turkish Servia, in Poland, even in Russia; the superstition, so we must call it, of the Vampire." As a demon and seductress, Carmilla has all the makings of a traditional vampire with the added distinction of bringing the lesbian vampire to the fore, a precedent that often appears throughout the history of female vampires. She also carries over a host of vampiric traits. Like Lord Ruthven and Sir Francis Varney, Carmilla is invigorated by the moon, has fangs, endures a "quiet" sleep with alleged sleepwalking tendencies, can hypnotize, and has the ability to shape shift.

Carmilla Karnstein stands as one of the most influential literary and cinematic vampires in history, and her presence cannot be understated. Simply put, she's the mother of all female vampires. Le Fanu's tempestuous portrayal of Laura and Carmilla's tense relationship is seething with sexual undertones that no doubt would've proved shocking to the Victorian contingent. In Chapter V, Laura says: "I am sure, Carmilla, you have been in love; that there is, at this moment, an affair of the heart going on." To which Carmilla whispers: "I have been in love with no one, and never shall . . . unless it should be with you."

Sheridan Le Fanu died in 1873, having penned fourteen novels of which the story "Carmilla" is arguably the most renowned. In crafting his haunting tale, Le Fanu, as did Polidori and Rymer and a handful of other writers of the day, greatly contributed to the evolution of the vampire. But it wasn't until another Irishman submitted a novel, originally called *The Undead*, that the figure of the drawing room vampire became set in stone as a permanent fixture in the cryptic vampire realm.

THE OBSCURE ROAD TO FAME

The great irony of Bram Stoker's phenomenally successful effort in creating his incredible and immortal character is that during his lifetime he would never realize the impact *Dracula* would have on millions of mesmerized readers and moviegoers. During much of his adult life, Stoker remained a relatively obscure figure who regularly brushed shoulders with the famous and near-famous, but it would only be after his death that he would gain distinction as the mastermind of one of the most celebrated characters in the world.

Learning to Walk

Bram Stoker's life began with a shaky start on November 8, 1847, in Dublin, Ireland, as the third of seven children. Stoker was sickly and bedridden with a variety of childhood ailments until he reached the age of seven, when he made a seemingly miraculous and complete recovery. Although little more is known about his early years, Stoker appears to have been a bright student and entered Trinity College in Dublin at the age of seventeen, graduating with honors as a science major and returning for a masters degree in mathematics. During his college years, he became involved with literary, philosophical, and dramatic groups, setting the stage for his fascination for theater and literature.

Flair for the Theatrical

Bram Stoker's first career choice was to follow in his father's footsteps as a civil servant, with a job as a junior clerk at Dublin Castle. However, he quickly took an unpaid position as the drama critic for a local newspaper. After writing a favorable review in 1876, praising actor Henry Irving during a tour by Irving's acting troupe in Dublin, Irving invited Stoker to dinner. A long and lasting relationship was born from that first meeting, and Stoker's life would begin changing forever. Two years later, in 1878, Irving had taken over the Lyceum Theatre in London and invited Stoker to join him as stage manager.

A Wilde Proposal

Before Henry Irving's business proposal, Stoker met Florence Balcombe, a beautiful woman with many admirers in Dublin, and began courting her. A fellow Irishman named Oscar Wilde also fell head over heels in love with Florence. At the age of twenty-four and recently graduated from Oxford University, Wilde had yet to reach the great fame he would see in later life as a playwright, poet, and author. Much to Wilde's utter dismay, Florence accepted Stoker's marriage proposal. Brokenhearted at losing the first love in his life, Wilde wrote to Florence to announce that he was leaving Ireland forever. Bram Stoker and Florence Balcombe were married in 1878 and moved to London, where Stoker would take Henry Irving up on his offer.

Oh Henry!

Henry Irving became one of England's pre-eminent classical stage actors during the late 1800s, after giving up an early career as a merchant's clerk and taking on a ten-year acting apprenticeship with various touring groups. In 1871, Irving began working with the Lyceum Theatre in London and gradually turned the failing stage into a highly successful venue with a series of brilliant performances that made him the most respected actor of the era. After the death of the Lyceum's manager, Irving took over the position and quickly assumed full control in 1878. This was the same year that he brought Stoker on board as his new stage manager.

Fangtastic Folklore

Henry Irving was one of the most unique actors of the English stage and was so highly regarded he was awarded with honorary degrees from the universities of Cambridge, Dublin, and Glasgow. Irving made another groundbreaking achievement in 1895 when he became the first actor in England to be knighted by the Crown for his enormous contributions to the arts.

THE DARK SIDE

Now in London with his new bride and a new career, Bram Stoker threw himself headlong into the acting world. At the same time, he began actively pursuing his second career as a writer, publishing the novel *The Snake's Pass* in 1890. Stoker had cut his teeth on an earlier nonfiction work written during his clerical days, with the utterly dull title *Duties of Clerks of Petty Sessions in Ireland*, and a collection of children's fairytales entitled *Under the Sunset*, published in 1881. The macabre themes of Stoker's fairytales were often criticized as being too frightening for children, but the tone of the book was an early illustration of Stoker's interest in unearthly topics and the boundaries of mortality. The same year his first novel was published, Stoker began writing *Dracula*, an endeavor that would take him seven years to prepare for publication.

FORMULATING DRACULA

Much has been written and debated over the past century about the inspiration for the character of Count Dracula and his horrific proclivities for drinking the blood of all measure of humanity. Although there's little doubt that Bram Stoker appropriated his villain's name from Vlad Dracula of Wallachia (see Chapters 5 and 6), the physical characteristics of Dracula are commonly believed to have been inspired by none other than his business associate, Henry Irving. The great actor's stature, grace, and facial features are found in Stoker's account of the gruesome literary Count, and it's probable that Irving's fiery temperament provided more than a little inspiration for Dracula's forbidding nature. Of equal interest in Stoker's novel are the band of characters who played into Dracula's scheming and who eventually prevailed in bringing the epitome of evil to a deservedly ghastly end. Those characters, as we present them in the following chapter, are arguably some of the most mimicked in cinematic history.

Fangtastic Folklore

With more than a bit of coincidence, Bram Stoker's family home was next door to the estate of young Hamilton Deane's family. Deane eventually came to work as a bit actor for Sir Henry Irving's Vacation Company, an acting troupe that toured extensively throughout Europe and America after the closing of the Lyceum Theatre in 1899. Deane would play an integral role in rewriting the successful stage play for Stoker's *Dracula* in 1924, even revamping the role of Van Helsing for himself (see Chapter 14).

ESTABLISHING VAMPIRIC LEGACY

As we've already learned, Bram Stoker's interests, reflected in his writings about the surreal side of mortality, acted as a precursor to his development of *Dracula* and all its characters, which have become as equally immortal as the black devil himself. From whence Stoker actually drew inspiration for his characters is anyone's guess, though the majority of speculation is based on Stoker's notes and various rumors and studies over the decades. What is known is that vampires in both fictional and historical accounts would likely have been of great interest to Stoker, for his was not the first vampire to be fictionalized as we've learned by examining the works of John Polidori, James Malcolm Rymer, and Sheridan Le Fanu.

What Stoker can lay claim to is the fact that his Count Dracula ultimately became synonymous with the word "vampire" in that his portrayal struck a chord in the collective conscious of society in Victorian England and, eventually, the entire world. Replete with drama, romance, graphic horror, supernatural occurrences, and punctuated by the underlying subtext of sexual repression, the politics of the aristocracy bleeding the lower classes, and the ultimate religious fight of good versus evil, *Dracula* stands on its own as the most recreated and popular novel in history. In the next chapter, we take a closer look at Stoker's legendary characters and the tenacity and verve that gave each of them in their own right a distinctly human immortality.

CHAPTER 4

DEAR DIARY . . .

Few novels in history contain an ensemble of characters who become forever embedded in our minds. *Catcher in the Rye, To Kill a Mockingbird, The Color Purple, Gone with the Wind*, and the works of William Shakespeare are but a few of the fictional writings where one can recall each and every character, their traits, their emotions, their turmoil, and everything encompassing their personal journey. Bram Stoker's *Dracula* is among those select few, with characters so often mimicked in vampire lore as to become questioned if they're not included. Here now we introduce to you the unforgettable cast of *Dracula*.

To Live and Die in Romania

One of the more unique aspects of Bram Stoker's *Dracula*, aside from the preternatural pretentiousness of his immortal fiend, is the format in which he chose to tell the tale. In *Dracula*, Stoker relied on the literary device of presenting excerpts from the journals and diaries of his key players (excluding Dracula), interspersed with other bits of crucial information such as letters, newspaper articles, phonograph recordings and the like, which gives *Dracula* the distinct advantage of portraying fictional firsthand accounts of the drama and horror as it takes place from Transylvania to Victorian London. What follows are descriptions of the major characters in the novel, each immortal in their own right as over the decades they've been used outright or adapted as characters throughout the vampiric genres of fiction and film. While it's unlikely that Stoker could've ever dreamed of such longevity for his creations, it's certain he'd be overwhelmed in the knowing that all of them have withstood the test of time. We begin with their origins as created by Bram Stoker.

SCREEN SCREAM Actor Edward Van Sloan gave us our first film portrayal of Van Helsing in the 1931 *Dracula* and again in 1936 in *Dracula's Daughter*. From there, the king of all vampire hunters became commensurate with legendary actor Peter Cushing, who played Van Helsing in many films, bringing new intelligence and physical capacities to the character (see Chapter 15). In 1992, Sir Anthony Hopkins gave a memorable turn as Van Helsing in *Bram Stoker's Dracula* (see Chapters 15 and 17), as did Hugh Jackman in the 2004 film *Van Helsing* (see Chapter 17).

Abraham Van Helsing

Next to Count Dracula himself, Abraham Van Helsing is considered to be the second major character in *Dracula*. Alternately cited as both doctor and professor in various presentations, Van Helsing is the true protagonist to Dracula's antagonist. Van Helsing first enters into the tale in Chapter Nine, when his friend and former pupil, Dr. Seward, is confounded by Lucy Westenra's deteriorating condition. Van Helsing is a Dutch professor based in Amsterdam and as Seward writes, he "knows as much about obscure diseases than any one in the world."

Van Helsing is also described as a metaphysician and philosopher with an open mind, attributes that Stoker no doubt granted his protagonist so as to offer extreme latitude in dealing with the supernatural. With Van Helsing's arrival in England, the story of Dracula begins to unfold and accelerate as the dear doctor turns vampire hunter, setting into stone the fact that for every vampire that stalks the earth, there is to be an individual who hunts him with relentless abandon—and who uses any means necessary to destroy him (see Chapter 10).

There exists a wide range of opinions as to the origin of Van Helsing's first name, the most obvious being that Stoker used Abraham as a tribute to his own name, the shortened version being "Bram." Others note that the name pays tribute to Stoker's father, who was also named Abraham, or even to Stoker's friend Arminius Vambery, a renowned Hungarian historian, scholar, and author. It's speculated that Vambery made Stoker's acquaintance in 1890 after a theater performance, and that it was he who may have introduced to Stoker the history of Romania's Vlad Dracula (see Chapters 5, 6, and 10).

Fangtastic Folklore

As a well regarded historian, Arminius Vambery was particularly interested in the Ottoman Empire and spent years in Constantinople during the mid-1800s where he tutored Islamic students and learned dozens of Ottoman dialects. As a Westerner, Vambery was constantly under threat, but he was so adept at passing himself off as a native, he was able to travel freely through much of the Middle East. His experiences within the very countries Vlad Dracula had warred with could easily have exposed Stoker to legends of the man thought to have inspired *Dracula* (see Chapter 5).

JONATHAN HARKER

As one of the primary heroes of *Dracula*, young, handsome solicitor Jonathan Harker is perhaps the best representation of the "perfect" English gentleman, one who's thrust into a situation beyond his imagining and forced to literally fight to the death to save his love and eventual wife, Mina Murray. The novel indeed starts with Harker and his trip to Castle Dracula. From minute one, Harker is tested, beginning with his leaving for the castle on the eve of St. George's Day, which as told to him by the hotel purveyor is when "all the evil things in the world will have full sway." Forcing a rosary with a crucifix upon him for safety, the stage is set for the true horror Harker is to face when imprisoned by the devil and confronted with a rapture of emotion, superhuman occurrences, Dracula's brides, humiliation, and his own survival, escape, and return to London.

Harker in many ways epitomizes the average man whose proper belief system and morals are challenged to the very brink of his sanity. Complying to some measure of internal revenge, it is Harker who first steps up to the plate to volunteer his services to Van Helsing in destroying Dracula. Indeed it is Harker who in the final confrontation at the Castle slits Dracula's throat before Quincey P. Morris stabs the fiend with his Bowie knife. What's of particular interest about Harker is that his is the first character that in many vampire films is either primarily featured or quickly eliminated. For example, as in the novel, Harker is the one who visits Castle Dracula in the 1922 film *Nosferatu* and the 1992 *Bram Stoker's Dracula*, but in the 1931 *Dracula*, based primarily on the Hamilton Deane/John Balderston stage play, it is Renfield and not Harker who makes the journey and becomes Dracula's servant.

Still other films use Jonathan Harker as well as the other characters in various measure. In Hammer's seminal 1958 film *Horror of Dracula* starring Christopher Lee, Harker makes the trip to the Count's castle, but not as the simple librarian he claims to be. Instead, he's working in league with Van Helsing (Peter Cushing) and arrives with the intent to kill the fiend. Unable to accomplish his task, he becomes a vampire himself and is very quickly staked by Van Helsing. The rest of the story revolves around

Arthur Holmwood, his wife Mina, and his sister Lucy. Dr. Seward is but a minor character, and Renfield and Quincey Morris are nonexistent.

MINA MURRAY

By all accounts, the character of Wilhemina "Mina" Murray is the representation of all things good and moral in Victorian society, standing forth against the legacy of evil that so permeates *Dracula*. Pure and virtuous in her thinking and behavior, it's ultimately this assistant school mistress who becomes the object of Dracula's obsession and with whom he shares his blood in an attempt to make her his bride. The hypnotic bond that Mina and the vampire share is both strong and elusive to all but Van Helsing, who uses Mina's telepathic link to track Dracula's whereabouts and set in motion the plan to destroy him. During his final erotically charged attack on Mina, Dracula made clear his intentions:

"And so you, like the others, would play your brains against mine. You would help these men to hunt me and frustrate me in my design! ... Whilst they played wits against me, against me who commanded nations, and intrigued for them, and fought for them, hundreds of years before they were born, I was countermining them. And you, their best beloved one, are now to me, flesh of my flesh, blood of my blood, kin of my kin, my bountiful wine-press for a while, and shall be later on my companion and my helper."

What many scholars derive of Mina's character is that she's in direct contrast to that of her childhood friend Lucy Westenra. Mina is a pure soul of modest means who by rights has no intention of succumbing to evil. Indeed, though she is indoctrinated into the undead by virtue of exchanging blood with Dracula, she manages to survive and goes on to give birth to a child, which she and Jonathan name Quincey, and who was born seven years later on the very day Quincey died.

Lucy Westenra

Another major character in the first half of *Dracula* is Lucy Westenra, who in many respects stands as the antithesis of Mina Murray. A woman of wealth, Lucy is delighted to be the object of affection from a trio of potential suitors who all propose to her on the same day, including Dr. Seward, Quincey Morris, and Arthur Holmwood (later known as Lord Godalming), who ultimately becomes her fiancé. Lucy resides in Whitby, and it is there that Mina joins her and witnesses firsthand the effects of Lucy's sleepwalking and subsequent mysterious illness. Providing opposition to Mina in the metaphorical sense, Lucy is the "bad" girl in that it is she who becomes a vampire by Dracula's bite and turns to the dark side. Following her death, and the denial by all but Van Helsing that she's now a vampire, the *Westminster Gazette* reports that several local children went missing and later asserted that they were with "the bloofer lady." Each of the children have been "slightly torn or wounded in the throat."

Lucy's nocturnal hunting—especially of small children—adds a wicked twist to the predatory nature of her character. First she's looking for a husband, then she's looking for victims. Whereas Mina fights the evil that is Dracula and all he represents, Lucy embraces it. Mina ends up living happily ever after, and Lucy is staked, decapitated, and has garlic stuffed in her mouth. Whether intentional or not, Stoker's handling of these two women reflects the subtext of the evils of aristocracy. Lucy and Arthur's wealth couldn't save lovely Lucy, but Mina, with only modest means, was able to survive.

Dr. Jack Seward

As a rejected suitor to Lucy, the affable Dr. Seward remains unwavering in his care of her when she becomes ill. In *Dracula*, he's described by Lucy as a twenty-nine-year-old doctor who's clever, handsome, well off, and of good birth. He's also in charge of his very own lunatic asylum and has under his care none other than the bug-eating madman, Renfield. It's Seward who brings Van Helsing into the gothic horrorfest, and indeed the good doctor is often featured in films and usually survives. During the final battle with Dracula, it's Seward who holds off the gypsies while Harker and Quincey destroy the Count. The musings of Dr. Seward throughout the book make him a very likeable character, which is why, perhaps, he's often part of Dracula cinema. In that respect, however, he is typically portrayed as an older man, with Lucy being his daughter instead of his romantic interest.

Quincey P. Morris

If ever you want to impress your friends with cocktail party trivia, ask them which character in the novel *Dracula* actually dealt the demon its final blow. Chances are they'll answer Van Helsing, Harker, or even Mina. In truth, it's Quincey P. Morris who dispatches Dracula to hell by plunging his Bowie knife into his heart, after which the king of all vampires' "whole body crumbled into dust." It's a sad fact that in most vampire films, and even in the Hamilton/Balderston adapted stage play, that the character of Quincey Morris is entirely eliminated. As a close friend of both Arthur Holmwood and Dr. Seward, Morris is the sole American in the novel, a sturdy, well-traveled Texan who's one of Lucy's ardent suitors. Even after Lucy chooses Arthur over Quincey and Dr. Seward, both men remain steadfast in their pursuit of Dracula. Why Quincey is often missing from future vampiric renditions is anyone's guess. In some ways, Stoker made him the quintessential American caricature, replete with American slang, humor, and adages that often break the seriousness of the impending horror. Fortunately, Quincey was given his due credit and ran close to the novel in the 1992 film *Bram Stoker's Dracula* where he was played by Bill Campbell.

ARTHUR HOLMWOOD

Of all the three suitors pursuing Lucy Westenra, the Honorable Arthur Holmwood is the most aristocratic. Partway through *Dracula*, in fact, he becomes Lord Godalming after the passing of his father. With the knowledge that Lucy is to become his wife, Holmwood is, next to Harker, the most motivated to kill Dracula in the name of revenge. It is, in fact, Holmwood who is the last to believe that his beloved Lucy has become a vampire and ultimately the one who must put a stake through her heart to give her peace. Like Quincey Morris, the character of Holmwood has oftentimes been eliminated from film and stage plays, appearing only as the central character in the 1958 *Horror of Dracula* and again in *Bram Stoker's Dracula* in 1992.

SCREEN SCREAM

Bram Stoker's last novel, *The Lair of the White Worm*, was published in 1911, just a year before Stoker's death. Although the book is one of Stoker's lesser known works, it was made into a film in 1988 by director Ken Russell, with Hugh Grant as the leading man. Russell's version of *Lair* is an intentionally campy take on Stoker's final horror story involving a huge snakelike creature that's fed human flesh by a psychotic woman. The film tanked at the box office but over the years has become a cult classic.

R. M. RENFIELD

In many of the Dracula-based films it is R. M. Renfield who is quite literally the loony in the asylum, a fact that makes him one of the more intriguing characters in Stoker's novel. He's initially described by Dr. Seward as fifty-nine years of age, with a "sanguine temperament, great physical strength, morbidly excitable, periods of gloom, ending in some fixed idea which I cannot make out." Seward later mentions that his "homicidal maniac is of a peculiar kind" and that he must invent a new classification for him—a "zoophagous" for his life-eating propensities, including spiders, flies, and small birds. What is made obvious is that as soon as Dracula arrives in London, Renfield becomes more engaged in helping "the master," and thus acts as a conduit by which Dracula's hunting party can learn more about the fiend and by which he can ultimately gain access to the asylum. The importance of Renfield is the obvious parallel between his mortal lust for taking lives and Dracula's immortal lust for doing the same.

DRACULA UNLEASHED

Bram Stoker's *Dracula* was released in 1897 to mixed reviews, with some critics considering the subject matter too repulsive for casual readers. During Stoker's life *Dracula* never sold well, and there's no evidence that Stoker himself thought the book was remarkable in any way. For a novel that would become one of the most popular works in literature, *Dracula* received a shockingly inauspicious debut, and that disinterest would last for over twenty years.

Fangtastic Folklore

Soon after the publication of *Dracula*, the Lyceum Theatre went into a financial spiral as tastes in entertainment changed in London, and Sir Henry Irving's health began to fail. By 1899, six years prior to his death in 1905, Irving turned the theater over to a business syndicate. Stoker continued writing novels, and managed to eke out a moderate living from book sales, but *Dracula* was never a major player in the book market during his lifetime.

Florence Stoker's financial situation changed dramatically after she sold the film rights to Universal Studios for their 1931 production of *Dracula*. Although the estimated $40,000 she received for the rights may seem paltry by today's standards, the truth is that Florence Stoker got lucky. When Bram Stoker filed for copyright protection in the United States. for *Dracula* in

1897, he failed to deliver the required two copies to the U.S. Copyright Office as required by law. Technically, *Dracula* has been in the public domain in America since it was first released, and no permission from Florence Stoker would've ever been required.

DEATH AND IMMORTALITY

Bram Stoker's own health began failing in 1905 after he suffered a stroke and developed a long-term and malicious kidney disease. With Florence at his side, Stoker's final novel, *The Lair of the White Worm*, was published in 1911, a year before he passed away. Florence retained the copyrights to her husband's work and continued receiving a very modest income from book royalties. But it wasn't until a German filmmaker, Friedrich Murnau, made the film, *Nosferatu*, in 1922 as an unauthorized adaptation of *Dracula* that Stoker's novel would get noticed. Florence Stoker's lawsuit against the makers of *Nosferatu* triggered enormous interest in a public who wanted to know what all the legal fuss was about (see Chapter 14). Within a decade, *Dracula* would become the standard by which horror fiction is measured, and it has never been out of print since its first publication. The tragedy is that Bram Stoker was never able to appreciate that his masterwork of surreal immortality would itself become immortal.

What must now be investigated is the hotly debated legend of what many claim is the "real" Dracula, or what experts more commonly realize as the true-life men whose combined exploits Bram Stoker is thought to have used as inspiration for creating his legendary monster—Prince Vlad Dracul and his notorious son, Vlad the Impaler. Where did these legends emanate? How did Stoker allegedly mold his black devil after two of Romania's legendary leaders and the exploits leading to their immortality in the annals of European history? And more importantly, what's the *real* story behind these two notorious historical figures?

CHAPTER 5

VLAD THE IMPALER

Of all of the very human influences on the modern concept of vampirism, no single historical character has played a more significant and hotly debated role than Romanian prince Vlad Dracula, one of the most menacing, misconstrued, and misunderstood eastern European rulers to haunt the history of the walking dead. Bram Stoker's brilliantly innovative approach to the horrors of vampirism in *Dracula* reshaped Western concepts of the legendary creature of the night and brought the undead into the libraries and drawing rooms of Victorian England. At its core lay the resurrected heart of a legendary living monster.

A TALE OF TWO VLADS

The life and times of Vlad Dracula often reads like a convoluted gothic romance, with character switches, confusingly similar names in politically opposed roles, and plot twists and turns that would have given Shakespeare a migraine. Were it not for the appropriation of the Dracula name by Bram Stoker, very little of this history would mean much in the scheme of Western historical study or to the average reader, but this background is part and parcel of the modern Dracula legend and adds immeasurably to the expertise of the vampire aficionado. That said, we now delve into the terror and tyranny of a pair of men named Vlad.

THE REAL DRACULA

The question of whether the anecdotal horror and history of the fifteenth-century Romanian prince, Vlad Dracula, was the dominant factor in Bram Stoker's conception of *Dracula* has triggered innumerable books and films and has attracted the attention of scores of literary and historical scholars over the past century. There's little question that the efforts of several prolific authors and researchers have attempted to seal an intrinsic relationship between the life of Vlad Dracula and the character of Stoker's frightening construction of the fundamental bloodthirsty creature in modern lore. The parallels between Dracula the vampire and Romania's Vlad Dracula are often perceived as unmistakable. But one thing is for certain: If, in some past incarnation of fact or fiction, you'd ever stumbled upon the paths of either one of these ruthless beings, you'd have been in for the fright of your life.

Birth of a Tyrant

Vlad Dracula was born into one of the most contentious eras in the struggle for domination of eastern Europe during the fourteenth and fifteenth centuries between the empires of Hungary and the Ottoman Turks. The regions of modern Romania that encompass the principalities of Wallachia and Transylvania were keys to that struggle, and rulers would often find themselves playing a political chess match of diplomacy and military intrigue in order to appease conflicting doctrines and to maintain regional power. Much of Vlad Dracula's life would be spent as a pawn in the maneuverings of desperate and often duplicitous leaders on both sides.

The Prince of Wallachia

The man who would become inseparably tied to the most unnerving character in horror was descended from Basarab the Great, the fourteenth-century ruler of Wallachia, who gained his homeland's independence from Hungary in the mid-fourteenth century. Basarab established a lineage that became the House of Basarab and from which the rulers of Wallachia would be chosen. During the ensuing decades, Basarab's descendants were forced to alternately cooperate with the Christian authority of Hungary and negotiate periodic sovereignty to the rapidly expanding Ottoman-Turkish Empire. Essentially, they were caught in the geographical metaphor of the rock of Christian Holy Roman Hungarian authority and the hard place of Ottoman-Turkish muscle in a struggle for dominion over the region that would last for generations.

VAMPIRE BITE

Although the name *Vlad Tepes*, or *Vlad the Impaler*, is the most common description of Vlad Dracula today, there's no evidence that he ever used or even recognized the sobriquet. The third in his family's line to bear the name *Vlad*, Vlad Dracula is often technically, and correctly, identified as Vlad III. As the son of Vlad Dracul, Vlad Dracula translates to "Vlad, Son of the Dragon," and there are existing documents drawn during his life on which he signed the infamous and instantly recognizable name, "Dracula."

DRAGON TALES

One of the confusing points in the lineage of the House of Basarab is the name association between his descendants, Vlad Dracul and Dracul's son, Vlad Dracula. Vlad Dracul's father, Mircea cel Batrin, or Mircea the Old, was revered in Wallachia for his adamant determination to rid Wallachia of the

Ottoman-Turkish regime. After Mircea's death, the elder Vlad came to power as a military leader under the auspices of the Hungarian Empire and was stationed in the Transylvanian town of Sighisoara to continue fighting off the repeated incursions of the Turks, while Vlad Dracul's half-brother, Alexandru I Aldea, assumed full control of Wallachia.

It was during this duty in 1431 that Vlad was summoned by Sigismund, then the Holy Roman Emperor in Hungary, to receive initiation into the Order of the Dragon, which had been created as an institution of military and religious loyalty to defend the Holy Roman Empire from the threat of Turkish encroachment. This fortunate honor would become a pivotal point in Vlad's life, and he attached the Wallachian word for "dragon" to his own name, becoming Vlad Dracul, which translates to *Vlad the Dragon*. Vlad's illegitimate son, born in Vlad's military post of Sighisoara in approximately 1431, by birthright became known as "Vlad, the son of the dragon," which, serendipitously for Bram Stoker and millions of vampire enthusiasts, effectively translates into Vlad Dracula.

THE CAPRICE OF POWER

Far more influential than the relatively diminutive principality of Wallachia, Hungary wielded enormous power in eastern Europe that lasted for decades, and at its helm for a half-century was the crafty king, Sigismund. Sigismund's reign culminated in his being elected as the Holy Roman Emperor in 1433, a title that carried the political leverage and blessings of the Pope, whose own authority over the Christian world was beyond measure. Sigismund's own life was rife with mystery and intrigue, and he came into power through a series of shrewd deceptions and political scheming. Born into Polish royalty, Sigismund's early maneuverings cost him any opportunity to gain the Polish throne. Through marriage, he fell into a position of power in Hungary, and although he was defied by much of the nobility there, he had himself declared king in 1387.

Although the principal enemy of all of Christian Europe was the expanding Ottoman-Turkish Empire, Sigismund was equally threatened by houses of nobility in Hungary and its outlying principalities which disputed his right to the throne. It was with this background of internal quarreling and the external threat of Turkish invasion that Sigismund created an order that would develop its own life and legend in the pages of vampiric history.

The Order of the Dragon

The influence of the Order of the Dragon on Vlad Dracul, his son, Vlad Dracula, and its impact on the concept of Bram Stoker's *Dracula* is incalculable, but there's little doubt that without this organization of nobility in eastern Europe, our vision of Dracula and our mythology of vampires in general would be much different than it is today. For Vlad Dracul, the Order of the Dragon was a badge of honor and would become symbolic of his extraordinary efforts to gain control of his homeland. The Order of the Dragon was originally conceived by Sigismund of Hungary in 1308 as a select group of initiates from the feudal regions of the Hungarian Empire. The Order of the Dragon was an honorific to be bestowed on Sigismund's most trusted and loyal vassals and was a highly respected and much sought after title. The concept of the order was also politically and militarily advantageous to Sigismund on several levels. As a feudal state, the power that Sigismund wielded over Hungary was inextricably linked to the support of relatively disconnected landowners and military leaders in the far-flung regions of the empire. At its very core, Sigismund's motives for creating the Order of the Dragon were entirely self-serving, and he effectively swore his initiates to complete loyalty and trust in support of *his* regime. In return, they were expected to respond to any threat to his sovereignty.

Bad Blood and Ascension

The death of Vlad Dracul's half-brother in 1436 advanced Dracul's eldest son, Mircea II, to the throne of Wallachia, and the death of Sigismund the following year in 1437 left Dracul with the political leeway to negotiate a peace treaty with the Turks. Just five years later, the new regime of Hungary launched an all-out attempt to drive the Turks from Europe, and Hungarian general Janos Hunyadi demanded that Dracul fulfill his sworn obligations to the Order of the Dragon and join the battle. It was an invitation that Vlad Dracul—perhaps wisely—declined, although he later sent his son Mircea II with a token contingent of Wallachian warriors into the crusade to placate the Roman Church.

The crusade was a series of decisive victories and dismal failures over the next two years, and the Christian army was finally routed by the Ottoman Turks in the Battle of Varna in eastern Bulgaria in 1444, bringing an end to the campaign of Janos Hunyadi, but not to his bitter hatred of the Turks. Although Hunyadi escaped the carnage, the stage had already been set for animosity between Hunyadi and the family of Dracul that would have a lasting effect on the still adolescent Vlad Dracula, who would enter his teens in the midst of conflicts over which he had, as yet, no control. After the Battle of Varna, internal power struggles within the Ottoman Empire forced the sultan, Murad, to negotiate a peace treaty with Hungary in an unsteady arrangement that would boil over into battle during the coming years.

VAMPIRE BITE The dominant political and social system of medieval Europe during Vlad Dracula's lifetime is known as *feudalism*. Under feudal rule, landowners were invariably considered nobility who operated under the auspices of the reigning Crown, and to whom they pledged military support. Although the word itself doesn't describe active feuding among opposing powers, there's no question that quarrels between the nobility of the realm were common and often led to bloodshed.

The Intrigues of Infidels

It's recorded that Vlad Dracul actually relinquished control of Wallachia to his eldest son, Mircea II, in 1442 and traveled to the Ottoman-Turkish court to negotiate a separate treaty in order to maintain his regency. While Vlad Dracul was away, Hungarian leader Janos Hunyadi attacked Wallachia and drove Mircea from the throne, installing Basarab II as his own chosen regent. With the aid of Ottoman-Turkish military might, Vlad Dracul retaliated and regained the throne within a year, and in a diplomatic negotiation that required the Wallachian principality to pay annual tribute to the Turks, Vlad Dracul was also compelled to leave his young sons, Vlad Dracula and Radu, as an insurance policy to confirm Wallachian loyalty. In the hands of the Ottoman-Turkish sultan Murad, the two sons were seen as serving dual purposes: they ensured an alliance with Vlad Dracul in the short term, and they were of royal Wallachian blood and could be groomed into puppet rulers of Wallachia for the Ottoman Empire.

Fangtastic Folklore

Popular author Karen Chance remolded the historical figure of Mircea II into the handsome and horrific antihero of her *Cassandra Palmer* series of vampire fantasy fiction novels. In an interesting twist, it's Mircea, rather than his little brother Vlad Dracula, who functions as the primary instigator of vampiric villainy.

Throughout the period of Turkish confinement suffered by Vlad Dracula and Radu, their father Vlad Dracul continued a series of political gamesmanship with the Ottoman Turks and the Hungarian regimes. Meanwhile, in the hands of the Turks, the young Vlad Dracula learned the military skills and the statesmanship of limitless power, all the while developing an increasing resentment for the perceived betrayal of his father and an abiding hatred for his captors. As would be proven in his later years, Vlad Dracula took full advantage of his Turkish education, not to become a vassal of the Ottoman Turks, but to use his knowledge to exact bloody retribution. For his younger brother, Radu, the Turkish experience was much different. It's estimated that Radu was around eight years old when he was handed to the Turkish court, and was much more impressionable at such an early age. Radu, who would become known as Radu the Handsome, was a beautiful boy and quickly became a popular addition to the court of Sultan Murad. During his years with the Turks, Radu was a willing convert to Islam and rapidly shed the appearance of being a diplomatic hostage. Radu in essence became exactly what Murad had intended him to be—a minion of the Ottoman Turks.

DECEPTION BY DECREE

Vlad Dracul's various games of pretense in dealing with Hungary and the Turks reached a breaking point in 1445 when his son, Mircea II, attacked the Ottoman-held fortified city of Giurgiu on the strategically located banks of the Danube River in southern Wallachia. In Dracul's imprudent concept of diplomacy, he could use the assault to indulge the Holy Roman Empire while simultaneously claiming to the Turks that Mircea had essentially gone rogue and was out of his control. The duplicity backfired, and Dracul was quickly compelled to return Giugiu to Ottoman control and reaffirm his treaties with the Turks to avoid an all-out confrontation. The outcome proved to be a diplomatic success with the Ottoman Empire and a tactical disaster with Hungary.

The Fall of Dracul

Janos Hunyadi, the sworn enemy of the Ottoman Turks, was elected as regent of Hungary in 1446, giving him full authority to conduct military campaigns at will. This was a troubled time for the Hungarian Empire, with the Ottoman Turks looming from the south and east, German threats from the west, and political enmity within the nobility of Hungary. Despite this turmoil, Hunyadi launched a punitive assault on Wallachia in 1447, defeating the forces of Vlad Dracul and Mircea II and driving Dracul into hiding. In Romanian history, it's said that Mircea was captured by members of the Wallachian nobility, or *boyars*, near the capital of Targoviste (sometimes spelled *Tirgoviste*) who'd fostered pro-Hungarian sentiments and tired of Dracul's regime of flip-flopping his loyalties with the Turks and the Christian world. The boyars blinded Mircea with the tip of a red hot poker and buried him alive. Vlad Dracul himself was hunted down and killed near the Romanian city of Balteni, leaving the throne open to another of Janos Hunyadi's personal choices as regent of Wallachia—Vladislav II—who was considered unrelentingly loyal to the authority of Hungary.

In 1448, Janos Hunyadi's armies, with the aid of Vladislav II, launched an attack against the Turkish stranglehold on the strategically vital Danube River near Kosovo. The ensuing battle was a disaster for the Christian armies and resulted in the flight of both Vladislav and Hunyadi. En route home, Hunyadi was taken prisoner by Serbian ruler George Brankovic, who had no love for Hunyadi's authority and whose Hungarian principality of Serbia had been estranged from Hungarian rule. Hunyadi was forced to barter for his release by arranging marriage between his son, Matthias Corvinus, and Brankovic's daughter-in-law, Elizabeth Cilli, in a matchup of purely political purposes.

Moldavian Exile

Janos Hunyadi's imprisonment and Vladislav's military trouncing presented Vlad Dracula with the opportunity to finally own what he felt was his birthright—the crown of Wallachia. With the aid of the Ottoman Turks, Vlad Dracula assumed the throne. His exceptionally short-lived reign lasted just one month. Backed by neighboring feudal warlords, Vladislav took back Wallachia and drove the frustrated Dracula once again into the relative safety of the Turks. From there, and later with his uncle Bogdan in Moldavia, Dracula plotted his return to power for eight years. During this time, a most surprising relationship developed between Dracula and the mastermind of his father's overthrow and death; Janos Hunyadi himself. When Bogdan was assassinated by a rival in 1451, Dracula was forced to flee once again—this time to Hungary and into the hands of Hunyadi.

VAMPIRE BITE

The term *boyar* describes the landholding gentry of eastern Europe, who were considered nobility by birthright and were the ruling class of most countries and principalities. By custom, the *boyars* normally elected their own monarchs with selections from specific ruling families, or *houses*. *Boyars* ruled their own land with relative autonomy but were expected to show loyalty to their rulers and set aside common disputes and power struggles in defense of the kingdom.

The Doorway to Power

The unlikely combination of Vlad Dracula's guile and Hunyadi's political savvy soon proved advantageous to both men. After years of captivity, training, and failed indoctrination with the Turks, Dracula knew the mindset and inner workings of the Ottoman-Turkish Empire, which made him an invaluable resource to Hunyadi. No doubt, Dracula's hatred of Turks was instrumental in the arrangement, and Dracula became one of Hunyadi's most trusted advisors. Much to Dracula's benefit, tensions began developing between Hunyadi and Wallachia's Vladislav II. New threats from the

Ottoman Turks forced Hunyadi to the defense of the city known today as Belgrade in Serbia, and Dracula was entrusted with his own troops to protect the borders of Wallachia. The battle for Belgrade in early 1456 was a convincing victory for Hunyadi and his forces, but just three weeks after the Turks relinquished their ground and retired from the war, Hunyadi's own life was taken, not by battle, but by plague. With the flight of the Turks and Hungarian power in flux after Hunyadi's passing, the doorway to Wallachia was now wide open for Vlad Dracula.

VAMPIRE BITE

Impalement was a hideous form of torture and execution, and it became Vlad Dracula's hallmark death sentence. A sharpened stake was forced through a victim's body, often with the use of ropes and horses, and then mounted into the earth vertically with the body dangling from above. Although the shock of such horrific abuse was enough to kill almost instantly, Dracula's minions took great care to perfect the "art" of impaling in order to prolong the agony as long as possible—sometimes for days.

Sticking It to the Masses

Dracula invaded Wallachia the same year Hunyadi died and subsequently overran the defenses of Vladislav's forces. It's said that Dracula himself dispatched Vladislav in hand-to-hand combat and took his head to ensure a permanent ending to Vladislav's reign. Dracula's primary objective for gaining absolute control of the throne was to undermine the power of the boyars, for whom he had little use and who'd been so instrumental in the deaths of his father and brother. During the Easter festival in 1457, Dracula called the boyars of Targoviste to assemble for a grand feast. Dracula questioned each of the noblemen, asking how many princes of Wallachia they had known during their lives. According to the German minstrel, Michel Beheim, who wrote the poem *Story of a Bloodthirsty Madman Called Dracula of Wallachia*, the oldest boyars thought there had been at least thirty princes, some thought twenty, and the youngest responded with seven. Dracula's response to their answers was decisive:

> "How do you explain the fact that you have had so many princes in your land? The guilt is entirely due to your shameful intrigues."

Legend has it that Dracula then seized 500 of the boyars and had them impaled. Although the number is undoubtedly exaggerated, there's little doubt that the oldest were executed in sufficient numbers to gain Dracula's reputation and the permanent appellation, *Vlad Tepes*, which translates into English as the unmistakable "Vlad the Impaler."

SCREEN SCREAM

In an interesting twist of historical character use in cinema, the name of Hungary's Matthias Corvinus was partially appropriated for the vampire films *Underworld* and *Underworld: Evolution*, in which the male protagonist, Michael Corvin (Scott Speedman), was imbued with a genetic immunity to an undisclosed plague. Corvin's fifth-century ancestor, Alexander Corvinus (Derek Jacobi), developed the immunity after his village was wiped out and was described as a Hungarian warlord who was effectively the first true immortal.

Vlad Dracula replaced the boyars he disposed of with personal choices from the lower classes in a clever and efficient effort to ensure loyalty. For these recently endowed boyars, any attempt to replace their new monarch with another ruler would undoubtedly mean that their questionably gained powers would be stripped away by the established nobility. Dracula's intense suspicion of the boyars of Wallachia was well-founded, and he used every means at his disposal to keep the pack at bay. He altered the makeup of his royal court to eliminate the older and more hostile boyars and replaced them with boyars of his own choosing. The established boyars were also economically tied to merchants of

German origin in Transylvania. Dracula dealt a financial blow to the aristocracy by establishing trade sanctions against the merchants and regularly raided key trade communities.

Maintaining law and order in Wallachia became a prime focus of his regime, and virtually every sentence for any crime—no matter how large or small—was death by impalement. Dracula showed no mercy for miscreants. One of the most famous legends about his intolerance illustrates his no-nonsense position. It's said that Dracula placed an ornate golden cup in the shallows of a stream near Targoviste from which passersby could freely quench their thirst. For the length of his rule the cup remained in use, but never stolen, for no one dared incur the inevitable wrath that would follow.

War with a Vengeance

The pressure on Vlad Dracula to maintain civil law in Wallachia was equaled by the continuing threat of the Ottoman Turks. Hungary's nobility raised Matthias Corvinus to the throne of the country in 1458, and one of his primary objectives was to go to war with the Turks. Dracula's hatred for his former captives knew no bounds, and after hearing of Corvinus's intentions, he assembled an army of about 20,000 and marched across the Danube River toward the Black Sea, where they attacked and pillaged town after town in a months-long campaign of terror. In response, Mehmed II, the new sultan who'd succeeded Murad, raised an enormous force, often estimated to number well over 100,000 men, to crush the Christian assault. Badly outnumbered, Dracula retreated back to Targoviste employing a "scorched earth" tactic of destroying and burning every village, town, and food supply, and poisoning the water wells along the way—including the communities of his own people.

Fear and Loathing in Transylvania

Dracula retreated to Targoviste with the Ottoman Turks in hot pursuit, but what the Turks found on the outskirts of the city cemented Dracula's reputation for cruel vengeance. According to Greek historian Laonicus Chalkondyles, Mehmed and his troops came upon a field of impaled Turkish prisoners nearly one-half mile wide and two miles long that numbered over 20,000 victims, including women and babies skewered together. The stunned sultan and his horrified army surveyed the hideous carnage, after which Mehmed exclaimed that he could *never* conquer the land of a man who would do such things.

Fangtastic Folklore Some historians and psychologists have suggested that part of Vlad Dracula's interest in impalement as a means of torture and execution was rooted in his younger brother, Radu the Handsome, having been the popular recipient of homosexual advances in the Ottoman-Turkish court. The truth of that conjecture will forever remain a mystery, but it's likely Sigmund Freud would probably approve of the speculation.

With Dracula virtually at their fingertips, the Turks withdrew—but they were hardly finished with the man who had created such a shocking spectacle. Mehmed's response was to leave part of his army under the command of Vlad Dracula's brother, Radu the Handsome. With the aid of seditious Wallachian boyars and their forces, Radu chased his brother to his remote fortification near the village of Poenari. (See Chapter 6.) Under siege and on the run, Vlad made a narrow escape into Transylvania where he was taken prisoner, not by the Turks, but much to his surprise by his former ally, Matthias Corvinus. As Radu assumed control of Wallachia, it appears that Corvinus had seen the short-term political simplicity of letting it be so. Dracula was stripped of his authority and held captive for two years.

Rebirth and Sudden Death

During Vlad Dracula's incarceration, Radu the Handsome died from syphilis, and the throne of Wallachia was taken by Bassarab the Elder, another vassal of the Ottoman Empire. Dracula himself had gained a level of trust with Matthias Corvinus, and after converting to Catholicism was encouraged to marry into the Corvinus family. With his conversion, Dracula was given command of a contingent of troops in 1475 and went once again to war with the Turks—and to retake the crown of Wallachia. The following year, Dracula drove Bassarab from the throne and regained the position that he'd struggled to achieve for so many years. In power for only a month, Dracula was again besieged by a new Turkish force led by the deposed Bassarab. In December of 1476, Dracula was finally killed. Accounts vary as to the circumstances of his death, but it's likely that he was killed in battle near Bucharest. There is documentation that Dracula's head was removed and sent to Istanbul preserved in a jar of honey. There, Mehmed ironically placed Dracula's head on a stake as the final trophy in a long and bitter battle for domination.

HERO OR HERETIC?

Vlad Dracula's legendary status as a real-life monster takes on several incarnations, depending on who's telling the story. In much of Romanian folklore, Dracula was a patriot and hero who fought and died in his attempts to protect his homeland from Ottoman-Turkish invasions. Even his harsh and unrelenting treatment of criminals and his ruthless death sentences are put into the historical context of a man who tried to correct the inherently corrupt system of the ruling boyars. From the German perspective, Dracula was vilified in lore and literature as a monster of inconceivable proportions. It's likely that most of the atrocities attributed to Vlad Dracula were either wildly exaggerated or simply invented as propaganda. One of the most retold stories about Dracula's horrors relates that he impaled over 500 German merchants during a raid in Transylvania. On the flipside of the same story, a contemporary account of his action put the number at forty-one. Nevertheless, although there's a big difference in the numbers, even the unembellished figure would still present a horrific picture.

Few authentically accurate historical documents exist of Vlad Dracula's life, but there's little doubt that he was fueled by savage revenge, a lust for power, and the determination to spill the blood of every one of his enemies. As the namesake of Bram Stoker's famous novel and the legend that followed, neither history nor fiction could have provided a more perfect candidate than Vlad Dracula. In the next chapter, we take a closer look at the fact and fiction of the infamous Romanian leader and the search for the real Castle Dracula.

CHAPTER 6

In Search of Dracula

In the previous chapters, we learned of the remarkable history of Vlad the Impaler, legendary author Bram Stoker, and the characters who comprise one of the most famous novels in history. Now it's time to take a closer look at the fact and fiction of Dracula as well as examine the faraway lands that Dracula purportedly hails from. Both topics have, over the century, been the subject of great debate. Was Vlad Dracula a hero or a horror? Was he really a vampire? And where exactly *is* the legendary Castle Dracula?

FIENDISH FACTS AND FABRICATIONS

Imagine for a moment what it would be like knowing that your country is saddled with most of the civilized world believing that its most famous resident is also the most nefarious renowned vampire in history. What most of us are likely unaware of is that to the people of his homeland in Romania, the legacy of Vlad Dracula is generally considered to be symbolic of national pride and patriotism. Although Dracula was a harsh and unforgiving monarch, he vented most of his wrath on the enemies of his principality of Wallachia, as well as the richest and most dominant nobles in the country. Traditional wealth and influence was treated with utter disdain and contempt by the unorthodox prince, and he despised the traditional corruptions of commerce and power that bled his beloved homeland dry.

Fangtastic Folklore

During Vlad Dracula's relatively brief rule that totaled only seven years, he abolished the economic privilege and power of the German merchants in Transylvania, whose stranglehold on trade and merchandise from the more industrialized western countries of Europe prospered there, primarily because Transylvania was a far more compliant vassal state of the Hungarian Empire.

Eliminating criminal behavior of any sort was also a primary objective of Vlad Dracula, who hated corruption in any form or perpetrated by anyone—be they petty thieves and pickpockets or wealthy noblemen with their own legacies of political and economic power in Wallachia. Dracula treated malefactors with the his consistent and universal death sentence of impalement, no matter whose life was—quite literally—at stake. Many of the legends that followed him through the centuries support the conclusion that his efforts were feared, respected, and effective. For his brief reign, Wallachia experienced less criminal behavior than any other principality in eastern Europe.

There's also the valid counterpoint that Vlad Dracula may have been a cruel and despotic ruler, just as were so many rulers of the medieval era who followed traditional patterns of abusing their power in order to maintain complete authority. Some of the legends of Vlad Dracula suggest that he had little respect for any life other than those who loyally supported his desire for total control. Still, it can be argued that Dracula had clear-minded political and idealistic opinions of how his country should be run in the midst of the voracious opposing powers on the doorstep of every border. The extreme measures that Dracula employed to establish his dominance over Wallachia made him a figure of fear and a fair target as the instigator of a litany of legendary atrocities.

Was Vlad Dracula Really a Vampire?

Through the magic of fictional literature and cinema, Vlad Dracula and his legacy, along with his association to Transylvania, are inextricably linked in the Western world to the fictional Dracula and vampirism. From the publication of *Dracula* in 1897, to modern times, Romanians have made about as much sense out of this connection—and have been just as offended—as Americans would be if we were to discover that according to foreign legends, George Washington was the origination of Bigfoot, resulting in camera-toting tourists showing up in droves demanding to search for the lair of the hairy beast at Mt. Rushmore.

Despite Vlad Dracula's alleged cruelties, it must be said that there's no evidence or suggestion in Romanian history or lore that equates Dracula's life or death with vampirism. Even the Ottomans, who hated Vlad with a fierce passion, never suggested that "the Impaler" was one of the undead. They loathed and despised him enough in life, and were more than a little relieved to have taken his head as a trophy, thereby bringing a permanent cessation to his unbridled hatred and harassment of them in their endeavors to control the fate and fortunes of his homeland.

The Name Blame

An interesting anomaly concerning references to the historic Wallachian ruler is that Romanians invariably detest the name Vlad "Dracula," primarily because of the association between him and the vampire of Bram Stoker's novel. In Romania, the preferred name is *Vlad Tepes*, or even the English translation of Vlad the Impaler, despite the probability that their historical sworn enemy, the Ottoman-Turkish Empire, had endowed him with the title. To modern Romanians, the transformation of Vlad Dracula into a vicious vampire by Stoker bears an offensive similarity to the slanderous stories of their national hero by the Ottomans and Germans hundreds of years ago and is simply reminiscent of legends that vilified a cherished champion of Wallachian and, ultimately, Romanian independence.

VAMPIRE BITE

Some historians suggest that Vlad Dracula, who would become better known as Vlad the Impaler, or in Romanian terms as *Vlad Tepes* (Tse-pesh), actually derived the "Impaler" sobriquet from the Ottoman nickname for the Wallachian ruler. Because of the horrors Dracula inflicted on his enemies by impaling them on poles and planting them into the ground, the Ottomans began referring to their archenemy as *Kasiklu Bey*, or "the Impaling Prince."

The Power of the Pawn

That Wallachia and Transylvania were treated as puppet states and mere pawns in the battle for supremacy between the Ottomans and the Christian states is of little doubt. Given the fact that Wallachia was a fraction of the sizes and populations of the Hungarian Empire and the Ottoman Empire, Vlad Dracula was able to assemble an army of many thousands, most of whom were untrained peasants who obviously believed in the sovereignty of their homeland. On more than one occasion, the relatively tiny forces of Wallachia faced down the incredible strength of two of the most powerful empires in all of Europe thereby giving them a reputation as a fiercely independent and stubborn foe. Because of his exploits and conviction in the face of overwhelming odds, Vlad Dracula earned a well-deserved respect in eastern European history. Given the odds against "the Impaler," it's more than a little surprising that Wallachia and Transylvania weren't completely engulfed by outside forces of much greater strength.

From a military perspective, Vlad Dracula was an innovator of psychological warfare in stifling Mehmed II's Ottoman intention to stamp out Wallachian rule. His extreme measure of impaling thousands of Ottoman prisoners effectively convinced the sultan that he was dealing with not only a man, but an entire people who were loath to make concessions in any conflict and against any antagonist. Those tactics not only broke the will of the Ottomans to overrun his country, but gave the rest of Europe the conviction to stand against the growing Ottoman territorial expansion. Although Dracula ultimately met his demise toward the end of the Ottoman campaign against him, the main invasion force of the Ottoman's left Wallachia unoccupied by their vast armies, and they effectively abandoned the concept of sucking the principality into the Ottoman Empire.

DRACULA UNDER FIRE

The relationship between Vlad Dracula and Bram Stoker's vampire was solidified in 1972 by the publication of *In Search of Dracula*, written by Raymond McNally and Radu Florescu, two respected history professors at Boston College in Massachusetts. McNally and Florescu's work has been a staple of Dracula aficionados for over thirty-five years and continues to influence the perceptions of both scholastic authorities and casual researchers alike. Since the book first came out, both authors have revised their early findings and perhaps softened what at first appeared to be conclusive evidence that Stoker based the vampire Dracula directly on the legends of Vlad Dracula. There's no question that the pair of historical detectives changed public perception of Dracula's heritage and conception, and brought the real Vlad Dracula into the light of public interest and scrutiny.

The Flicker of Controversy

McNally and Florescu were hardly the first researchers to make a link between the two Draculas. Very likely, the first scholar to make that connection was University of West Virginia professor, Bacil F. Kirtley, in 1956. A renowned anthropologist, folklorist, and historian, Kirtley wrote a seminal essay describing one of the earliest chronicles of Vlad Dracula, found in the Kirril-Belozersk monastery (now spelled, Kirillo-Belozersky) in northern Russia. Dated to 1490, the essay is a copy of the original chronicle penned by Russian Orthodox monks in 1486—just ten years after Vlad Dracula's death. This historical document is known to have been copied and circulated widely among eastern European monasteries and eventually made its way into Germany. It appears to be the primary source of many of the horrific legends—often repeated as fact—that have dogged Vlad Dracula throughout the centuries. Along with Kirtley's early studies in 1956, Florescu and McNally were in part inspired by the 1962 publication of Stoker's first biographer, Harry Ludlum, who made the same connection in his long out-of-print book *A Biography of Dracula: The Life Story of Bram Stoker.*

Fangtastic Folklore

Bram Stoker discovered the book *An Account of the Principalities of Wallachia and Moldavia*, from which he took the name, "Dracula," at the library in Whitby, England. A small fishing village on the Esk River near the North Sea, Whitby became a favorite vacation retreat during the years Stoker worked on his famous novel. The ruins of an ancient stone abbey with its towering facades, and St. Mary's Cathedral—which both loom over the town—are believed to have helped inspire Stoker's vivid architectural descriptions.

HE DID WHAT?

As with all legendary leaders and politicos of any era, there comes a rash of outrageous tales meant to enhance or undermine an individual's reputation. Vlad Dracula is no exception to that rule. The 1486 Russian chronicles of Vlad Dracula's various exploits and atrocities have been a staple of Dracula "facts." At their best, these legends are generally considered to be gross exaggerations of actual occurrences, and at their worst, they're outright fabrications. Nevertheless, they're very much a part of the story of Vlad Dracula, if only because they describe the intense fear and grudging respect afforded the famous Wallachian ruler by his enemies. Intriguing in their very telling, all of these so-called Vlad Dracula "facts" have been revised and elaborately embellished throughout the centuries:

✝ Turkish ambassadors sent to negotiate with Dracula failed to remove their fezzes in his presence, claiming that this was not their custom. In response, Dracula had their caps nailed to their heads.

✝ Dracula is said to have summoned the poor, aged, and sick of his homeland to a feast inside a large hall. After asking his guests if they wished to be freed from all earthly cares, Dracula had the building burned down around them.

✝ Two Hungarian monks visited Dracula to beg for alms. Separately, Dracula showed them a number of criminals impaled upon stakes. When he asked if he'd behaved correctly with his executions, one said "no." The other said that a ruler was ordained by God to punish the wicked and reward the righteous. Dracula had the first monk impaled, and gave fifty gold ducats to the second.

✝ A merchant had 160 gold ducats stolen from his cart and appealed to Dracula for justice. Dracula assured the merchant that he would find the stolen money within one night. The next day Dracula caught the thief and returned the merchant's money to him, with the addition of a single ducat. The merchant counted the money and returned the excess, after which Dracula told him that had he not displayed such honesty, Dracula would have impaled him along with the thief.

✝ A peasant attending one of Dracula's feasts had the audacity to hold his nose at the stench of corpses in the courtyards. Dracula had him impaled to elevate him *above* the odor.

✝ After King Matthias of Hungary captured Dracula and imprisoned him, Dracula whiled away his time by catching mice and impaling them on sticks, and plucking the feathers from live birds.

Objective Origins

Of all the scholars to take on the quest for the origins of Bram Stoker's *Dracula*, none have approached the subject with as much academic and intellectual zeal as Professor Elizabeth Miller of the University of

Newfoundland in Canada. In Miller's quest for Stoker's inspiration, she has relied on Stoker's book notes as the only reliable factual evidence of his approach to the invention of the world's most famous vampire. The gist of Miller's conclusions is that Stoker undoubtedly appropriated the name "Dracula" from William Wilkerson's book *An Account of the Principalities of Wallachia and Moldavia*. Stoker's notes refer to the book, which Stoker had borrowed from the Whitby Library in northern England, and from which he copied a footnote describing (incorrectly) the term "Dracula" as being Wallachian for "devil." Other than that, there's no evidence that Stoker knew the names "Vlad Tepes" or "Vlad the Impaler," nor is it anywhere apparent that Stoker was aware of the many legends that had been attributed to Vlad Dracula so many centuries earlier.

As Miller points out in her works, the argument is often made that Stoker's description in *Dracula* of the madman, Renfield, and his obsession with taking the lives of flies, spiders, and birds was adapted from a Vlad Dracula legend. The unlikely tale relates that Vlad passed time by torturing and impaling mice and birds on sticks while he was incarcerated by Matthias Corvinus in Hungary in 1462. That association is tenuous conjecture at best, particularly given that Renfield didn't impale his tiny victims—he ate them raw.

Hungarian Homage

Another argument offered by several *Dracula* researchers is Van Helsing's coy reference in Chapter Eighteen of the novel to a colleague named "Arminius." The mention comes after the group resolves to destroy Dracula and pays heed to Van Helsing's telling of the fiend's history:

> "Thus when we find the habitation of this man-that-was, we
> can confine him to his coffin and destroy him, if we obey
> what we know. But he is clever. I have asked my friend Armin-
> ius, of Buda-Pesth University, to make his record, and from
> all the means that are, he tell me of what he has been. He
> must, indeed, have been that Voivode Dracula who won
> his name against the Turk, over the great river on the very

frontier of Turkey-land. If it be so, then was he no common man, for in that time, and for centuries after, he was spoken of as the cleverest and the most cunning, as well as the bravest of the sons of the 'land beyond the forest.'"

What some experts surmise is that Van Helsing's so-called Dracula expert is a tribute to suggestions made by Arminius Vambery, a noted Hungarian and Ottoman historian and linguist who Bram Stoker knew socially (see Chapter 4). The probability certainly exists that Stoker's "Arminius" may well have been an homage to the real-life Vambery, who had the perfect name and background for a fictional characterization, but the sticking point in the theory is that none of Stoker's notes refer to Vambery, nor to *Vlad Tepes* or "the Impaler," as Vambery would likely have known him.

In much of the research literature surrounding Vlad Dracula, the term *voivode* is often used to describe his position as the ruler of Wallachia. The word was originally meant to describe the leaders of military forces in Slavic countries and gradually came into common usage to denote the rulers or princes of principalities in much of eastern Europe.

Unintentional Infamy

The brutal life and audacious exploits of Wallachia's Vlad Dracula are unquestionably worthy of the scores of manuscripts devoted to him over the years and have provided a springboard to countless hair-raising narrations in film and fiction in the world of vampirish horrors. Despite Vlad Dracula's relatively recent contributions to vampire legend in regard to intense study, it's likely that his sole influence on Bram Stoker's vampire was a fortuitous and unforgettably perfect name for the world's most frightening creature of the night—Dracula.

SURVEYING THE LANDSCAPE

Bram Stoker's choice of Transylvania as the site for the origination of his vampiric creation is a timeless blending of geographical reality into fanciful literature. Even the name of the principality, "Transylvania," is so simultaneously eerie and purely poetic, it's inconceivable that any fictional novelist could have possibly concocted a more enduring location. It's arguable that as well known as the character of Dracula is, his homeland has easily achieved the same ageless international recognition, and certainly holds as much spine-chilling mystique. Bram Stoker's descriptions of the countryside of Transylvania were deadly accurate, with its surreal and densely carpeted forests, sinister bogs fading into the mist, and ethereal mountain ranges that stretch into infinity and then, without warning, materialize menacingly to absorb the wayward traveler into their unfathomable chasms.

Fangtastic Folklore

Despite Stoker's apparent grasp of the landscape and mystery of his leading villain's homeland, it's known that he never set foot on Transylvanian soil, or any other part of the Balkan region. Stoker gleaned virtually every bit of his knowledge of Transylvania from travel guides and geography books found in London libraries and at the British Museum.

Where the Heck *Is* Transylvania?

The principality of Transylvania is situated in what is now central Romania, with Wallachia located on its southern borders through which run the Carpathian Mountains. On its western edge, also bordered by the Carpathians, is modern Moldova (Moldavia), through which the Ottomans often conducted military raids. The eastern border was the post of Vlad Dracula's father, Vlad Dracul, where he was charged with protecting the vital economic resources of Transylvania from Ottoman incursions. During the twelfth century, German Saxon merchants were invited by the Hungarian Empire to settle in the sparsely populated region, both to ply their trades and to help defend Hungarian dominion. The Germans prospered in Transylvania and developed commercial strangleholds on trade across the Carpathians and into Wallachia—an economic superiority for which the younger Vlad Dracula had little respect and which ignited his nationalistic fury.

The Carpathians and Borgo Pass

The descriptions of Transylvania presented by Stoker in *Dracula* would have meant little without his inclusion of the forbidding Carpathian Mountains on the borders of Transylvania. Running through central and eastern Europe for over 600 miles, the Carpathians are the largest mountain chain in Europe, and—fortunately for the apprehensive tone of Stoker's novel—are also home to the largest populations of bears, lynx, and of course, wolves in all of Europe's wild habitats. The mystique of *Dracula* was exponentially enhanced by Stoker's enduring reference to the Borgo Pass, which is where Jonathan Harker encounters the menacing blue flames and howling wolves and over which Dracula's pursuers travel to bring him to a ghastly end. Historically, the Borgo Pass, known in Romania as the Tihuta Pass, has long served to connect Transylvania to the eastern route through the Carpathians to Moldova and on to the Black Sea.

The Real Castle Dracula

The international popularity of Dracula and the character's association with Vlad Dracula led to an inevitable public demand to visit the legendary homeland of the world's supreme nightcrawler, and in particular to tour the vampire's spooky castle. Of course, the fictional Dracula's castle near the Borgo Pass is just that—a figment of Stoker's imagination. Located in central Wallachia, the Poenari Castle near the Arges River is considered to be the primary stronghold to have been fortified and used by Vlad Dracula in the 1400s (see Chapter 5).

Located in a remote region and virtually inaccessible, Poenari Castle lies in ruins at the top of a forbidding abutment. The "castle" can be more accurately described as a small fortress and wasn't large enough to house more than 100 troops for any length of time. Vlad Dracula was known to have escaped to Poenari to avoid invasions, but it was primarily a military outpost and was never designed as a residence. The Wallachian capitol city of Targoviste was the historical center of monarchy for Vlad Dracula, and for a brief time during the end of his short reign, Dracula resided at the court in Bucharest.

Fangtastic Folklore

The Romanian tourist industry has made a thriving cottage industry out of passing off Bran Castle located in the community of Bran, Romania, as Castle Dracula, because it's readily accessible and offers tours, and it has a place in Romanian history as most recently having served as the summer home of Romania's beloved Queen Marie. It's said the castle is currently up for sale.

BITE ME!

Now that we've captured the rich history of Dracula—both true and imagined—it's time to get down to the basics of vampires and vampirism, including their creation, the symbolism of blood and their quest to obtain it, and that naughty little habit they have of mesmerizing us, among other things, so we bend to their every whim.

CHAPTER 7

VAMPIRES UNBOUND

Amid *Le monde merveilleux des vampires*, or *the wonderful world of vampires*, there exists a modicum of fact buried amid an amalgam of folklore, historical accounts, fiction, and film. To comprehend the core elements of a creature of the damned, one must study the elements of a vampire's making; its thirst for blood and how it's acquired; the tools—such as fear and hypnosis—the fiend employs to create an environment that's secure; and how the creature assures loyal servitude to ease its assimilation into society.

How Vampires Are Created

The most obvious answer to the question of how vampires are created is that they become a member of the undead by being bitten by another vampire. Right? While in the majority of cases that may hold true, a vampire's making is infinitely more complicated than that, with many varieties of transformation put into effect depending on the type of vampire and whether the demon is a beast of legend, mythology, literature, or film. Some outer space suckers, for example, vampirize a human's energy by mouth-to-mouth contact rather than biting. It must be noted that the term "vampire" wasn't typically used in folklore but was said to have first appeared in English references in the late 1600s. Renowned author Katherine Ramsland notes that an explanation of vampires as "reanimated corpses" appeared in 1810, in *Travels of Three English Gentlemen from Venice to Hamburg, Being the Grand Tour of Germany in the Year 1734*.

Throughout folklore there are many varied references to the ways in which an individual could become a vampire. In Chapter 2, we make mention of potential candidates for becoming the undead, including children born out of wedlock, those who lead sinful or criminal lives or commit suicide, women who allow vampires to gaze upon them, and even the seventh son of a seventh son. But that's just the tip of the iceberg. Depending on the culture and its superstitions and beliefs, vampires might also be those who are born with teeth or who, like witches, possess a third nipple. Individuals who are not baptized or who are born on holy days are also at risk, as are those who practice black magic or die violently.

No Drain, No Gain

If you happen to be the obsession of a typical drawing room bloodsucker, then chances are you're intended to become his bride or partner rather than his blue-plate special, in which case said vampire would technically become your *maker*, or *parent*. One thing that most vampires have to learn is how much blood to take from a victim. Taken in small doses, a victim can sustain a vampire's bite for quite some time before either dying or, should the vampire chose, enter the world of the undead. The act of consuming blood is for the vampire a matter of restraint, as the action generally triggers sexual arousal and a frenzy that if not carefully controlled usually kills the victim.

Depending on the type of vampire, *bringing* or *crossing over* a victim, that is to say making them a vampire, can trigger various actions. Some vampires gain the memories of their maker; others are left to discover their newfound powers and bloodlust for themselves. In Anne Rice's *Interview with the Vampire*, Louis tells of his making by Lestat's hand in 1791, describing being "weak to paralysis," complete panic, and the inability to speak. This was punctuated by the foreplay of the act: ". . . the movement of his lips raised the hair all over my body, sent a shock of sensation through my body that was not unlike the pleasure of passion." Once initiated with Lestat's blood, Louis roamed free to see the intensity of the world for the first time with preternatural eyes.

Night of the Living Dead

As we've learned, the majority of vampires of folklore aren't the pristine, white-skinned, radiant preternaturals created by Anne Rice. As a collective, most are reconstituted corpses in various states of disarray and decay. All measure of humanity, from plague victims to nobles to ordinary farmers, have been exhumed and burnt to a crisp in order to expunge their alleged vampirism and keep them from feeding on the living. Which is to say that given the lack of understanding of decomposition, many of those poor souls were unjustly convicted of being in league with the undead. In the case of Arnod Paole and the Medvegia Vampires, some of his victims weren't even attacked by Paole. They'd fallen victim to the fact that they'd consumed cattle that Paole had allegedly vampirised (see Chapter 11).

THE FEAR FACTOR

As a species that's trained to fear all things that go bump in the night, it would seem obvious that, to humans, a vampire would prove to be anyone's worst nightmare. Fear is a powerful proponent within the human psyche, one that—like a vampire—feeds off our imagination and lays patiently in wait in the dark corners of our minds like so many sordid demons trapped behind the gates of hell. Vampires thrive on fear and the power they have in controlling it through hypnosis, seduction, or any physical means necessary (see Chapters 9 and 10).

Given that the vampiric creatures of lore were often insipid and hideous beasts, it's easy to see why the mere thought of them instantly elicits fear. Vampires in literature approach the aspect of fear with carefully measured words meant to evoke specific imagery and emotional reactions. Silver screen vampires have arguably given us the most nightmares in that regard. To actually see a vampire encircle its prey in a frenzied attack or enact a slow, macabre courtship, then ultimately watch as its fangs pierce through exposed skin, leaves a lasting impression both literally and figuratively. Among the many swirling tales of vampirism there are several major factors that play into the terrifying grip these malfeasants have on our psyche, including, among other things, plagues and epidemics.

EPIDEMIC PROPORTION

Throughout history mankind has been burdened by all measure of incidents deemed epidemic, be it a loss of livestock, crops, accidents, uncontrollable weather, unexplainable deaths, insane behavior, and, of course, various forms of plague. For all of those occurrences there's typically a need for blame to be placed and retribution taken. In areas of the world where superstition or strict religious adherence is the law of the land, this approach has been historically prevalent. When plagues strike, the inevitable ensuing hysteria quite often includes accusations of paranormal or supernatural occurrences in order to explain the spreading sickness, or alternately, that the sickness itself causes vampirism. For example, the very stench of the dying was often considered what we in the modern-era term an airborne illness. To ward off the stink and alternately repel evil demons, people would surround themselves with pungent odors such as garlic, juniper, incense, perfumes, animal manure, and even human feces (see Chapter 10).

Vampires, witches, werewolves, and all types of mythological creatures were easily blamed for epidemics, as were outcasts of society, and even children, pregnant women, midwives—practically anyone who by today's standards would in some areas be considered out of society's norms. Naturopaths or other types of medicinal healers, or anyone who lived on what was then considered to be the fringe of society, often fell under suspicion. Likewise, any stranger who had the misfortune of arriving in a village around the same time people became ill would be highly suspect. In ancient times, folkloric creatures were easy to blame, for example, the Indian *bhuta* (see Chapter 2), malevolent spirits who feed on the living and dead and who appear as mist or lights, or the Ashanti *obayifo*, a West African vampire who sucks the blood of children as well as life out of crops. And lest we forget, many epidemics were believed to be brought upon mankind as a punishment from God.

SCREEN SCREAM

The bubonic plague, which is said to have begun in Asia in the 1340s and quickly spread to Europe by 1347, is speculated to have wiped out one-third of the population. Commonly called the Black Death or Black Plague for the dark swelling of glands as a result of the sickness, it is in some respects considered a form of vampirism, a fact that many science fiction vampire writers and filmmakers have taken advantage of, for example Richard Matheson's novel turrned film *I Am Legend* or the 2006 film *Ultraviolet*.

During the plagues of the Middle Ages, whether they were bubonic (transmitted by the fleas from rodents), septicemic (blood poisoning), or pneumonic (lung related and therefore airborne), the undead were among those highly suspect in initiating the illness or becoming undead as a result of it. Under such circumstances, steps would be taken to identify the culprit (the earliest infected individual) and stake or burn the corpse, or both, along with various measures taken to spread the ashes in rivers or consecrated grounds. What could also contribute to vampiric hysteria is the way in which plague victims were buried: in mass graves, shrouded, without coffins, and some even prematurely. Suffice to say, whatever the illness, be it widespread or localized, it was easy to blame it on a vampire.

BLOOD IS THE LIFE

In Chapter Eleven of Stoker's *Dracula*, Dr. Seward tells of his altercation with Renfield, who after attacking Seward with a knife and cutting Seward's wrist, licked the blood from the floor and began repeating over and over: "The blood is the life! The blood is the life!" An oft-used phrase in vampiric film and literature, "the blood is the life" is indeed a concept intrinsically linked to the vampire realm on all accounts, from folklore to modern society. Blood *is* what keeps us functioning. It's the elixir common to all mammalian life forms—one that's cherished, sought after, sworn by, studied, shed, exploited, diseased, spilled, and donated, ultimately revered for its ability to rejuvenate both in a spiritual and physical capacity. Blood is unique in that it can be offered on many levels: as sacrifice, in absolution, revenge, or in exchange for saving a life or alternately used to take a life. Blood has a rich history that has evolved from our earliest beginnings and continues to flow in all types of creative ways. What must also be stated before embarking on the symbolism of blood is the fact that a contigent of vampires are not intent on sucking blood but crave psychic or spiritual energy. An individual's life force, spiritual energy, and soul are all equally enticing to a sucker, depending of course on the type of creature he or she is (see Chapter 19).

Historic Symbolism

The symbol of blood in all realms, be it spiritual, physical, scientific, religious, supernatural, or metaphorical, has been immortalized and analyzed since the dawn of man. For starters, there are endless accounts and legends of blood rituals and sacrifices throughout history from the early pagan beliefs in eastern Europe to the ancient Mayan civilization to centuries of warriors, tribes, practitioners of magic, serial killers, and scientists done in the name of progress, religion, or any number of causes or beliefs. Warriors, for example, have been known to ingest the blood of their enemies in order to increase their own strength. Likewise, in the modern era, the Masai warrior tribe of Kenya exsanguinate blood from the jugular of their cows and consume the blood with milk in the belief that it will give them extra strength.

Many deities are also associated with blood in regard to practices and sacrifice. The Egyptian goddess Sekhmet, whose name translates to that of "mighty or powerful one," is a woman bearing a lion's head. According to legend, Sekhmet became the punisher of men, breathing fire and killing relentlessly, and nearly wiping out humanity with her bloodlust. She is closely associated with the color red. India's goddess Kali (literally translated to mean "black" or "the black one") is the Hindu goddess of destruction and death and the overseer of plagues and annihilation among other things. A woman possessing four arms, Kali is often depicted as having fangs or a protruding tongue and ominously sports a garland comprised of corpses or skulls. Her legendary battle with the demonic Raktabija, during which she speared him and drank his blood, contributes to her vampiric reputation. Worshippers of Kali often sacrifice goats in her name.

Perhaps the best-known manifestation of metaphorical blood is wine in relation to the blood of Christ. This particular aspect of blood symbolism is arguably the most relevant when it comes to vampires, given the underlying subtext of the vampire as the devil; its practice of usurping blood, which is equated to life; and its typical aversions to holy artifacts like the crucifix, holy water, churches, consecrated ground, and the Eucharist wafer, which is symbolic of Christ's body (see Chapter 9). The blood representation that Bram Stoker used in *Dracula* is evidence that he likely intended to link its meaning to biblical sources, and many authors over the decades have followed his lead. The phrase "the blood is the life" is from Deuteronomy 12:23 and reads: "Only be sure that you do not eat the blood: for the blood is the life; and you may not eat the life with the flesh." As a black devil and symbolic opponent of God, Dracula in many ways uses blood as revenge against God.

Blood and Immortality

In much of history, the concept of blood as life is the ultimate physical manifestation of sustaining existence. Humans cannot survive without blood coursing through their veins. Within folklore, and especially in the vampire realm, blood is inextricably linked to mortality, and thus immortality. Deprived of blood, a traditional vampire, as well as many other types, would likely starve. This fact alone accounts for their predatory nature and plays to the vampiric creatures of folklore, many of whom—like the Greek *lamia*, Indonesian *pontianak*, Indian *rakshasa*, Ashanti *obayifo*, Malaysian *langsuyar*, and Romanian *striga*—prey upon children, women, and pregnant women, perhaps out of revenge, pure survival, or in an effort to gain eternal youth and vitality (see Chapter 2). This mythology could relate to another strong symbol in the vampiric blood realm, that of menstruation, an event that would serve as a double enticement to a vampire by furthering its underlying sexual conquest.

Fangtastic Folklore

Given the obvious complications of obtaining genuine human blood, modern-day practitioners of vampirism find other ways of maintaining their hemodynamic dietary requirements. Always looking for ways to replicate the consistency of real blood, they often use tomato juice as a base, adding to it any number of pulpy ingredients such as orange juice to act as clotting agents whereby they can satisfy their immortal "thirst."

Individuals suffering an attack from a vampiric creature typically endure several fates. In many instances, enough blood is sucked by the creature as to cause its victim to perish. Still others lose a substantial amount of blood and develop a prolonged illness that eventually ends in death. At its worst, victims of vampires have enough blood drained from them that they are turned into one of the undead. In literary and cinematic traditions, the ever-present aspect of vampirism as a twisted fountain of youth is often employed by vampires in an effort to assure their victims that immortality is a gift rather than a curse. Such is the case with Miriam Blaylock, Whitley Strieber's vampire protagonist in *The Hunger* (see Chapter 15). In Chapter 8, we delve into the characteristics of the vampire, but there is one trait that arguably stands above the rest in regard to the overall persona of the bloodsucker and its relation to the procuring of blood. Therefore, we introduce here a discussion of hypnosis and the way in which a vampire uses mesmerization to his or her best advantage.

THE POWER OF HYPNOSIS

One of the more insidious and most discussed characteristics of vampires is their ability to hypnotize their victims and even create a telepathic bond. More often than not, the transfixed gaze of a vampire results in the victim's full cooperation in surrendering freely and fully to the fiend's formidable dark gift. In truth, it's a clever tactic and animalistic in its execution. Interestingly, vampire bats impose a similar poise as part of their attack procedure. With the ability to walk upright, a vampire bat stalks its prey, mesmerizes it, and then heads for the nearest vein in order to pierce it and use its elongated tongue to lap up the blood. A vampire's hypnotic abilities cater perfectly to the strong sexual aspect of vampirism. Biting someone is a very intimate act, and compounded by the removal of blood in a commingling of fluids it is reminiscent of the sexual act itself. Of course, mesmerizing victims to perform acts against their will—regardless of their perceived cooperation—plays to the sexual deviancy of the vampire and vampirism in general.

 **VAMPIRE BITE** A threshold, meaning the bottom of a doorway or entrance, holds significance to vampires. In general, a bloodsucker is not allowed to cross a threshold unless invited to do so. Of course, once you've invited the devil inside your domicile, your life is in peril, as the black devil can do as he pleases.

Take Me to Your Bleeder

The greatest benefit of vampiric hypnosis is the most obvious—if you can will another to do you bidding, your ability to ultimately satisfy your sexual arousal or simply procure your food becomes infinitely easier. A compliant victim under a vampire's spell typically offers little resistance when the fiend moves to suck the life from the victim. This type of control also makes it easier for a vampire to move about society, travel, maintain living arrangements, and generally obtain whatever it is that he or she requires with minimal effort.

Mind Over Matter

The process of mesmerizing an individual first came to prominence with Franz Anton Mesmer during the late 1700s. When Bram Stoker wrote *Dracula*, the "science" of hypnotism would've been known to him, and as such he made good use of it in his novel. Many experts attribute the vampire's hypnotic ability to Stoker's creation, where it appeared on several occasions, the first of which Jonathan Harker discovered when attempting to strike the sleeping Count with a shovel and was hypnotically driven to flee. Lucy also falls victim to Dracula's remote telepathy as he bids her awake and to walk out into the dark night. During the scene in which Dracula baptizes Mina with the blood from his chest, Van Helsing declares that: "Jonathan is in a stupor such as we know the Vampire can produce." But it's Mina who's ultimately the one who establishes a mind link to the dark devil, a fact that's confirmed after Van Helsing hypnotizes Mina and learns through their telepathic link that Dracula is aboard a ship sailing for home for Transylvania.

Establishing a Lair

Part of being a successful vampire requires a well-honed survival instinct, and where residence is concerned, the same principles that apply to humans apply to vampires: location, location, location. That, and trusted servants, proper lodging that traditionally includes native soil stuffed in a comfy coffin or crate, and a top-of-the-line security system that would make Fort Knox seem like a Circle K. Of course, that elaborate setup is for the more affluent bloodsucker. For the average vampire, one who's always on the move (or in case of emergency) a decrepit old crypt, mausoleum, cemetery, or abandoned building would surely do. In the television series *Forever Knight*, for example, detective Nick Knight made ample use of the trunk of his car if the coming dawn found him far from home.

Servants and Security

By their very nature, vampires require a certain measure of privacy and security. Being in possession of a creepy remote castle is obviously ideal, or in the case of the modern vampire, a mansion or luxury apartment that affords easy access, maximum security, and foolproof escape routes when the pesky vampire hunters come calling. In *Dracula*, Stoker used Renfield as a tool, his lunatic persona giving valuable insight to Dracula's London pursuers. Only when the evil fiend arrives in England does Renfield begin to show servitude to the "master." In the decades that followed *Dracula's* publication, the character of Renfield has alternately been downplayed or highlighted. Quite often in cinema, it's Renfield rather than Harker who travels to Castle Dracula and becomes Dracula's servant, and the one who brings him to London on the *Demeter* (see Chapter 4).

The tricky bit with having servants who are unaware of one's vampiric condition is the necessity of cloaking the basics of normal existence, namely the lack of conventional food consumption, sleeping during daylight hours, victims being dispatched at one's home and the disposal of said victims, and the inevitable trickles of blood running down one's chin after a meal or leftovers dried on the face during sleep. Of course, much of this can be remedied by putting servants under hypnosis or, in some cases, using them as an occasional midnight snack so as to retain their zombielike state.

Now, that isn't to say that all servants and friends of a vampire are placed under the fiend's spell. Many vampires in both fiction and film have human companions who are well aware of their condition. In the case of most vampire romance novels, like Stephenie Meyer's young-adult tales, you often find human/vampire romantic connections. Meyer's Bella is a young human in love with the immortal Edward (see Chapter 13). In the aforementioned *Forever Knight*, Nick's coroner friend Natalie was in the know, and despite the fact his second partner Tracey *didn't* know, she was actually in love with one of Nick's undead compatriots and was well aware her paramour was a vampire (see Chapter 18). From a writing or filmmaking point of view, the complications and love stories that arise from having the two species intermingle makes for a more interesting storyline—one that usually ends brilliantly or very bloody.

Fast Food

A vampire's need for sustenance is both inevitable and obsessive, and like most creatures in need of food, there must be accessibility, be it the bar down the block, or in the case of a traditional bloodsucker, bleeding dry the inhabitants of a nearby village, town, or city where those feasted upon are unlikely to be missed. In folklore, many of the creatures, such as the Indian *bhuta*, feed on corpses and therefore spend their time foraging graveyards and cremation sites. Many others, like the Greek *lamia* and other so-called birth demons, focus their undead revenge on newborn children or pregnant women (see Chapter 2). For the average vampire, meaning those who don't fall into the reluctant vampire category, blood *is* the life and must therefore be procured no matter the risk of exposure. Modern-day vampires have a much better chance of their killings going unnoticed if victims are properly chosen and disposed of. It also helps if vampire slayers and various medical personnel and detectives and the like remain blissfully unaware that an immortal bad boy or girl is on the prowl.

Fangtastic Folklore

In the majority of fictional works and film, a vampire's servants are nothing more than a vehicle for accomplishing the tasks one expects of hired help: arranging travel, monitoring security, and, in some cases, helping to lure the unwary fly to the web of a famished fiend. Travel is, of course, of grave concern to the traditional vampire as many, such as Dracula, are hindered by the confines of traveling with earth or native soil packed into a crate or coffin.

SMOOTH OPERATORS

Whether they operate independently or in clans, vampires retain their fearsome reputation largely because of the host of eccentric, evil, and superhuman characteristics they possess. In the next chapter, we discuss the traits most prized by the black devils including their manner of dress, physical transformations, powers, and the fangtastic dental work that serves to punctuate their immortal mischief.

CHAPTER 8

VAMPIRE CHARACTERISTICS

As a species, vampires are quite an extraordinary race with abilities—though basically evil in their construct—that must be admired for their efficiency, intelligence, and self-preservation. To understand vampires is to learn of their characteristics: how they appear, where they sleep, why they become one with the bat, wolf, and mist—all these peculiarities that give us a bigger picture of why vampires are the way they are. And bear in mind that while these powers may seem attractive, they may also become passé after centuries of overuse.

FANGS, COFFINS, AND HELLSPAWN HABITS

When you think of the physical appearance of a vampire, what do you see? A tall, dark stranger with a pale and pasty complexion? A long opera cloak? Slicked-back hair with a widow's peak and a rather intimidating set of canines that make your toes curl? All that we perceptibly know—or think we know—about the vampire in regard to his or her typical characteristics and powers is born of the vampiric triad of folklore, fiction, and film. The first two render a historical legacy of vampires and vampirism that, save for the occasional artistic rendering, is primarily left to our respective imaginations. The third, film, gives us a whiz-bang shot in the jugular by actually *showing* us vampires.

Everything speculated upon by historians, folklorists, scholars, vampirologists, authors, and filmmakers surrounding various legends is primarily the result of intense study, educated guesswork, and the interpretation of information gathered since the time of ancient civilizations. Film, on the other hand, gives us our most powerful picture of the vampire, the physical body, actions, and reactions more permanently embedded in both our conscious and unconscious minds. Thanks to vampiric cinema we see the fangs extending and piercing the skin, hear the wolves and rats, feel the mist, and watch the blood flow in all its crimson glory.

Vampires as a species vary depending on what one sees or reads (see Chapter 19). A characteristic that may be prevalent in film and literature, for example, may not appear in folklore and vice versa. But one thing is certain—all three of these disciplines play off one another and provide inspiration in their presentation of the vampire as a complete picture. What's commonly asserted when discussing vampiric traits is that many of them are derived from Bram Stoker. For example, the notion of sleep and resting on native soil, coffins, and transforming into mist evolve from his conception of *Dracula*. That said, it's time to examine the various characteristics of the average vampire, including its dental characteristics, sleeping preferences, various transformative talents, supernatural powers, and its sense of fashion. Given that the traditional drawing room vampire can generally pass for a human save for the pallor of its skin, it's fair to say that if vampires do exist, we'd likely remain blissfully unaware that there's a predator in our midst. Until, of course, it's too late.

Fangs

When one thinks of vampiric figures, it's quite naturally a set of frighteningly sharp pearly whites that first comes to mind. After all, from a purely functional standpoint, fangs are the mechanism by which most vampires ultimately consume their food. In the traditional sense, a vampire's fangs are sharp, elongated canine teeth, which when bared are a gruesome and intimately brutal way to achieve sustenance. At their best, fangs most obviously equate vampires to animals, in particular, wolves, rats, and snakes. At their worst, they act as an efficient mechanism for tearing apart their meals.

Symbolically, the biting of one's neck is a highly erotic act, which is in keeping with the vampire's portrayal as a sexual predator. Interestingly, fangs don't often appear among the vampires of folklore, with many of the deities and monsters using their tongues for exsanguinations. It's speculated that the concept of using fangs has some basis in regard to the crossover of vampires and werewolves and the idea of the monsters of folklore ripping into victims with their teeth.

Fangtastic Folklore	Individuals who consider themselves modern-day vampires or who engage in blood fetish practices sometimes wear fangs as part of their ritual. Still others file their teeth to emulate fangs or subject themselves to costly dental work to have implants replicating fangs. For the morbidly curious, it's unlikely that dental insurance covers that procedure.

Early films such as Bela Lugosi's *Dracula* in 1931 and even the 1922 silent film *Nosferatu* didn't show Dracula actually biting the necks of his victims. Hammer Films, on the other hand, had no issue in boldly showing Christopher Lee's dental demons. Over the decades, both literary and celluloid bloodsuckers have punctured necks with fangs of varying sizes ranging from pin pricks to holes the size of softballs. Stoker described his Dracula as having "peculiarly sharp white teeth," and later in the tale, when Lucy Westenra is first bitten, Mina describes the bite as "two little red points like pin-pricks." Indeed, they were so inconspicuous that poor Mina believed she caused the wounds with a big safety pin when securing a shawl around Lucy's neck.

In James Malcolm Rymer's 1847 penny dreadful *Varney the Vampyre*, Sir Francis Varney is described as having "fearful looking teeth—projecting like those of some wild animal, hideously, glaringly white, and fang-like." In many modern-day vampire films, the black devils retain all measure of killer fangs, with some that completely mutate and dominate their faces when bared. In *Blade II*, bloodsuckers infected with a vampire virus become "Reapers," who feed indiscriminately on both the living and the undead. With the lead vamp taking the ratlike features of Max Shreck's *Nosferatu* one step further, Reapers are quite possibly some of the most frightening and voracious vampires ever imagined—they don't just have fangs, they have multiple eel-like tongues that slither out when their chin splits apart, opening up their face to accommodate spikes within their cheeks that latch onto their victims necks and faces. Very tongue and cheek, and definitely innovative in regard to vampiric dentistry.

Fingernails

The first sign of a vampire in desperate need of a manicurist was Count Orlock in *Nosferatu*, whose demonic digits are intentionally and abnormally long and gruesome, which adds dramatically to his rodentlike appearance (see Chapters 14 and 16). Other than various B-movie bloodsuckers sporting exceptionally long and hideous nails while in their transformed states, most traditional Draculas are shown to have some measure of length to their nails, which are usually well manicured. In Chapter Two of Stoker's *Dracula*, Jonathan Harker includes in his initial description of the Count that his hands had first seemed rather "white and fine" but that upon closer inspection, "I could not but notice that they were rather course, broad, with squat fingers. Strange to say, there were hairs in the centre of the palm. The nails were long and fine, and cut to a sharp point." By contrast, Anne Rice's preternaturals have fingernails that are translucent as glass.

Bring Out Your Dead!

When it comes to burial practices there's enough information to fill an entire book, as customs and technology have evolved since cavemen roamed the planet. Early methods of burial didn't make use of coffins as we know them today. Instead, the dead were left to the elements, placed in caves, buried under rocks, set afire, or simply wrapped in a shroud and interred in shallow graves. Naturally, this left corpses vulnerable to the attack of the vampires of folklore like the Hindu *vetala*, a mythological spirit that lurks in burial grounds and takes possession of corpses. The concept of having a coffin, funerary box, or crate is generally believed to have been a logical necessity in keeping animals, or in the case of folklore, all measure of vampiric creatures, from disturbing the dead. No doubt the existence of cemeteries, mausoleums, and crematoriums evolved from this thinking as well as the basis for profit in the funeral industry.

SCREEN SCREAM

True vampire aficionados will likely never forget the eerie yet slightly comical emergence of *Nosferatu's* Count Orlock from his rat-infested, soil-filled coffin aboard the ship *Demeter*. In one swift movement, the stiffened vampire arose from his coffin—a maniacal unblinking mannequin from the bowels of hell. Since that classic silent film, the cinematic and literary vampire have both been characterized as snoozing in coffins and typically shown emerging from them with sinister fingers slowly opening the lid.

Coffins

Traditional coffins as we know them likely evolved during the 1600s in the form of boxes and later as increasingly more elaborate caskets for anyone who could afford them. As such, coffins were a common practice in the late 1900s, and the concept was of use to Bram Stoker in creating a resting place for Dracula. During Jonathan Harker's imprisonment at Castle Dracula, he happened upon fifty boxes piled atop newly dug earth, and it was in one of those boxes he discovered the sleeping Count—who didn't necessarily require a coffin per se but did need to rest amid native soil. The aspect of all future vampires needing a coffin likely arose from Stoker's initial premise. Even some practitioners of modern-day real-life vampirism prefer to sleep in coffins.

As a result of requiring such specific sleeping quarters, the vampire is also restricted to lugging a coffin around wherever he or she goes. This is evident in early vampire fiction and film. Given that it's not the easiest bed to transport, the use of a coffin is one that many modern authors and film-makers have modified, or even dropped, in their vampire sagas. Anne Rice's bloodsuckers, for example, don't need coffins (though when they use them it's more for show than substance), instead simply requiring a dark sanctuary such as a crypt, a basement, or even a place in which they can bury them-selves for up to centuries at a time when hibernating, as Lestat does from 1929 to 1984 before awakening to become a brash rock star in *The Vampire Lestat*. Likewise, Whitley Strieber's vampires in his 1981 novel *The Hunger* have no aversion to daylight, and therefore slumber comfortably in beds.

Native Soil and Sleep

When it comes to sleep, the vampire, in general, is relegated to slum-ber just like the rest of us mere mortals, which is one of a vampire's few consistent vulnerabilities. The only difference is the vampire's rest is more trancelike and affords various levels of awareness depending on whether it's a creature of folklore, fiction, or film. That awareness is often instilled so as to give the dozing fiend a method of defense in case of an unwel-come intruder. In *Dracula*, Harker's journal entry describes Dracula's sleep during Harker's incarceration at Castle Dracula:

"There, in one of the great boxes, of which there were fifty in all, on a pile of newly dug earth, lay the Count! He was either dead or asleep. I could not say which, for eyes were open and stony, but with-out the glassiness of death, and the cheeks had the warmth of life

*through all their pallor. The lips were as red as ever. But there was
no sign of movement, no pulse, no breath, no beating of the heart."*

Given that the creatures of folklore and Bram Stoker set into motion the
idea that vampires must rest between dusk and dawn, it's fair to say that it's
a practice that's endured in traditional vampire legends. The primary reason would suggest that vampires need rest in order to rejuvenate themselves
and perhaps as a peaceful respite to fully digest their liquid lunch. Following
Harker's initial discovery of the Count, he documents an attempt at hitting
Dracula with a shovel while at rest, but as the shovel is about to strike, Dracula's turns to avoid full impact. This action reinforces the concept of awareness during vampiric sleep and a certain measure of hypnosis that caused
Harker to flee the scene (see Chapter 7). The above excerpt also suggests
the alleged importance of resting on native soil.

Fangtastic Folklore

In her historical horror series, author Chelsea Quinn Yarbro—who
many credit with revolutionizing vampire romance—concocted a
unique way for her vampiric protagonist Count St. Germain and his
minions to stay in touch with their roots. Rather than sleep in native
soil, they place it in a hidden compartment within the heels of their
shoes (see Chapter 13).

Throughout vampire lore there also exists the concept of *consecrated
ground*, a term primarily associated with various religious sanctities whereby
an individual is buried within lands considered holy, for example a churchyard. The practice is most common in Catholicism and significant in the sense
that certain deaths, such as suicides, are deemed unacceptable for holy interment. For vampires, the practice of sleeping on native soil can pertain to the
soil of their homeland or, in some cases, the earth in which they were originally buried. Of course, if they were originally interred in consecrated ground
that creates an issue because a vampire wouldn't be able to tolerate holy soil.
Thus is the conundrum created by Bram Stoker in asserting that Dracula didn't
need to actually sleep in a coffin but did require a bed of native soil.

While many early literary vampires made use of the practice, others did not. Neither James Malcolm Rymer's fiend Sir Francis Varney nor John Polidori's Lord Ruthven or even Anne Rice's Lestat and company require a coffin or the native soil. What Stoker created with the trapping was a plot confinement whereby Van Helsing could gather his troops and search for Dracula knowing that he could be found in one of fifty earth-filled boxes that could then be filled with Eucharist wafers to pollute the soil. For some of the folkloric vampiric creatures native soil was a necessity, though the majority who were shape shifters could easily enter and exit their grave via a hole dug in the ground. For the most part, modern-day vampires are rarely hindered by the confines of native soil.

SUPERHUMAN POWERS

As a physical presence, vampires on all accounts are, without question, entirely intimidating. And they have every right to be given the varying range of "superpowers," if you will, that they can possess. The vampire as evolved from Dracula has some of these abilities, including superhuman strength, physical agility, acute vision, a magnified sense of smell, vision, and hearing, hypnosis, and shape-shifting capacities. Add to that what's been introduced in literature and a range of films, including vampires who can fly, levitate, become invisible, time travel, start fires, employ telekinesis, use telepathy, self-heal, move with extreme speed, cast spells, withstand sunlight, or even cause spontaneous combustion.

Strength

One of the characteristics common to most vampires is superhuman strength coupled with extreme physical agility. After all, they need those abilities in order to overpower their prey, fight attackers, and elude capture. In the Hammer films, for example, it's quite common to see Christopher Lee tossing an attacker across the room with the strength of a dozen men. More modern-day vampires, like *Blade*, Violet in *Ultraviolet*, and Selene and her kind in *Underworld*, not only possess otherworldly strength, but the ability to perform *Matrix*-like jumps and acrobatics across great heights and distances. Still other vampires are able to spend some time in daylight, though their powers may be greatly reduced. Stoker's Dracula also had the ability to scale walls like Spiderman, a tradition carried on in the 1992 film *Bram Stoker's Dracula*. Romance novelist Linda Lael Miller's bloodsuckers have the freedom to time travel at will, while some of Anne Rice's ancient vampires have, in addition to strength, the gift of flight, and in the case of Akasha, Maharet, and Marius to name a few, the destructive ability of setting afire and obliterating inanimate objects or immortals.

Fangtastic Folklore

Given that traditional vampires are creatures of the night who have an extreme aversion to sunlight, it would only make sense that they would possess extraordinary night vision superior to mortals. Theories and speculation of how vampire vision came to be are inconclusive, but some say it relates to the acute vision possessed by bats and wolves. In addition, they often have a heightened sense of smell and hearing.

As the vampire genre continues to evolve in the literary and cinematic realm, so too do the powers that vampires possess. Because of the growing list of vampiric powers, there must also be new means of destroying them. For example, in the *Underworld* films, vampires can be vanquished with the clever use of ultraviolet ammunition in liquid form, with the lycans likewise succumbing to bullets filled with liquid silver nitrate. The one thing, however, that remains consistent in regard to a typical vampire's strength, and ultimately all of his superpowers, is blood, or in some cases energy. As their life force, vampires must maintain their blood or energy consumption or risk losing everything. The blood is the life, and without it, a vampire will weaken to the point of starvation.

Play Misty for Me

In the 1931 film *Dracula*, Mina Harker describes to her husband John Harker a terrible dream she had, and that when the dream came: "It seemed the whole room was filled with mist. It was so thick, I could just see the lamp by the bed, a tiny spark in the fog. And then I saw two red eyes staring at me and a white livid face came down out of the mist." In the same film, Renfield describes a similar encounter: "A red mist spread over the lawn, coming on like a flame of fire. And then he parted it, and I could see that there were thousands of rats with their eyes blazing red like his only smaller." The two scenes brilliantly illustrate the apparent concept that Dracula possesses the ability to become mist—a power that preys upon our debilitating fear of that which we cannot lay eyes upon. Who knows what lurks within the fog? And worse yet, how easy is it for mist to creep under doorways and seep through small cracks and crevices?

VAMPIRE BITE The term *sanguinarian*, which originates from the Latin word *sanguineus*—meaning bloody, reddish, or bloodthirsty—refers to an individual who believes he requires the ingestion of blood to retain proper health. Sanguinarian vampires are part of an alternate lifestyle subculture that practices blood consumption (see Chapter 19).

The use of mist as a harbinger of evil in the vampire realm is quite common and has been effectively used in both literature and an abundance of films. In Stoker's *Dracula*, the doomed ship *Demeter*, carrying the vampire on-board, becomes awash with mist and Van Helsing himself asserts that: "He can come in mist which he creates, that noble ship's captain proved him of this, but, from what we know, the distance he can make this mist is limited, and it can only be round himself." In *Dracula*, it's Mina Murray who's most plagued by the mist, whereby in Chapter Nineteen, while safely stowed in her quarters, she writes that during what she perceives to be a dream she notices a white mist creeping toward the house with "almost perceptible slowness," a whirling mist that enters her room forming a cloudy pillar with lights that "seemed to shine on me through the fog like two red eyes." For Mina, that would be the last time the fiend appeared to her by means of mist.

There's no doubt that Stoker made great use of mist as well as elemental dust as two of Dracula's powers. It is, and most likely shall remain, a permanent fixture in the horror genre, but Stoker wasn't the originator of the vampire as mist. Creatures of lore and legend were often tracked and identified by means of grave markers and any unusual characteristics of their final resting place. In some cases, the sign of a vampire would be suspected if small holes were noticed around her burial site, indicating that an evil creature had the means to possibly become mist and move freely in and out of her grave without disturbing it.

Altering Weather

Many superstitions and rituals throughout history have been based on controlling or predicting weather. Think Groundhog Day, Native American rain dances, and the fact that your crummy knee joint can predict an upcoming frost. In the vampire realm, controlling weather has little to do with superstition and everything to do with it being a supercool power to have. In truth, Stoker's study of superstitions is likely what caused him to make mention of Dracula's ability to alter weather patterns, an ability that's shown up in a number of vampire films, quite blatantly in Coppola's *Bram Stoker's Dracula* in 1992.

WHAT'S IN A NAME?

As we learned in Chapters 5 and 6, it's a logical assumption that Bram Stoker came across the word "Dracula" as part of his research of Transylvania and learning of Prince Vlad Dracul and his son Vlad the Impaler, aka Vlad Dracula. *Dracula*, meaning "son of the dragon", would seem an apropos name for a predatory preternatural mythical creature who can fly. And one also has to wonder how coincidental it was (it wasn't) that protagonist Van Helsing bears the name of the author—Abraham—its shortened version being Bram (see Chapter 4). In an attempt at trickery, the name *Alucard* has also been used on numerous occasions, Alucard, of course, being Dracula spelled backwards. This was used by Lon Chaney Jr. in the 1943 film *Son of Dracula* as well as other films including *Dracula A.D. 1972* and the animated *Hellsing* trilogy. Author Sheridan Le Fanu employed a similar tactic to his vampiric lesbian ingénue Carmilla, who is also known as Countess Mircalla Karnstein.

DRESSING THE PART

Vampires in folklore, fiction, and film have many commonalities and just as many obscurities and eccentricities. For most of us, the mere mention of the word *vampire* conjures up the traditional Dracula ensemble of a black tux and/or tails, a long opera cloak, and the occasional hint of red so as not to end up on Mr. Blackwell's worst-dressed list. While this image of Dracula is almost entirely attributed to Irish playwright Hamilton Deane and his 1924 adaptation of Stoker's novel (see Chapter 14), it has also been reinforced by a number of films, not the least of which is Bela Lugosi's *Dracula*. Whether he's known as a Count or Prince, the mere designation of Dracula as royalty—as with many other fictional and celluloid vampires—lends itself to his wearing attire befitting an aristocrat. After all, who would suspect an impeccably dressed vampire to be a deviant, bloodthirsty jugular junkie?

Fiendish Fashion

In literature, especially in historical horror and vampire romance, that trend continues, with vampires ranging from Count St. Germain to Lestat costuming themselves with the styles of their era, as any intelligent undead predator would do in order to blend in with the general public. Some vampires, however, refuse to go with the flow. Anne Rice's Marius, for example, wears rich velvet jackets no matter the era. Where vampires tend to get more specialized with their attire is in film, especially in the action crossovers. In the *Underworld* films, Kate Beckinsale's Selene is a cool drink of water in her black skintight leather unitard and long coat with accentuated capelike flow. In *Ultraviolet*, Milla Jovovich does her comic book alter ego justice with her instantly interchangeable slick attire and haircolors reminiscent of Sydney Bristow in the series *Alias*. Even Van Helsing has rolled with the fashion punches. In the 2004 blockbuster *Van Helsing*, dashing protagonist Hugh Jackman is fabulously clad in an ensemble harkening back to the heroes of the Wild West with a black hat and a long, black leather coat and duster.

What's with the Cape?

One of the most instantly recognizable traits of the vampire, aside from the gleaming, blood-dripping fangs, is its cape. Typically long, heavy, and black with the occasional red lining, the cape is highly symbolic in its representation of the bat. As previously mentioned, the adding of a cape to the Dracula persona is the brainchild of playwright Hamilton Deane, who no doubt felt that such a cloaked gentleman fiend would make for great impact in theatrical performances. He was spot on. The cape has become an iconic part of the Dracula legend, its long swishy fabric allowing him to move with ease and giving rise to one of the vampire's most famed positions—that of pulling the cape up to his face and over his head so as to completely hide himself and blend into the shadows. It's a brilliant concept made more permanent by Bela Lugosi's performance on stage in 1927 and in the 1931 film.

VAMPIRE BITE For those who have an aversion to vampire bats, here's one more thing to give you the willies. Meet *Calyptra thalictri*, otherwise known as the vampire moth. No lie. It's said that a bite from the moth gives it the ability to fill its stomach with human blood, leaving swelling and pain in its wake. No doubt a bug zapper might help drive off the latest and greatest in vampiric predators.

ANIMAL INSTINCTS

The vampires and vampiric creatures of folklore are a decidedly mixed bag of humans, zombies, animals, and various hybrids and mutants. In many ways, the creatures of lore are more primal in their conception and definitely more animalistic in their hunting and killing of victims than vampires turned from humans. While vampires are often associated with a number of different animals, among them cats, dogs, birds, and various insects, they are most commonly linked to bats and wolves. And while many animals can become vampires, they can also be used to combat vampires. Horses, for example, are used in graveyards because they refuse to step near vampiric graves.

Going Batty

It's no small mystery that the vampire bat is associated with the legendary bloodsucker. As luck would have it, there's a good reason for that. In total, there are three species of vampire bat from the *Desmontidae* family and *Desmondus* genus: the common *Desmodus rufus,* the *Desmodus rotundus,* and *Diphylla ecaudata.* Primarily found in areas of Central and South America and a few areas of the southern United States, the vampire bat is small in size but bears a particularly frightening appearance that lends to its feeding habits, including an erect stance, large eyes, teeth that are incredibly sharp, and a lower lip possessing a cleft. As mentioned earlier, it is indeed a blood drinker with tactics similar to that of a vampire in that it feeds at ground level and attempts to hypnotize its prey before glomming itself to a vein and lapping up blood with its long tongue. With saliva containing an anticoagulant, the bat is able to keep blood flowing until it's sated. Like vampires, they must maintain blood intake or face rapid deterioration.

The bat has appeared in legend and lore for centuries but didn't become famous until Bram Stoker brought it to the forefront. Stoker made free use of the bat in *Dracula,* as it appeared at the windows of Renfield, Lucy, and the Harkers. Subsequently appearing in Bela Lugosi's *Dracula* (in what many still dub the "yo-yo bat" for its jerky movements), it quickly became one of the most definitive icons of the vampire.

Hungry Like the Wolf

In Chapter Two of *Dracula,* when Jonathan Harker sits with the Count after his arrival at Castle Dracula, there is, in the background, the sound of wolves howling. It's at that point the black demon utters arguably the most famous line of the novel: "Listen to them, the children of the night. What music they make!" By all accounts, it's a chilling statement, one that over the decades has been repeated many times with varying alterations. Dracula's almost gleeful acknowledgment of the wolves is a devilish way of paying homage to folkloric beasts while also hinting at his ability to become a wolf himself.

Fangtastic Folklore

One possible explanation for individuals allegedly becoming were-wolves is the fungus *ergot*, which most commonly pollutes rye, barley, and wheat crops. During Medieval times these were the grains typically used in bread. One of the common byproducts of ergot is that it can cause convulsions, psychosis, and hallucinations. Experts have speculated that contaminated bread is a possible explanation for lycanthropy and even the hysteria of the Salem witch trials.

Like witches, vampires and *lycanthropes*, or werewolves, have also been connected throughout lore, fiction, and certainly in film, largely as a result of their ability to shape shift, their predatory urges, and their quest for survival. They are, after all, hunted beasts. The Slavic interpretation of the vampiric Greek *vrykolakas* is that of a wolf (see Chapter 2). Throughout history there have also been many documented accounts of werewolves, though there have been equal accounts analyzing the causes of alleged lycanthropy affecting humans. Suffice to say that the most prevalent human/wolf hybrids have been those featured in circuses and freakshows and are in general overly hairy humans.

FEAR NO EVIL

As is evidenced throughout vampiric folklore, there are a wide range of mechanisms, rituals, superstitions, weaponry, and religious implements employed in an effort to rid the living of the undead. Some of those deterrents remain in common use by vampire writers, filmmakers, and the occasional modern-day vampire hunter, while other new and advanced techniques have evolved with various films and fictional works. In the next chapter we take a practical view of the vampire, introducing methods of how you can protect yourself from the onslaught of a bloodsucker and, more importantly, what you can do to destroy them.

CHAPTER 9

PROTECTION AND DESTRUCTION

L et's say for a moment that you're being stalked by a vampire. How do you protect yourself from the undead fiend? What weapons do you need in your supernatural arsenal? Most importantly, how can a vampire be destroyed? Fortunately, there are many different methods and implements that are purported to work, ranging from a vampire's abhorrence of garlic and its fear of certain religious items to decapitation and driving a stake through the creature's heart and burning the corpse. In this chapter, you'll learn how to battle a black devil, and hopefully keep your jugular intact.

COMBATING AN IMMORTAL

When it comes to the legendary triad of witches, lycanthropes, and vampires, there's never a fun or easy way to rid yourself of their malevolence. Witches can call upon black magic, spells, and all measure of sorcery. Werewolves have all the creature comforts afforded a wild animal and can strike and stalk with zero inhibition. Vampires have a bit of both, but their circumstances are hindered by a multitude of deterrents and relatively well established ways to die. In the case of many fictional and cinematic vampires, they often succumb to death and wait until they can be resurrected through magic, blood ritual, or all sorts of imagined reanimation recipes.

While it is possible to destroy a vampire, keeping them at a distance—if only temporarily—is a much safer option. Over the course of centuries, through folklore, fiction, and film, we've become well acquainted with a host of items that can be used to deter creatures of the night and keep them away from their potential victims. Some of these objects, for example garlic or crucifixes, may not necessarily kill an immortal, but they are thought to offer some protection against them. After all, no vampire hunter worth her salt would fail to have crosses, garlic, holy water, stakes, a few memorized biblical passages, and a way to create fire readily at her disposal (see Chapter 10).

Now in qualifying the items and methods we discuss, it must be said that much of this applies to the traditional vampire. As society has evolved, so has the vampire and its aversions, perversions, and the ways we can destroy it. What may repel or kill the bloodsucker of legend may prove ineffective on a wide range of modern fiends—from the soul suckers and plague vamps to the exotic, erotic, and predisposed blood drinkers on PETA's hit list. The bottom line with any vampire who doesn't fit the traditional mold is the good old trial-and-error method of discovering what it's repelled by and what its weaknesses are. For starters, that would still include the basics, and the tried-and-true methods of yesteryear. With that in mind, let's begin by taking a look at what might help in your quest to protect yourself from a dastardly demon of the night.

PRACTICAL PROTECTION

Speaking from a highly logical and practical standpoint, there are several items that you might simply have around the house that can, in many cases, repel the traditional vampire or act as a testing ground for a modern-era vamp. Garlic, salt, candles, incense, and even bells, among other items, have in the past been proven effective against vampires. Most of these methods are steeped in folklore and used by early writers of vampire fiction including John Polidori, James Malcolm Rymer, Sheridan Le Fanu, and, of course, Bram Stoker.

Garlic

If you're of Italian ancestry or just a fan of spaghetti bolognese, then it's likely you have garlic in your kitchen. We're not talking the crusty, dried-up powered stuff at the back of your spice cupboard. We mean nice fat bulbs of the stinking rose. Garlic is one of the most commonly thought of items used to ward off the majority of vampires, and a it's a protection device against evil that's existed since ancient times. In fact, so prominent is garlic that in the vampire realm it's commensurate with repelling the demons.

A member of the lily family, garlic contains natural healing powers and has long been used for medicinal purposes as well as herbal uses. As a vampire deterrent it's arguably second to none as a first line of defense. It's also used in the destruction process. Throughout much of folklore and in Stoker's *Dracula*, a vampire's mouth is stuffed with garlic after beheading or a corpse's mouth is similarly filled to prevent its joining the undead. In *Dracula*, Van Helsing fills Lucy's entire room with garlic flowers and bulbs, even rubbing it all over the door jamb and fireplace to keep Dracula from entering.

Vampiric folklore is rife with individuals making use of garlic as a repellant. Given that a vampire's senses are heightened, particularly its vision, hearing, and smell, it stands to reason that garlic, whether it's worn around the neck as a wreath, strewn around a house, rubbed onto a human, animal, or object, or even liquefied and sprayed would be enough to keep the undead at bay. During times of plague, it was often believed—with a logical basis—that smells could not only ward off evil and the stench of death, but disease as well. In the case of airborne germs such as pneumonic plague, this did prevent some individuals from succumbing to illness. In light of the fact that vampirism in itself is often considered a plague (see Chapter 7), other odiferous means were often employed, including incense, juniper, manure, human feces, and all types of perfumes.

Fangtastic Folklore

One theory of why garlic repels vampires is born of the similarity between vampires and mosquitoes, both of which bite their victims and drink their blood, and both of whom can spread disease through their bites. Mosquitoes and other insects are known to be repelled by garlic. As of this writing, however, no one has as yet manufactured a bug spray for vampires.

Salt and Seeds

As a matter of superstition, there are still many of us who subscribe to several practices including knocking on wood, avoiding stepping on a crack, or tossing salt over one's shoulder for luck or to ward off evil. In the case of the latter, there's good reason to keep it on hand in case of vampiric incursion. Sodium chloride is a staple of ancient and modern history especially in regard to the supernatural, paranormal, religious, and, of course, the culinary realms. Throughout history, salt has been used as a means of preservation both with food and in the form of natron, which Egyptians used for perfecting mummification processes. Salt also serves as a symbol of purity and a means by which one can repel evil. In some legends, the undead cannot cross a line of salt, in which case windows, doors, fireplaces, and entire houses were often surrounded with an unbroken line of salt if vampires were thought to be on the prowl.

Like salt, seeds are often used as a vampire repellant. While mustard seed is the most prominent—possibly for its religious connection as mentioned in one of Jesus's parables—other small seeds and grains like poppy, oats, millet, and carrot to name a few, can also be used, as can the thorns gathered from wild roses. One theory is that if a vampire encounters the seeds, he is required to count each seed before coming to a village to procure victims. Some folkloric tales mention that the vampire can count only one seed per year, so even a small handful of the seeds would keep evil at bay for long periods of time. Another speculation is that a vampire would become so caught up in obsessively counting the seeds that he would lose track of time and be forced to retreat as the sun begins to rise. Seeds as well as salt can also be sprinkled in and around corpses and coffins to prevent vampirism or keep a vampire from rising from the grave.

HALLOWED WEAPONS

In many legends of vampires, religious icons play a strong role in defending against the undead. As a representation of evil, as Bram Stoker injected into his fiend, it makes sense that "good," as represented by such items as a crucifix or holy water, holds sway over them. Stoker used this underlying theme prominently in *Dracula*, but not all writers have continued this tradition, and the effectiveness of religious weapons against the vampire varies. In the film *Interview with the Vampire*, Louis de Pointe du Lac flat-out tells his interviewer that he's rather fond of crucifixes, a common theme among modern vampires who often mock and scorn frightened mortals who attempt to fend off attack using a holy artifact. To some, the power of a crucifix or holy water exists only if *you* believe—and the undead would be unlikely to believe. Nonetheless, hallowed weaponry such as crosses remain, much like garlic, intrinsically linked to vampirism.

Crosses and Crucifixes

One of the most oft-used weapons against a vampire is a *cross* or *crucifix*, which is a cross bearing the figure of Christ hanging from it that represents Jesus's crucifixion on Good Friday. The crucifix is primarily a Roman Catholic symbol, with other Christian religions preferring a plain cross, representative of Christ after the crucifixion. It's said that a crucifix has more power than a cross, but again, in both cases its energy is largely dependent on how strongly the person holding it believes in its symbolism. In *Dracula*, Stoker brings the crucifix into the mix beginning in Chapter One, as a confounded

Jonathan Harker has a rosary with a crucifix forced upon him by a villager as he awaits his departure for Castle Dracula. Harker, of course, being an "English Churchman" believes the crucifix to be somewhat idolatrous.

SCREEN SCREAM

In the 1960 film *The Brides of Dracula*, Van Helsing (played by Peter Cushing) makes innovative use of a windmill against David Peel's evil Baron Meinster. Van Helsing jumps on the windblade, carefully turning it so as to create the giant shadow of a cross which on the ground below confines and effectively helps destroy the Baron.

In traditional lore, the crucifix will burn the skin of the vampire when pressed against it and mark the flesh of a person who has been bitten but not yet fully transformed into a vampire. Additionally in some legends, the crucifix or cross will steal the creature's source of strength, rendering it less powerful. Some stories claim that crosses or crucifixes hung on a door will keep a vampire from entering a room or that a cross placed on a gravesite will render a vampire's entering the grave impossible. Perhaps the best thing about crosses is that they're easily improvised using items such as candlesticks, swords, random bits of wood—anything that can replicate its crossed positioning. As is the case with more contemporary vampire caricatures, however, crosses and crucifixes, while typically used in some measure, often present no threat to a vampire's existence.

Holy Water

As one of the primary symbols of life, water retains its power as a spiritual and physical cleansing mechanism and one of the strongest proponents of life itself. We spent our first nine months immersed in water, and our bodies are almost entirely composed of water. That said, revenants who are no longer among the living or the dead have little use or respect for water—especially that which has been blessed. Used in many religious ceremonies such as baptisms and absolution rites, holy water, which is blessed and made sacred by the clergy—especially in the Catholic and Eastern Orthodox churches—is believed to have special powers and uses. Among them is the ability to repel most unholy creatures—including vampires.

Because holy water is pure and blessed it's said to burn the flesh of the demons like acid burns human flesh, causing extreme pain and peeling burns. In the case of newly created revenants, this could prove fatal. Throughout vampire lore, when bodies of suspected vampires were exhumed, holy water was often used in the rituals meant to keep the undead from rising. In the same vein, it was also sprinkled atop a grave or over a coffin to prevent its inevitable return. Much like salt, holy water can also be sprinkled or poured onto window sills and doorways to prevent a vampire from entering. In film and fiction, holy water is typically tossed onto a bloodsucker from a vial or flask.

Eucharist Wafer

The Eucharist wafer is yet another religious symbol that is thought to offer protection against vampires, though it's not as commonly mentioned as crosses or holy water. The wafer, which is a thin piece of blessed bread, represents the body of Christ in the Holy Communion ceremony. Like a crucifix, the wafer can burn the flesh of a vampire and leave a mark if pressed against the skin of its victims. In Chapter Sixteen of *Dracula*, Van Helsing, after finding Lucy's empty coffin, shocks his cohorts by finely crumbling up wafers, combining them with putty, and using the mix as a sealant around the door to Lucy's tomb. When asked what the mixture is, he replies that it's "the Host," which he brought from Amsterdam. In Chapter Twenty-Two, he again makes use of the wafer on several occasions, the first in an effort to keep Mina from further harm. When he touches the wafer to her forehead, however, she screams as her skin becomes seared as if touched by "a piece of white hot metal." After that incident, the hunting party proceeds to Carfax and are faced with Dracula's boxes of earth. Again, Van Helsing produces the consecrated Host:

"And now, my friends, we have a duty here to do. We must sterilize this earth, so sacred of holy memories, that he has brought from a far distant land for such fell use. He has chosen this earth because it has been holy. Thus we defeat him with his own weapon, for we make it more holy still. It was sanctified to such use of man, now we sanctify it to God."

Van Helsing then proceeds to open the soil-filled boxes, lay the wafers upon the earth, and reseal them to prevent Dracula returning to them. Stoker's use of the Eucharist speaks to a range of issues, including good versus evil, moral versus immoral, and dark versus light. No doubt the religious significance of the wafer is a religious reinforcement to the spiritual turmoil of the Victorian era. One possible reason that the wafers aren't as popularly used as holy water is likely due to accessibility. As a powerful representation of the body of Christ, wafers are typically locked away in tabernacles within churches and chapels and not easily acquired. In the 1992 film *Bram Stoker's Dracula*, Francis Ford Coppola paid homage to Stoker's Eucharistic ploy, including the searing of Mina's forehead and the subsequent disappearance of the burn when the curse of Dracula is lifted upon his destruction.

Fangtastic Folklore

While the power of moonlight is more closely associated with werewolves, and primarily used in film and fiction as a matter of creating ambiance, it has played a factor in bringing vampires to life. In John Polidori's *The Vampyre*, Lord Ruthven is reanimated after he gives the order that his corpse "be exposed to the first cold ray of the moon that rose after his death." No doubt this gives new meaning to the term "moon walk."

MIRROR, MIRROR ON THE WALL

One of the more shocking aspects—or at least one that was until it became commensurate with drawing room vampires—is the concept that bloodsuckers cast no reflection in a mirror. If the eyes are indeed the window to one's soul in a metaphorical sense, then the inability to see one's own reflection speaks to a lack of soul. This begs the question of whether or not vampires even have souls, other than ones doomed to eternal damnation or to ultimate absolution once their curse is lifted. In the film *Bram Stoker's Dracula*, the latter concept seems to apply upon Dracula's death, an appearance of final absolution, if you will, as we don't actually see the black devil carted off kicking and screaming to the bowels of hell. His face at the time of death is flooded in white light, suggesting a heavenly ending. On the other hand, in Stoker's novel, the destiny of eternal damnation is more likely, as one can argue that Dracula is more deeply entrenched as an evil figure rather than a romantic one, and his death results in his crumbling to ashes.

The mirror aversion likely spawns from Stoker's *Dracula*, and after it was published, it quickly became an accepted part of the vampire legend. In Chapter Two, Jonathan Harker makes note in his journal that Castle Dracula is void of mirrors. Later in that chapter comes one of the more chilling scenes of the book, whereby Harker is shaving using his small shaving mirror when the Count comes up behind him. He casts no reflection, a fact that does not go unnoticed to Harker, who has cut himself, nor to the dark devil who reacts to the blood running down Harker's chin, the rosary he wears, and the mirror:

> "Take care," he said, 'take care how you cut yourself. It is more dangerous than you think in this country.' Then seizing the shaving glass, he went on. 'And this is the wretched thing that has done the mischief. It is a foul bauble of man's vanity. Away with it!' And opening the window with one wrench of his terrible hand, he flung out the glass, which was shattered into a thousand pieces on the stones of the courtyard far below."

How to Kill a Vampire

Vampires, as with all revenants, exist in a strange dichotomy. They're no longer living, and they're no longer dead—they're undead. So, if you're stuck in a *Night of the Living Dead* situation and you lack the ubercool weaponry that a cinematic Van Helsing possesses, what do you do? For starters, you have to know what kind of vampire you're dealing with. Is it a traditional stake-through-the-heart preternatural fiend, an outer space soul sucker, or a genetically mutated biological-warfare-gone-horribly-wrong plague pusher?

If it's the latter two, you may have to do a bit of experimentation to ascertain a method of destruction, but what's curious about all types of fictional and cinematic vampires is that almost always there exists a way of killing them by traditional means, even if they may be somewhat disguised.

What's at Stake?

Perhaps the most common method associated with destroying a vampire is staking it through the heart. No doubt, it's a procedure that's been well-used throughout literature and film, as it makes for a spectacular end to an unearthly villainous rampage. After slaughtering half a village, who wouldn't want to see Dracula taking a snooze and then screaming as Van Helsing raises his mallet and pounds away, sending a hefty splurch of blood all over Drac's lovely tux. Though the practice of staking was introduced in early literature, particularly Sheridan Le Fanu's *Carmilla* (see Chapter 3) and Stoker's *Dracula*, the concept of using a sharpened stake is entrenched in not only vampiric folklore, but the legends of numerous other revenants as well. The idea of driving a stake through a corpse was born of the typical folkloric propensities devised for dealing with the undead and the efforts undertaken to make certain they didn't rise from the grave. In some traditions a buried body would have a stake driven completely through it to hold it into the ground, with some cultures going so far as to drive spikes or thorns through the tongue to prevent the alleged vampire from using it to draw blood.

Traditionally, stakes are handmade, finely sharpened, and usually made of local hardwoods felled from trees such as juniper, whitethorn, hawthorn, ash, wild rose, or buckthorn. Curiously, some legends make mention that a stake is only to be hammered into the chest in one blow, for if it's struck twice, the revenant can reanimate and return to its vampiric state. One of the benefits of staking, aside from the obvious relief that one can at last get a night's rest, is that in many instances it's reported that after the staking, the screaming, and the inevitable blood spurting, the corpse's face often relaxes to show relief. In folklore, and throughout film and fiction, this is the quintessential signal that the afflicted individual's spirit and soul is finally at peace. But staking a vampire doesn't necessarily mean he or she can't be resurrected.

In the 1970 film *Taste the Blood of Dracula*, Christopher Lee's Dracula is burned to cinders. Later that year, in *Scars of Dracula*, said ashes are bled upon by a leaky, blood-engorged bat and lo and behold, it's enough to resurrect the king of all immortal bad boys. The same principle applies to Blacula in the 1973 sequel *Scream Blacula Scream*, whereby Shaft's answer to vampirism coupled with a bit of voodoo results in Blacula's bones acting as a conduit to his groovy resurrection (see Chapter 15).

Fangtastic Folklore

In some legends, stakes were pounded in the ground above a grave to ensure a reanimated corpse was staked if it attempted to arise from the earth, or its head was staked to secure it to the ground. A few legends call for a corpse to be staked through the back and buried face-down to prevent it digging its way up and out. Some corpses, in addition to staking, were also beheaded, their mouths stuffed with garlic, or their hearts removed and burned to cinders.

Let There Be Light

Another common form of vampiric destruction is, of course, sunlight. Given that vampires are reanimated undead corpses who in most cases have no beating heart and are cold as ice, the warmth of the sun stands in direct contrast and therefore provides an easy mechanism for vampiric destruction. But that convention doesn't always apply. A host of folkloric vampires were able to move about during daylight hours as well as both traditional and modern-day vamps in both fiction and film. The Bulgarian *vampir*, for example, is a reanimated corpse that moves to a new village. As many serial killers, it lives normally by day but becomes a monster by night. In *Dracula*, Bram Stoker twice allowed Dracula to appear during daylight hours, though his powers were greatly diminished. Whitley Strieber didn't even go that far with his immortals in *The Hunger*. They had no issue whatsoever functioning in daylight, as does Blade, in part due to his hybrid human/vampire disposition.

Where sunlight as a destructive mechanism came to public prominence is in F. W. Murnau's 1922 landmark silent film *Nosferatu*, where Count Orlock fell into a trap set by Ellen Hutter (aka Mina Harker) after she reads *The Book of the Vampires*. Keeping Orlock in her bedroom and occupied with her bloodletting until cock's crow resulted in his exposure to the sun and his spectacular disappearance into a wisp of smoke (see Chapter 14). Since that time, many cinematic and literary vampires have alternately suffered from a daylight aversion or been given the power to embrace it, or in the case of Anne Rice's vampires, in particular, Armand, the choice of flying into the sun to commit suicide.

SCREEN SCREAM

Arguably the most evil twist to the destructive capabilities of sunlight is the fact that it's quite often used by vampires to kill other vampires. In *Interview with the Vampire*, Anne Rice makes use of this, assigning the fate to Claudia and her keeper, Gabrielle, for Claudia's attempt to kill Lestat. In the film *Underworld*, vampire elder Viktor bestowed the same fate on his daughter Sonja for carrying a child conceived with lycan leader, Lucian.

Fire

As far as fire is concerned, it's one of the mainstays of human history since the dawn of man. It keeps us warm and aids in food preparation. It also is used as a method of destruction and the byproduct of both accidents and Mother Nature. Even further, fire is often used by witches, sorcerers, shamans, holy men, and all measure of conjurers for both good and evil. In the metaphorical realm, fire, like water, is a characteristic means of cleansing or purification. Biblically speaking, fire is entrenched in symbolism, not the least of which is God appearing to Moses in the form of a burning bush. With all of that history behind it, fire has both a good and bad reputation in what it provides. In vampiric folklore it's often used as one of the means for combating evil, though how it's used is largely dependent on its effectiveness.

Folkloric creatures were often exhumed and their bodies burned to ashes. For the most part, this is the safest way to assume a vampire is indeed dead. But in the modern era, that's most definitely not a sure bet. More than a few fictional and cinematic vampires have been resurrected despite having been reduced to a pile of ash or with even a small portion of their ashes serving as the catalyst. The same goes for threatening a vampire with fire.

Given that many vampires have regenerative capacities that allow them to quickly recover from things such as stabbings and gunshot wounds, setting one on fire doesn't provide a guarantee of destruction. In the 2004 film *Van Helsing*, for example, Dracula is violently thrown into a huge burning fireplace by Frankenstein, only to walk out of the flames to have his burnt face quickly return to normal. As a rule, cremating a revenant is always worth a try, but be warned that the ashes-to-ashes and dust-to-dust rule should be heeded with extreme caution. Err on the side of caution and release the ashes into the nearest river.

Fangtastic Folklore

Some folkloric legends have it that vampires and other revenants can be banished to remote islands surrounded by water, thereby assuring they have no means of interacting with society and could even die of malnourishment. Salt water in those instances provides a twofold measure of protection as vampires are also repelled by salt.

Waterways

As previously discussed, water is one of the primary symbols of life, and while holy water can do damage to a vampire, unblessed water has a different set of benefits, many of which apply to other revenants such as witches as well. One commonly held folkloric belief is that vampires cannot cross over running water, nor can they swim across it. As we've seen in Stoker's *Dracula* and many other incarnations, they can be carried over water by means of a ship. That vampires can actually drown is debatable, as some legends suggest that though a vampire cannot swim, it would suffer no ill effects if pulled from the water. One film in particular, the 1966 *Dracula: Prince of Darkess*, made good use of this legend by having Christopher Lee's bloodsucker become submerged in icy waters, only to be resurrected in *Dracula Has Risen From the Grave* (see Chapter 14).

Off with Your Head!

As folklore and common logic would dictate, it would seem that decapitation would be the most obvious and permanent means of destroying a vampire. For the most part, beheading a dark devil does indeed do the trick, but there are a few caveats. In the case of modern vamps, the same rules sometimes apply as with fire. If a vampire possesses the power of regeneration, then it's conceivable that it's able to reposition its head upon its neck and allow everything to reattach itself. Throughout folklore, corpses were very often beheaded with the head being burned along with the body or removed and even buried separately with the mouth stuffed with garlic. Many suspected vampiric corpses were also treated to a garlic stuffing. However, the concept that those exhuming and burying the corpse had to pay heed to is the fact that if you decapitated a vampire, the head should be placed nowhere near its neck or especially its arms, which could conceivably move the head back where it belongs.

Watch Your Ash

As we've learned, vampires are infinitely more complex creatures than one might expect, each one possessing its own powers and capabilities that are largely drawn from folkloric revenants, early vampire literature, and cinema. Of course the only way one can protect oneself from a vampire and uncover its weakness and potentially destroy it is to learn how to detect and slay it. In the next chapter we take you into the world of vampire hunters and what it takes to actually deal with the devil.

CHAPTER 10

VAMPIRE HUNTERS

Amid vampiric film and fiction we've been given the image of a vampire slayer as one who, despite any reluctance, must step up to fight all measure of bloodsucking demonic creatures. Though glamorous in its conception, especially if one has a supply of modern weaponry, vampire hunting is not for the faint of heart. To fight evil is to dive into the abyss, to truly understand what one is fighting, and hopefully emerge unscathed. In this chapter, we examine the vampire hunters of history, the tools of the trade, and famous vampirologists whose insights shed light where there's perennial darkness.

THE QUINTESSENTIAL SLAYER

In the vampire realm, there is but one name, and one name alone, that's associated with the vampire hunter—Van Helsing. While Dracula himself is one of the most popular literary characters in history, it goes without saying that he would be nothing without a protagonist to decipher his origins and weaknesses, and work to destroy him using intellect, science, religion, psychology, and weaponry befitting the execution. As far as heroes go—and make no mistake, Abraham Van Helsing *is* indeed the hero in *Dracula*—one finds in the Dutch professor all the ingredients a larger-than-life hero should have (see Chapter 4). That is not to say that vampiric cinema and literature hasn't benefited from the garden-variety reluctant hero, because it has, but what Bram Stoker needed to counter his preternatural fiend was not the average Joe.

With Jonathan Harker, Quincey Morris, Dr. Seward, and Arthur Holmwood serving as the metaphorical mules to his cart, and with Mina acting as his muse, Van Helsing has a base upon which he can execute his plan. By making him a renowned progressive Victorian scientist, philosopher, metaphysician, and man of God, Stoker opened the door to Van Helsing having the open-mindedness necessary to fight what God-fearing folk would consider the spawn of Satan. It's an epic battle rife with spiritual, mental, physical, and metaphorical symbolism that has, over the decades, led to Van Helsing gaining powerful immortality.

Dealing with the Devil

Though there's much to be said about Van Helsing's character, what we focus on here is a key point in *Dracula*, where Van Helsing, who throughout the novel abides by the rule that discretion is the better part of valor, pulls together all he knows to be true about the black devil and reveals it to the now-allied hunting party. Through the vast knowledge he possesses, Van Helsing acknowledges many of the characteristics associated with the majority of vampires and vampire hunters that follow in Dracula's fiendish footsteps, including garlic, the crucifix, beheading, confinement to his native soil, and the Host. Here is the crux of the matter, according to Van Helsing:

"The vampire live on, and cannot die by mere passing of the time, he can flourish when that he can fatten on the blood of the living. ... He can grow even younger, that his vital faculties grow strenuous . . . He throws no shadow, he make in the mirror no reflect . . . He has the strength of many of his hand . . . He can transform himself to wolf, he can be as bat . . . He can come as mist which he create . . . He come on moonlight rays as elemental dust . . . He can become small . . . He can come out from anything or into anything, no matter how close it be bound or even fused by fire . . . He can see in the dark . . . He may not enter anywhere at first, unless there be some one of the household who bid him to come . . . He can only pass running water at the slack or the flood of the tide . . ."

SCREEN SCREAM

In the 2004 film *Van Helsing*, an intriguing final confrontation takes place when Van Helsing (Hugh Jackman), who possesses a divine measure of immortality, learns of a way to ultimately destroy Dracula (Richard Roxburgh). In this instance, the deliciously wicked bloodsucker can only be killed by a werewolf—an affliction Van Helsing acquires in order to get the job done.

The Holy and the Horrific

For all the wonderful embellishments that film and fiction have added to the vampiric legacy, the basics all harken back to Stoker and his scholarly hero. Perhaps Van Helsing, ultimately, is best described by his former pupil Dr. Seward, who states that his mentor possesses: "An iron nerve, a temper of the ice-brook, and indomitable resolution, self-command, and toleration exalted from virtues to blessings, and the kindliest and truest heart that beats, these form his equipment for the noble work that he is doing for mankind, work both in theory and practice, for his views are as wide as his all-embracing sympathy." In no uncertain terms, that *is* the description not only of a true hero, but one who's able to forgo the rationality of humanity in order to save it from an evil that they don't even realize exists.

LITERARY SLAYERS

Although Abraham Van Helsing has become the quintessential vampire slayer, Stoker's characterization was undoubtedly influenced by Sheridan Le Fanu's *In a Glass Darkly*, published twenty-five years earlier in 1872 (see Chapter 3). Designed as a collection of five encounters with the occult, left as posthumous accounts by Le Fanu's fictional narrator Dr. Hesselius, the five narratives include the novella "Carmilla," which is considered one of the first truly influential vampire tales and from which Stoker likely drew substantial inspiration. The parallels between the two characters are undeniable—and it's possible that Stoker even created the name for Van Helsing as an alliterate homage to Le Fanu's Dr. Hesselius. In their fictional exploits, Van Helsing and Hesselius were both imbued with extraordinary knowledge of the occult and possessed the same presence of mind in the face of demonic forces. Van Helsing is quite rightly considered to be the father of fictional vampire slayers, and Dr. Hesselius can certainly be considered the godfather.

Another argument can be made for General Spielsdorf serving as inspiration for Van Helsing, as it is Spielsdorf who turns vampire hunter in "Carmilla" after his niece is killed by the demon, and he ascertains Carmilla is a vampire and sets off to find her corpse and behead her. During the closing scenes of "Carmilla," Spielsdorf learns from a woodsman that Karnstein village became deserted as a result of a plague brought on by revenants in which many villagers perished. The revenants were detected, exhumed, and then extinguished "in the usual way, by decapitation, by the stake, and by burning." No doubt, Le Fanu was a student of vampiric folklore, as his description is very much in keeping with folkloric accounts of dispatching vampires. But that's not the end of it. According to the woodsman, a vampire slayer was involved as the killings continued: "A Moravian nobleman, who happened to be traveling this way, heard how matters were, and being skilled—as many people are in his country—in such affairs, he offered to deliver the village from its tormentor." To accomplish this, after seeing the fiend rise from his grave, the slayer lured the alleged vampire to the chapel and after a struggle, decapitated him. The villagers then impaled and burnt the demon.

You Slay Me

Through the long history of vampirism in folklore, particularly in the Slavic regions of eastern Europe, there are numerous references to those rare individuals who possessed the mysterious knowledge to detect and dispatch suspected vampires. Although there's a common belief, particularly in our relatively "informed" modern age, that those who purported to have the ability to see and kill vampires were simply charlatans bent on earning a few kopecks through the fears and ignorance of their neighbors, there's little evidence, anecdotal or otherwise, that this was the case.

A significant aspect of vampire hunting is that there was little visible evidence that slayers had indeed been successful in their efforts. Slavic vampire hunters were seldom expected to destroy a vampire that was actively on the prowl, and virtually all suspected vampires were terminated as they slept in their graves. While it's physiologically improbable that any of the human remains thought to be lost souls wandering about searching for midnight snacks in the moonlight were anything more than a pile of decomposing flesh, the fact remains that the services of vampire hunters were regularly called upon.

With the common belief that vampires were a part of everyday life, and that hired vampire hunters could do something about them, the obvious implication is that *something* was being accomplished, whether it was the eventual end of strange maladies, an epidemic, or the more common result that physical mischief, such as banging on walls, nervous livestock creating nighttime ruckuses, or any number of other odd happenings, ceased to occur.

SCREEN SCREAM

The 1985 *Lifeforce,* directed by Tobe Hooper features a trio of outer space vampires in human form who forgo the use of fangs and blood in favor of sucking out one's soul. After attacking a space shuttle, they arrive in London and initiate a plague of epic proportion. With the surviving shuttle astronaut, the vampires are hunted and it's discovered that they can be killed if a lead shaft or sword pierces their chest in an energy center just below their heart.

Most modern psychological interpretations of this phenomenon lean toward assertions of various forms of mass hysteria, as with the infamous Medvegia Vampires of the 1720s, where frightened villagers would begin a contagion of rumor and gossip that resulted in virtually every normally uncomplicated but inexplicable happenstance being attributed to the workings of the undead (see Chapter 11). By hiring a professional vampire hunter to drive a stake into the corpse of the most likely, and usually the most recently deceased suspect, fears would abate, odd sounds were just the wind, life would return to normal, and the hunter's mission was accomplished.

Healing the Dead

Given the powerful undercurrents of religious conviction, literary and scientific ignorance, and social dogma that pervaded the culture of early eastern Europe, there's every likelihood that the vampire hunter was the equivalent of a healer. It's thought that ancient medicinal healers were actually the forefathers of designated vampire hunters and performed the same tasks in much the same way. In dealing with the inherently disturbing issues of staking, decapitation, or setting rotting corpses alight, the vampire hunter performed a duty that was generally far too gruesome for the average individual, and the rituals of dispatching the body of a revenant were specific to local traditions and had to be carried out in perfect order. This was no job for the novice or the uninitiated, and bringing in the services of a professional vampire hunter was the equivalent of hiring a pest control company to rid your home of an infestation of creepy crawlies.

A Symbiotic Relationship

In Slavic cultures, the vampire hunter was usually "marked" in some fashion to differentiate him from the rest of society, and the most common of delineations was the *sabotnik*. *Sabotniks* are quite simply those people born on a Saturday, the traditional Jewish Sabbath, and a day that is rife with taboos. Although the Christian Orthodox Church differentiated itself early on from Judaism by declaring Sunday the Sabbath, the taboos of Saturdays became entrenched in tradition and spread throughout much of eastern Europe. In effect, *sabotniks* were considered to be tainted with associations to demonic forces and therefore held supernatural powers to detect evil.

The Fall Guy

Another common "marking" of the destined vampire hunter, or seer, was attributed to the individual born of sexual union between a widow and a deceased husband who had become a vampire. Such individuals were regionally known as *glogove, vampirdzii, vuperari,* or *vampirovici,* and they were attributed with much the same abilities to detect and destroy evil as the *sabotniks*, and for the same reasons—they shared supernatural powers with the undead.

The concept of the *glogove's* birth as the bastard child of a woman and a "vampire" illustrates a significant point in vampire lore. In scientifically ignorant eastern Europe, and indeed in educated modern times, inexplicable occurrences *require* explanation to pacify a nervous population, quell hysterias, and to maintain social unity. Culturally, women who lost their husbands were expected to remain chaste until they remarried. Should a recent widow become pregnant, her most effective line of defense was to blame her dead husband, who had clearly become a vampire and forced her into sexual relations. Through the ages, there has been a cultural requirement to seek out and exterminate suspected perpetrators of misdeeds, and that need placed the equally stigmatized vampire hunter in the unique position of having the ability to perform a distasteful, but necessary, function.

THE VAMPIRE HUNTER'S KIT

One of the most intriguing and continuing mysteries of the twentieth century involves the manufacture and sale of vampire-killing kits attributed to a Professor Ernst Blomberg of Germany, with antique percussion-style pistols made by gunsmith Nicholas Plomdeur of Liege, Belgium, supposedly dating from the late 1800s. A number of Blomberg's kits have turned up in recent years, and some have sold for rather astonishing amounts, including one at Sotheby's that went for $12,000 in 2003. The Sotheby's kit consisted of a walnut box with a hinged lid, housing an antique pistol, ten silver bullets, a wooden stake and mallet, a crucifix, rosary, several vials of garlic powder, and various demon-thwarting serums. The authenticity of Professor Blomberg's kits has come under a fair amount of scrutiny in recent years, with very few reliable results and even less hard evidence that he even existed.

There is, however, anecdotal evidence that vampire-killing kits became fairly popular in England and western Europe soon after the release of Bram Stoker's *Dracula* in 1897 that were supposedly made for nervous travelers to eastern Europe but were more likely concocted as souvenirs. Nevertheless, most of those kits were quite well made and expensive and designed for the well-to-do who had a penchant for unusual contemporary novelties.

Early vampire hunters in eastern Europe made do with shovels, hand-carved wooden stakes and a mallet, and an axe for decapitating the unsuspecting undead. The self-respecting vampire hunter of today, however, wouldn't be caught dead without an arsenal of demon-dispatching tools close at hand. That said, if you're planning on embarking on a career in slaying, there are a few mandatory items you'll need to assemble before facing off with a malevolent malfeasant of the night:

✝ **Wooden box**: Preferably made of ash or hawthorn wood with a cross carved into the lid so as to dissuade inquisitive vampires from snooping inside.

✝ **Stakes**: Just about any stake or sharp, pointed object should suffice, but according to lore, any local hardwood such as ash, hawthorn, juniper, wild rose, whitethorn, or buckthorn is ideal. In some cases, silver stakes can also prove useful depending on the type of revenant you're facing.

✝ **Crosses or crucifixes**: Keeping in line with your wooden box and stakes, crosses or crucifixes should be made out of ash or hawthorn wood to add to the aversion level. Remember to pack a couple of extras—vampire hunters are *always* losing their crucifixes at the most inopportune moments.

✝ **Holy water**: Most vampire hunters carry holy water around in vials or flasks. We'd suggest a spray bottle adjusted to squirt a steady, vamp-searing stream. If all else fails, enlist the help of an officially blessed team of holy firefighters and hose the bloodsucker all the way to Hades.

✝ **Fire**: Traditional vampire hunters typically rely on matches, candles, and torches. A few butane lighters, and maybe a small blow-torch, would seem a bit more reliable—and dramatic—assuming you can quickly grab your crème brûlée torch.

✝ **Mirrors**: A tried-and-true repellant—at least according to vampire cinema. The operative term here is "unbreakable." Irritated vampires are notorious for smashing up mirrors, so you'll definitely want something shatterproof and larger than a compact unless you're using it to reflect sunlight in a precisely-directed burn.

✝ **Garlic**: Vampires hate garlic with a passion. Garlic powder, garlic cloves, garlic anything. There's no such thing as too much garlic. In a pinch, you could even try garlic-flavored cooking spray, though it's unlikely to keep Drac from sticking to you.

✝ **The Bible**: Another vampire hunter favorite. Threatening a vampire with the Holy Book while reeling off a few choice verses is a standard vampire hunter tactic. Just hope he's not a Jewish, Hindu, Buddhist, or an atheistic bloodsucker.

✟ **Poppy or mustard seeds**: Because vampires traditionally have an obsession with counting grains, tossing a handful of seeds in his face should keep a vampire occupied for hours, which should give you enough time to fire up the torch. In a pinch, try sunflower seeds. Those take hours to pry open with fangs.

Be warned that the aforementioned items are the basic kit elements of the well-prepared vampire hunter, and nothing less will do in the face of a cranky vampire intent on slurping you dry. And don't forget to wear a scarf to protect your jugular, which will probably be pulsing at a delectably galloping rate. So, now that you've got the tools, how do you go about trapping a vampire?

HOW TO CATCH A VAMPIRE

In Wes Craven's 2000 film, *Dracula 2000*, Van Helsing (Christopher Plummer) came up with an innovative way to trap Dracula (Gerard Butler) by making use of the basics. Leading the demonic sucker into a dark London alleyway, Van Helsing disappeared into a doorway. Dracula, attempting to follow him, paused, sensing something was afoot. At that point, Van Helsing reappeared in Dracula's view as he reached out in front of him to discover that what he was staring at was a mirror. Given that he casts no reflection, Van Helsing was actually standing behind Dracula and immediately brought down iron bars around the fiend to form a prison cell. How clever is *that*?

Nailing a Nefarious Nightcrawler

For the most part, one of the best methods for catching vampires is to corner them in such a way that you can expose them to sunlight, torch them, or even drown them, as was done to Christopher Lee's Dracula in *Dracula: Prince of Darkness*. The key is making use of whatever weaponry or on-the-fly ingenuity you can conjure up at that very moment. In the 1979 *Dracula*, for example, Dracula's last stand in the hold of a ship gave Van Helsing the opportunity to entangle and hoist the sucker upward to the top of the mast to burn in the sun's rays. In *Dracula 2000*, a similar method was employed, with Mary Van

Helsing wrapping cable around Dracula's neck and falling with him off the edge of a building. She watched from below as Dracula (aka Judas Iscariot) dangled from the building and burnt with the rising sun.

 **VAMPIRE BITE** Like garlic, the rowan tree, commonly known as the mountain ash, is believed to repel the undead. Its wood is used to make crosses or in gravesites to keep a vampire at bay. Also, those who avoid going near mountain ash can be viewed as vampiric suspects.

Bait and Switch

For many literary and cinematic vampires, especially in classic films, the standard form of destruction is finding the vampire at rest and staking it through the heart. That tidy setup doesn't necessarily work on all modern-day vampires. The most important concept every vampire hunter needs to grasp, just like any hunter, soldier, or chess master, is how to assess and capitalize on your opponent's weaknesses. For the sci-fi nosferatu it may require a genetically self-mutating form of intergalactic Ebola. For the comedic berserker it could mean dressing like Bozo the Clown and shooting a holy water pistol. For the folkloric incarnation you might have to reanimate its natural predator. Whatever the situation, it's safe to say that there are no steadfast rules in destroying a nefarious neckaholic. The best you can do is start with the basics and go from there to find what works.

THE HIGHGATE VAMPIRE

When it comes to modern-day vampire hunting, there are a few instances where the perpetrator isn't typically a heinous blood-obsessed serial killer or a murderer using vampirism as a guise to justify his or her gruesome crimes. Although the modern vampire hunter is a relative oddity in comparison to the ubiquitous slayers of old eastern Europe, one of the most infamously well-known vampire hunts occurred at Highgate Cemetery in London in 1970, and it was conducted not by a single intrepid hunter but two competing "vampire slayers" who've repeatedly faced off to deal with the Highgate phenomenon. David Farrant and Sean Manchester were the combatants in this mortal, if not comic, crusade against the forces of evil and have vigorously defended their positions for over thirty years.

Grave Consequences

Strange doings at Highgate Cemetery began as early as the 1920s, when witnesses reported sightings of a huge batlike creature near the cemetery. According to the tale, investigating police later saw the creature roaming the grounds and chased it away. Soon after, several victims sought medical attention for bite wounds on their necks, and rumors of vampires quickly took off and remained entrenched for decades. In the early 1960s, several vampiric sightings were again reported in the cemetery, with depictions of hovering phantoms and bodies rising from graves. With an increasing volume of rumor and media attention, Highgate Cemetery drew the interest of a group of thrill-seeking occultists in 1969, among whom were David Farrant and Sean Manchester, who infiltrated the cemetery grounds to uncover the origins of the vampiric being.

Fangtastic Folklore Both Sean Manchester and David Farrant went on to create separate cottage industries out of their respective "encounters" with vampires and have written numerous books describing their exploits. Self-professed vampire experts and hunters, the pair have maintained the same melodramatic feuding that gained their initial attention and continue the theme to this very day.

Read All about It!

Verbal bickering between Farrant and Manchester proved irresistible to the headline-hungry British media, and when Manchester announced his intention to conduct a vampire hunt in mid-March of 1970, the press quickly televised interviews with both men. Within hours, a horde of curiosity seekers mobbed the cemetery, climbing over locked gates and walls for a first-hand glimpse of the notorious "vampires." Harried police officers finally emptied the cemetery grounds of looky-loos, but the historic die was already cast, with Highgate Cemetery's place in vampire lore officially secured.

Emboldened by the commotion at Highgate, Farrant was arrested several months later inside the cemetery carrying a crucifix, a mallet, and a wooden stake. Although acquitted for trespassing charges, Farrant's arrest again drew media attention. Manchester, by his own accounts, also visited the cemetery and claimed to have discovered the remains of a vampire, although a friend convinced him to let it rest. Years later, Manchester claimed that he discovered the corpse of the same vampire inside a vacant house nearby.

FAMOUS VAMPIROLOGISTS

Over the centuries there have been a number of scholars, historians, chroniclers, experts, and folklorists who specialize in the study of vampires and revenants. Some of these individuals have dedicated their lives to learning, revealing, and debating everything there is to know about the undead, basing their opinions and studies on everything from folklore to alleged accounts of vampirism to serial killers to modern-day blood fetish practices. Though there are many in the offering who've brought to light the intense legends surrounding bloodsucking revenants, there are a few who've staked their reputations in giving us a more well-rounded view of the vampire:

- ✝ **Leo Allatius:** A Greek Catholic scholar, Leo Allatius was one of the first historians to establish a connection between vampires and Greek history in his writings of the mid-1600s. Allatius' work was one of the first examples of the Catholic Church's acceptance of vampires as a reality.
- ✝ **Guiseppe Davanzati:** In response to waves of vampire hysteria in Europe, Italian archbishop Guiseppe Davanzati published an influential treatise in 1744 denouncing the vampire phenomenon as hysteria and delusion. He became known as a leading authority on vampirism within the Catholic Church and throughout Europe.
- ✝ **Dom Augustin Calmet:** A French Benedictine monk, Dom Calmet was among the first clerics to address vampirism and its relationship with witches and demons in his 1746 treatise on vampires and revenants, which lent a significant element of credence to their existence.

- ✝ **Franz Hartmann:** During the early 1900s, Franz Hartmann, a noted German physician and occultist of the era, wrote widely distributed and purportedly true incidents regarding vampires. Hartmann was an originator of the concept of *psychic vampirism*, explaining that while vampires didn't consume human blood, they did consume human energy and life force (see Chapter 19).
- ✝ **Montague Summers:** No list of vampirologists would be complete without the inclusion of Montague Summers. Despite Summers's notoriety as a respected expert and author of several vampire studies beginning in 1928, he's also known as an opinionated eccentric, and today it's generally accepted that he replaced careful research with often fanciful embellishments.
- ✝ **Raymond McNally and Radu Florescu:** The dynamic duo of vampirism, McNally and Florescu researched the origins of Stoker's *Dracula* and formulated the first generally accepted theories that *Dracula* was intrinsically based on the exploits Vlad Dracula—a concept that has come under fire since its inception in 1972. McNally is also the author of *Dracula Was a Woman: In Search of the Blood Countess of Transylvania*, in which he explores the myths, realities, and horrors attributed to notoriously bloodthirsty killer Erzébet Bathóry (see Chapter 11).
- ✝ **Elizabeth Miller:** A University of Newfoundland professor, Miller is internationally recognized as one of the world's leading experts on Vlad Dracula, Bram Stoker and his *Dracula*, and vampire history and lore. She has written dozens of articles and six well-respected books, including *Dracula, The Shade and the Shadow, Reflections on Dracula, Dracula, Sense & Nonsense,* and *A Dracula Handbook*.

KISS OF DEATH

Examining the world of vampire slayers and vampirologists now brings us to the issue of alleged "real" vampires and their exploits. As one might expect, this takes us back over a millennia, when the fact, fiction, and certainly the science of vampirism hadn't yet sealed its legendary coffin. But that didn't stop individuals from drawing on the revenants of folklore and the true-life exploits of several of the world's most sadistic and bloodthirsty killers.

CHAPTER 11

ONCE BITTEN, TWICE SHY

Throughout the centuries there have been numerous accounts of alleged encounters with vampires. Though the majority are the stuff legends are made of, there are a few documented incidents that have become renowned for their intrigue and the hysteria they caused among populations whose religious beliefs, superstitions, or just plain fear contributed to the tales gaining a distinct measure of immortality. In this chapter, we examine a few of the more well-known vampires and the chain of events surrounding their untimely deaths—and rebirth into the world of the undead.

THE CHRONICLES OF WILLIAM OF NEWBURGH

A careful chronicler of English history between 1066 and 1175, William of New-burgh is generally considered to be the most accurate contemporary authority of the twelfth century, having compiled the highly regarded *History of English Affairs* toward the end of his life in 1198. Newburgh was profoundly steadfast, and more than a little pompous, in his determination to record historically accurate events, and he vociferously denounced historians who relied on mythology and hearsay in their endeavors to educate the literate public. With Newburgh's unwavering dedication to historical accuracy, it's interesting to note that he included in his masterwork a series of events that he believed were passed to him by reliable sources. These are among the very few accounts found in English literature that were written by a distinguished historian to relate the existence of revenants—quite literally, the walking dead.

The Vampires of Buckinghamshire and Berwick

Newburgh's first account of the undead occurred in the English county of Buckinghamshire, where a deceased man returned to his wife's bed and laid upon her, nearly crushing her with his weight. After she fought him off, the man proceeded to terrorize the rest of his family and neighbors for many days. After insistent complaints to the clergy, the bishop Hugh of Lincoln, who would later be sainted by the Church of England, sent a written abso-lution to be placed on the man's corpse. Apparently, the religious curative worked, and the man's walking corpse ceased harassing the villagers.

Later, another deceased fellow in the town of Berwick, on the northern tip of England, who was reputed to have been very wealthy and graced with an evil temperament, reportedly began creeping from his grave to roam the streets at night with dogs furiously nipping at his heels. Within days the panicked townsmen solved their decomposing dilemma by digging up the corpse as it "slept" during the day and burning it to ashes.

The Cleric Vampire of Melrose Abbey

One of the most startling stories of the undead to come to William of Newburgh's attention was that of a chaplain who worked for a noblewoman near Melrose Abbey in Scotland, and who'd essentially ignored his religious duties during life, preferring to spend his days hunting with hounds on horseback. Shortly after the cleric's death, he began appearing at Melrose Abbey, but his attempts to enter were thwarted by the abbey's sanctity. Soon he appeared in the chambers of the noblewoman he'd failed to serve as a member of the clergy and haunted her with cries of anguish.

The frightened noblewoman beseeched a ranking monk from the abbey to put a stop to the corpse's nightly terrors, and he vowed to stand guard over the grave. As the tale goes, the man's corpse rose from the grave and attacked the monk, who responded with several panicked swings of the axe he carried. The defeated creature returned to his grave, which opened to receive him and then closed around him. The following day, a group of monks returned to the gravesite to exhume the disruptive corpse and burn it. When they recovered the body, they noticed with horror the slash marks of the axe and a growing pool of blood inside the casket.

VAMPIRE BITE

Even the Norse Vikings had legends of their own undead with the *draugar*, who were the human forms of mariners lost at sea and denied a proper burial. A *draug* (singular) would wander the shores of Norway seeking vengeance on any soul who dared cross his path. The Royal Norwegian Navy honored the legend with the production of their Draug Class destroyers, first built in 1908 as submarine hunters.

The Vampire of Alnwick

The final vampirish ghoul to appear in William of Newburgh's chronicles became known as "The Vampire of Alnwick" and had developed an evil reputation as a cruel and mean-spirited man during his lifetime. On his last night on earth in human form, this lost soul had crept onto his own rooftop in an effort to spy on his wife through the window of her chambers, with the apparent expectation of catching her in the act of an adulterous affair. He slipped from the roof and fell to earth, dying in agony the following day.

Soon after the man's burial, the people in the town of Alnwick began reporting the ghastly sight of his corpse wandering through the streets. Almost immediately, a plague began sweeping through Alnwick, and as the death toll mounted, an increasing sense of panic ensued. The revenant was held accountable for the disease and his corpse, enormously engorged with black bile and blood, was burned to ashes. Coincidence or not, the epidemic ceased, which was held as proof that the undead and damned had indeed plagued the people of Alnwick.

ERZÉBET BATHÓRY

Since the dawn of man there have been, and shall always be, heinous killers whose motivations and propensities provide scientists, scholars, psychologists, doctors, and historians with more than enough analysis, speculation, proof, and study to fill the Library of Alexandria a thousand times over. A number of those murderers possess an unquenchable obsession with blood among other unspeakable atrocities. Yet among those deviants is a sixteenth-century woman who stands alone in regard to her madness, sadism, and the sheer number of lives she destroyed for her own horrific hedonism. Though accounts of her crimes vary among experts, most generally agree that her blood obsession is part of vampiric legend, stained with the dubious fact that unlike many purported vampiric malfeasants—she was real. Her name is Countess Erzébet "Elizabeth" Bathóry, often known as the Countess of Blood or Blood Countess, who was born into Hungarian royalty in 1560.

The Family That Slays Together . . .

Alleged to be a woman of great beauty, it's speculated that Bathóry's malevolence may have stemmed from her suffering fits as a child, perhaps even epilepsy, while also being of a lineage rife with madness and close relatives purported to practice witchcraft, alchemy, and Satanism. This evil was perpetuated by her marriage at age fifteen to Count Ferencz Nádasdy, a man of equally unsound genetics who readily shared his allegedly torturous ways with Bathóry, making their castles and various homes literal houses of pain and torment. The majority of torture was handed out to poor servant girls, who the Count is said to have left outside, tied up, and covered with honey so as to endure the stings of insects. During harsh winters, another favorite practice saw naked girls left outside to the elements and water poured over them until they became human ice cubes. So strong was Bathóry's drive for torture and blood that she practiced all forms of supernatural arts and indeed accelerated her murders long after her husband died in 1604 and she'd holed up in one of her Hungarian estates.

SCREEN SCREAM

Ghost Hunters International, a popular Sci Fi Channel series that visits purportedly haunted sites throughout the world, visited the Bathory Ruins at Cachtice Castle in an episode that aired on August 18, 2008. Many visitors have claimed to feel the presence of Bathory while at the castle; however, the GHI team was unable to find any evidence of paranormal happenings.

The aristocracy of that era were the supreme class, and common throughout the caste was the practice of brutally mistreating and killing the lower classes with nary a soul batting an eyelash. This in part helped aid Bathóry in her personal pandemic, as few would dare oppose her, much less expose her proclivities lest they risk losing their own lives—despite the fact that for many years an unknown number of females, from children to women, simply disappeared. What's known from the writings and speculations of experts, accounts of the day, and the Countess' much heralded trials is that the alleged tortures that took place are even by today's standards so extreme so as not to be believed. Seemingly motivated by blood, the effect it had on her beauty and countenance, the sheer joy that torturing and watching girls die bestowed upon her is worthy of the devil's praise.

Cruel and Unusual

The unfortunate victims of both Bathóry and her cohorts endured a gamut of pain from removing and manipulating various body parts with scissors to biting, breaking bones, using hot pokers, draining their blood, burning them, eating their flesh or forcing them to consume their own flesh, and typically beating them until they mercifully died. What's often written about Bathóry is that she actually bathed in the blood of her victims in an effort to retain her youth and vitality, though this fact is never mentioned in her trial notes and cannot be established with considerable certainty. What's obvious, however, is her insatiable thirst for blood, coupled with the cruelty, sadism, and raw animalistic nature of the worst kind of predator.

The Price of Immortality

As with all serial murderers, there comes at some point an arrogance and invincibility afforded them as a result of not being caught. This trait befell Bathóry as well, at which time she erred in judgment by focusing her efforts less on lower class peasants and more on girls of various nobles under the guise of imbuing them to her as a Medieval Miss Manners. The act backfired, and in 1609 the Countess of Blood would at last be stopped. Her compound raided and victims found dead, tortured and dying, and even more imprisoned, Bathóry's despicable practices became horrifically apparent.

Two trials were held in an effort to convict or clear the Countess, with many victims and cohorts testifying the gory and brutal details of torture and murder. Estimates vary from the official court number of eighty victims to the unthinkable number of 650 as registered in writing by Bathóry herself. If accurate, that number is beyond astonishing. For her part, the Countess insisted upon her innocence, stating that the girls died from all measure of disease and other maladies. But that mattered little. Bathóry was found guilty and died over three years later, still allegedly isolated in the walled-up rooms of her castle, a Medieval Hannibal Lecteress who would, no doubt, still be up to her evil ways were she actually immortal.

HENRY MORE

A pre-eminent contributor to the study of metaphysics and to the *Cambridge Platonists*, an assembly of theorists at Cambridge University who defied Puritan dogma and promoted the concept that religion and rationality were harmonious, Henry More was a prolific writer of philosophical treatises. Among those was *An Antidote Against Atheism*, written at the age of thirty-nine in 1653, in which he discusses ghosts, witches, and, of course, revenants and vampires. Not since the distinguished works of William of Newburgh had a major English author attempted to chronicle the malodorous world of the undead, and More's book became an influential addition to their legacy. The ghoulish characters that Henry More documents offer an intriguing glimpse of the malignant malefactors who fouled the night air of early England.

VAMPIRE BITE

The term *poltergeist* has become inextricably linked with the trilogy of highly successful *Poltergeist* films made in the 1980s in which seemingly mischievous spirits become increasingly malevolent. The word comes from the German *poltern*, which means to rumble, and *geist*, meaning ghostly spirit. The nighttime nuisances of lost souls who roam the earth creating physical disturbances are the work of poltergeists, and the vampirish undead are part of the club.

The Shoemaker of Breslau

One of More's reports of the ghastly doings of the undead in 1590 involved a shoemaker in the town of Breslau, in the Lower Silesia region of Poland, who'd violated religious law by slashing his own throat. His relatives are said to have washed his blood-spattered body and covered his wounds with burial linens in an effort to convince the presiding priest that the man had died of natural causes. After being buried with Christian ceremony, rumors of the shoemaker's suicide began to circulate, and under pressure from the Church, the family confessed that he'd indeed committed suicide.

As the clerics pondered the contradictory situation of a suicide victim having been consecrated against Church custom, the shoemaker's corpse arose from its grave and began terrorizing the townspeople. The hauntings continued for several months until the church authorities ordered his body exhumed and placed on display for six days. Still, the stubborn shoemaker continued his nightly harassments, so his body was buried in an unmarked grave under the hangman's gallows in an effort to keep him still.

After suffering another month of nighttime rantings and disturbance through the city streets, the townspeople and authorities were completely fed up. They disinterred the shoemaker's corpse once again, and this time they cut off his arms, legs, and head, and cut his heart, which was recorded to be "as fresh and entire as in a calf newly killed." The shoemaker's dismembered body was cremated, and the soul of the man who would become known as "The Breslau Vampire" was finally at peace.

The Pentsch Vampire

Another of Henry More's historical tales relates the deathly emergence of an alderman, also in the region of Silesia in the Polish town of Pentsch in 1655. Johannes Cuntius (sometimes spelled Cuntze), a town alderman, had been severely kicked in the groin by a horse and succumbed after days of agony and complaining of his sinful life. On his deathbed, a black cat is said to have entered the room and scratched his face—a bad omen indeed. After Cuntius's burial, Pentsch was plagued with vicious poltergeist-like pranks, violent visitations on inhabitants, the attempted stranglings of elderly men, and horror stories of infants being bashed to death.

The frightened townspeople exhumed the corpses of several of the most recently deceased for examination and found that all had decomposed except that of the alderman's. His skin was said to be "tender and florid" and "a staff being put in his hand, he grasped it with his fingers very tightly." After nearly six months in the grave, Cuntius's still "fresh" corpse was burnt, putting an end to the misery of his malevolent vampiric wanderings.

PETER PLOGOJOWITZ

To the casual reader, the name Peter Plogojowitz may not ring a bell, but if you're a vampire aficionado you'll likely recognize the Serbian peasant as one of the most famous vampires in the folkloric realm. What's of particular interest in the Plogojowitz case is that his sordid tale is actually quite well documented, despite having taken place in the Serbian village of Kisilova in 1725. In his book *Vampire, Burials, and Death*, renowned author Paul Barber makes very astute and unbiased observations about Plogojowitz's antics, the repercussions taken by authorities, and what could have been a hysterical village population. But first, the account of what happened in 1725 to promote the hapless peasant into postmortem posterity.

Midnight Caller

In 1725, Peter Plogojowitz, by rights an average man of little distinction, passed away and was buried in the Rahm district of Kisilova. Just over a week later, a mysterious twenty-four-hour illness, which some report as involving a loss of blood, struck nine villagers of varying ages resulting in their deaths. Plogojowitz's wife claimed that her dearly departed husband had paid her a visit in order to collect his shoes (some accounts claim he visited his son for food on several occasions and when refusing dear old dead dad, the son died). This substantiated the reports—prior to their demise—from those who fell ill that Plogojowitz not only visited them but attempted to strangle them.

VAMPIRE BITE By definition, *decomposition* is the decay of a dead body or any organic matter. Where folkloric vampires and other corpses were concerned, little attention was paid or surmised that perhaps the bloating due to internal gasses and buildup of fluids accounted for the frightening groans and spurting blood that a corpse emitted as it was being staked.

As is often done in these situations, Plogojowitz was exhumed to ascertain if he bore typical vampiric signs, including a lack of decomposition, a ruddy complexion, fingernails and hair showing growth, and the presence of fresh blood. With the cooperation of authorities and military personnel, the poor man was dug up, and according to accounts did indeed bear the telltale signs of a vampire. Some of his skin had sloughed off to show new skin underneath, his hair and nails had grown, there was blood near his mouth, and he appeared relatively intact. It should come as no surprise that his appearance was cause for panic and anger.

A Grave Decision

The authority (as Paul Barber cites, the "Imperial Provisor") of the district and the clergyman who oversaw the exhumation were faced with villagers who took matters into their own hands—literally. Plogojowitz's corpse was staked through the heart, after which it was reported that fresh blood leaked from his chest and out the mouth and ears. The poor man's corpse was promptly set alight and burned to ash. Naturally, this gave cause for all of his alleged victims to also be exhumed and measures taken, such as garlic stuffed in their mouths, to make certain they would rest in peace.

Though accounts of the story vary depending on expert analysis, Paul Barber brings up what are rather typical consistencies and inconsistencies in these types of vampiric plagues. The first of those is that which we cover in Chapter 7, namely that it's typical that the first infected victim of a plague or epidemic is oftentimes blamed for its occurrence and the corpse is usually destroyed. Another commonality Barber mentions is that victims often complain of suffocation, which in Plogojowitz's case was mentioned by those who fell ill. What doesn't often make sense is the presence of fresh blood rather than coagulated blood. Unless he'd recently fed, then the blood would certainly clot and dry.

ARNOD PAOLE

Two years after the Peter Plogojowitz case came yet another incident that became even more famous, in part as a result of Austrian regimental field surgeon Johannes Flückinger's widely read report entitled *Visum et Repertum* (alternately translated as "Seen and Heard" or "Seen and Discovered"), which was published and presented to the Austrian Emperor in 1732. Flückinger's report, which states that vampires do indeed exist, focused on a Serbian vampire epidemic, the initial vampire in this instance alleged to be Serbian soldier Arnod Paole (also cited as Arnold Paul). Though accounts vary, the story goes that in 1727, Paole returned home to the village of Medvegia (also spelled Meduegna) on the outskirts of Belgrade. It's said that Paole himself told of an encounter he'd had with a vampire while stationed in

Greece, which was then known as Turkish Serbia (other accounts describe this incident as Paole having had a dream). The *Repertum* states that Paole "had eaten from the earth of the vampire's grave and had smeared himself with the vampire's blood, in order to be free of the vexation he had suffered." Unfortunately for the former soldier, his "cure" proved futile, and he allegedly spread his tall tale around the village—a seemingly harmless endeavor that would prove to be his unearthly undoing.

Fangtastic Folklore

In Chapter 7 we focus on how vampires are created, and Arnod Paole is a perfect example of the folkloric vampire who's blamed for initiating a vampiric plague, especially given the condition of his corpse. What's interesting is that Johannes Flückinger's investigation took place almost five years *after* Paole's death and destruction, thereby basing his report on villagers' accounts of what occurred at the time.

Stake Out

Not long after arriving home, Paole died as a result of falling off a hay wagon. A month or so after his interment, local villagers made known that Arnod Paole was not going peacefully into that good night. He was, in fact, troubling them and was allegedly responsible for four killings. As with Peter Plogojowitz, these accusations became grounds for digging up Paole to examine his corpse for signs of vampirism, which they did forty days after his burial. Again, the folkloric signs of the ultimate nightcrawler came into sharp focus. According to the *Repertum*, the villagers found that Paole was "quite complete and undecayed, and that fresh blood had flowed from his eyes, nose, mouth, and ears; that the shirt, the covering, and the coffin were completely bloody; that the old nails on his hands and feet, along with the skin, had fallen off, and that new ones had grown." As was customary, a stake was driven through Paole's heart, and he "gave an audible groan and bled copiously." After he was done scaring the knickers off everyone with his final death knell, he was burned to ashes.

The Medvegia Vampires

Whereas the Plogojowitz case ended with his burning, Paole's did not. The panic his alleged vampirism caused and the resulting exhumation, observation, and chain reaction destruction of victims afflicted by vampirism gave those victims the dubious title of "The Medvegia Vampires." The logic that ensued after Paole's destruction was such that the corpses of his four aforementioned victims should also be dispatched. But it didn't stop there. Common assumption dictated that Paole fed upon local cattle, and given that villagers consumed their cattle, *they* were also infected and in danger of becoming bloodsuckers. The *Repertum* states that within three months, seventeen individuals perished within two or three days as a result of illness. One even cited a fellow deceased villager as her attacker. Coincidence? Not bloody likely. As one would expect, all of the unfortunate deceased were exhumed, and the results of Flückinger's report are highly detailed in regard to the status of each corpse's condition, similar in many ways to that of Paole, with various traits that one in the modern-day might attribute to typical decomposition—or not. The few who were simply decomposed were reinterred; however, the majority of the Medvegia Vampires were summarily decapitated, burned, and their ashes released into the river.

THE VAMPIRE OF CROGLIN GRANGE

Because it's gained significant notoriety over the centuries, primarily as a result of its controversy, we'd be remiss in not mentioning the legend of the Vampire of Croglin Grange. Rife with intrigue, horror, and a bloodthirsty creature from hell, the story came to light in the late 1800s courtesy Augustus Hare, in his succinctly titled memoirs: *The Story of My Life*. The tale was told to Hare by Captain Fisher, the owner of a one-story country home called Croglin Grange in Cumberland, England. The Fishers rented the home to three siblings, two brothers and their sister, who were very popular among both the poor and wealthy of the community. One exceedingly hot summer night, the sister retired, though she couldn't sleep. Looking out the window, she noticed two odd lights in the distance—lights that came closer and closer until they manifested themselves into a horrific creature with a "hideous brown face with flaming eyes" staring and scratching at her window. Making its way inside, it attacked the poor woman, inflicting upon her a ghastly throat wound that quite nearly killed her. One of her brothers saw the beast retreat into the neighboring churchyard.

Justifying that the "creature" was an escaped asylum lunatic, the siblings recuperated for a time in Switzerland before returning to the Grange. However, months after their return, the creature reappeared at the sister's window. This time the brothers were prepared, with one shooting it in the leg as it again made for the churchyard. The following day, a group of locals opened an old vault at the churchyard, emptying the contents of each coffin until they at last came upon a creature described as "brown, withered, shriveled, and mummified." It had a gunshot wound to its leg. In true vampire fashion, the creature was burned.

Though far more dramatic and terrifying in its original publication, Hare's story provoked serious terror, while at the same time gathering a coffin-full of criticism citing the incident as pure fiction. It wasn't until the 1900s that a few intrepid souls set out—rather amusingly—to find the truth of the matter and debunk each other, beginning in 1924 with Charles G. Harper. Upon traveling to Cumberland, Harper discovered only a Croglin Low Hall and a Croglin High Hall and nary a church in sight for over a mile. In the 1930s, F. Clive-Ross set out to debunk Harper, coming to the conclusion that the Low Hall once had a chapel in close proximity.

Three decades later, in 1968, D. Scott Rogo came up with a different angle, suggesting that Hare's Croglin tale mimicked that of James Malcolm Rymer's 1847 penny dreadful *Varney the Vampyre*. Rogo's big revelation, however, was that in speaking with local villagers, Hare's Croglin Grange incident actually occurred in the 1680s and the late 1800s! And just in case this wasn't already a scholarly Peyton Place, renowned author Lionel Fanthorpe in recent years uncovered research showing that a vault near the Grange was destroyed during the Cromwell reign of England, thereby reaffirming the seventeenth-century timeframe. Whether the vampire actually existed remains uncertain.

FANGS FOR THE MEMORIES

No doubt the legends and accounts of alleged vampires such as Erzébet Bathóry, Peter Plogojowitz, Arnod Paole, and all of the other fiends we've discussed hold a significant, if not dubious, place in the vampire realm's Hall of Fame or Shame, as the case may be. In the next chapter, we further explore those deviants whose criminally vampiric exploits caused panic among modern-day populations and whose actions to this day remain unfathomable in their ferocity and bloodlust.

CHAPTER 12

Vampiric Crimes

Over the centuries, many criminals have committed or attempted murders using blood draining or drinking as a method of killing. Some truly believed they were vampires, others were looking for the thrill of the blood as a means of release. The Vampire of London, the Vampire of Hannover, and the Düsseldorf Vampire are a few of the infamous serial killers who used bloodletting and blood drinking to satisfy their murderous thirst. Whether these killers were truly acting as vampires or not is arguable, but their methods of carrying out their crimes is certainly drawn from vampire lore.

Early Vampiristic Crimes

There's much to be said about the nature of crimes committed by those individuals who for various reasons believed they were vampires, claimed influence by vampires, or simply used vampirism as an excuse for their heinous acts of torture, sadism, or murder. Over the centuries, especially in the modern era, these criminals and their acts have been analyzed, speculated upon, debated, and written about by all measure of expert, scholar, historian, and legal and psychiatric professional. There's no firm answer as to why an individual defiles another human being in the name of blood, but over time we've been able to ascertain certain commonalities that motivate the criminalistic vampire.

Gilles de Rais

One of the most notorious and shocking of the early European manifestations of bloodletting, torture, and murder—which included admissions of sadistic vampirism—centered on French nobleman Gilles de Rais, who had the distinction of having fought alongside Joan of Arc. In 1435, after inheriting a fortune, de Rais left the military at the age of thirty-one and retired to his estate, where he lived lavishly, delved into the occult and Satanism, and began a gruesome campaign of slaughtering at least fifty, and likely well over 100, young boys in hideously conceived, blood-soaked sacrificial ceremonies.

In 1440, de Rais was dragged before the French court after an ecclesiastical investigation showed evidence of his depravities, and he was forced to confess details of crimes so repulsive the magistrate ordered that the most disturbing revelations be struck from the record. News of the trial and the lurid tales of his blood drinking, cannibalism, and monstrous sexual perversions provoked public horror and outrage. The sadistic de Rais was found guilty and hanged, but the infamy of his barbarism earned him legendary notoriety as a living vampire with inhuman tastes in mayhem.

Vicount de Morieve

During the eighteenth century, French soil again became the focal point of heinous vampiric crimes when the Viscount de Morieve narrowly avoided the upswell of rebellion during the French Revolution that turned the nobility of France upside down. After the Revolution ended in 1799, however, de Morieve exacted his own form of retribution by arbitrarily executing many of the peasants who worked his estates. His capricious murders triggered his assassination, and soon after his burial a number of children began mysteriously dying in a steady series of occurrences that lasted for seventy-two years.

> ## VAMPIRE BITE
>
> *Hematomania* is a term identified with an individual who's psychologically obsessed with blood. Some modern-day "vampires" claim to suffer from this type of erotic bloodlust, which many would argue is more psychologically based than a medical condition such as hemophilia. One might argue that Gilles de Rais or Countess Erzébet Bathóry (see Chapter 11) were plagued by a type of hematomania spurned on by obvious psychological disorders.

In the early 1870s, de Morieve's grandson investigated the growing rumors that his grandfather had become a vampire and was responsible for the children's deaths. The vault containing de Morieve was opened and his remains appeared as fresh as the day he'd been interred, with soft, flushed skin, and grown fingernails. As a stake was driven into de Morieve's heart, it's said that his corpse uttered a last violent groan as blood gushed from the wound. De Morieve's grandson completed the ritual by having the corpse burned to ashes. As evidence that de Morieve's vampiric remains had been the cause of many decades of malevolent mischief, the mysterious deaths of children near his estate came to an end.

STAKING A CLAIM

As with all things historical and criminal there are always varying accounts of every crime that's ever occurred. When vampirism is involved, and the added incidents of cannibalism, necrophilia, witchcraft, and lycanthropy, it gets that much murkier. In Chapter 11, we discussed the evil torturer Erzébet Bathóry who's almost always included in the dark dungeons of the vampire realm. Sadly, she was not alone in her bloodlust, madness, and murder. Many sadists, cannibals, necrophiles, and torturers with no aversion to blood or consuming it have walked the planet, worst among them the infamous Marquis de Sade (for which sadism is named), the "Rostov Ripper" Andrei Chikatilo, Jeffrey Dahmer, and Ted Bundy to name a few.

A wide range of documented cases of vampiric crimes surfaced during the nineteenth and twentieth centuries, running the gamut from Frenchman Martin Dumollard, who was convicted and executed in 1861 for murdering several young girls and drinking their blood, to sixteen-year-old New Yorker and self-proclaimed vampire Salvatore Agron who donned a Bela Lugosi get-up and randomly stabbed two young boys in 1959. Typical of many of the cases involving alleged vampirism are a variety of psychological and behavioral disorders, including a lack of remorse, promiscuity, domination, childhood abuse, and all measure of perversion and deception in order to accomplish their bloody goals. Though there are dozens of cases of alleged vampires, a few stand out in regard to their bizarre nature.

Frenchman Joseph Vacher of Bourge, for example, undertook a walking tour of the country and along the way killed a dozen individuals by biting their necks and drinking their blood. He was convicted and executed in 1897. In 1920, Russian Baron Roman von Sternberg-Ungren wasn't convicted, or even charged with murder, but he was known for drinking human blood, presumably against his victims' wishes and with the motivation that he was Genghis Khan reincarnated. A change in government put him out of favor with the new regime and he was finally executed. In Argentina in 1960, Florencio Roque Fernandez was identified by fifteen women as the man who assaulted them in their bedrooms to drink their blood.

James Riva suffered from the common belief that consuming blood would give him immortal life. He also claimed to hear a vampiric voice. In 1980, Riva shot and killed his wheelchair-bound grandmother and then allegedly drank her blood. In 1998, Joshua Rudiger, a self-professed vampire residing in Oakland, California, became the "Vampire Slasher" by preying upon the homeless, attacking them and slashing their throats with a knife. He wounded three men and killed one woman in San Francisco. According to news accounts, he said of the killings that "prey is prey." Rudiger believed he was a vampire who was two millennia old, and that he needed the blood to "obtain vitality."

THE VAMPIRE OF LONDON

In March of 1949, the *London Mirror* ran a series of stories entitled *Hunt for the Vampire* that detailed the disappearance of several area residents and the arrest of the man believed responsible for their deaths. That man was John George Haigh, and shortly after his arrest, he confessed to killing six people and dissolving their remains in acid to hide the evidence. He claimed that his motive for the murders was a compulsion for blood, and the story he told portrayed him as a mentally ill individual who'd simply acted on his impulses. Authorities were inclined to believe otherwise, leaving the matter to be settled in court in a sensational, if not gruesome, trial that earned Haigh the title of "The Vampire of London."

Fenced In

John Haigh was born in 1909 in Wakefield, England, and raised by parents who were members of the Plymouth Brethren, which practiced extreme isolationism from society. Haigh's fundamentalist parents instilled in him an overwhelming impression of Christ bleeding on the cross and the saving grace of that very blood—an image that would haunt his nightmares, and which in turn would become the nightmares of his victims. During his childhood, Haigh's life was stifled and largely confined to the family home, surrounded by a ten-foot-tall fence to keep him from the outside world.

For years Haigh's life seemed uneventful until he reached the age of forty and lived in South Kensington. One day, he told a close female friend of sixty-nine-year-old Olive Durand-Deacon that Olive had missed a business meeting with him and hadn't been seen for a day. Haigh took the friend to the police to file a report, and once Scotland Yard received the report they quickly learned that Haigh had a lengthy record for fraud, forgery, and theft. While the mannerly Haigh calmly expressed his concern for Olive's well-being, the police launched an investigation into his business where he conducted so-called "experimental work." When searching the business, they found containers of sulphuric acid, a chemical-stained apron, rubber gloves and boots, a gas mask, and vats full of "sludge."

Fangtastic Folklore Known as the "Vampire of Sacramento," Richard Trenton Chase's six victims suffered from his delusion that he needed to drink and bathe in their blood, *and* eat their raw organs to prevent Nazis from transforming his own blood into powder. Chase was so certain of his Nazi theory, he asked renowned profiler Robert Ressler for a radar gun, with which Chase believed he could shoot down Nazi UFOs and force *them* to stand trial for the murders. Sentenced to life in prison in 1980, Chase committed suicide in his cell with an overdose of prescribed antidepressants.

Ticket to Ride

Haigh was finally arrested after pawning jewelry to a suspicious dealer, who took it to the police where it was identified as belonging to Olive Durand-Deacon. During his interrogation, Haigh surprised detectives by asking what the odds were of being relegated to the Broadmoor Asylum for the Criminally Insane. Assuming he'd discovered a loophole in the legal system, Haigh, utterly convinced that he couldn't be prosecuted without a corpse for evidence, confessed to murdering Durand-Deacon and dissolving her body in acid. As he dictated the gruesome details of Olive's death and the dissolving, Haigh was so self-assured, he confessed to the murders and disposals of eight more people using the same technique. By his own admission, he claimed that he had to kill to survive and slit the throats of all of his victims so that he could drink their blood.

The media sensation prior to Haigh's trial was one of pure hysteria, and the killer reveled in descriptions of his being a blood-crazed vampire. In his mind, he was untouchable and above the law, and he was certain he would be acquitted without bodily evidence, or at the very least, placed into a mental institution from which he would eventually be released. Haigh was wrong on both counts. Forensic examinations of the "sludge" found at Haigh's workplace provided intact dentures belonging to Olive Durand-Deacon. Olive's lipstick container and her bloodstained coat were also discovered, along with blood on knives, walls, and Haigh's own shirtsleeve. A team of psychiatrists—including those for the defense—established that Haigh was most certainly paranoid but faking his insanity, although there was little dispute that the monster's fascination with blood began during his youth with visions of a bloodied Christ. The jury found him guilty of murder in twelve minutes, leaving the "vampire" John Haigh to be hanged at the gallows on August 6, 1949.

Fangtastic Folklore

John Haigh's final questionable glory in life was answering a request from Madam Tussaud to fit him for a death mask before he was hanged, ironically, just a year before her own passing. The delighted mass murderer was more than happy to comply and even provided her with his own suit to clothe his wax figure likeness for display at Madam Tussaud's Chamber of Horrors.

THE VAMPIRE OF HANNOVER

During the devastated years of post–World War I Germany, the city of Hannover was the hunting ground of Fritz Haarmann, one of the most notorious vampiric serial killers of all time—and it would take years before it was discovered that the fiend had been committing his grisly crimes right under the noses of the police. The first evidence of Haarmann's butchery emerged on May 17, 1924, on the banks of the River Leine, which runs through the city and where a growing number of human bones and skulls began washing onto the riverbanks. These savage discoveries coincided with a groundswell of rumors that human flesh was being peddled on the flourishing black market—a fact that sent the community into a frenzy of public outcry to find the brutal beast who was littering their city with human remains.

A Match Made in Hell

At the age of forty-one, Fritz Haarmann was only one of a long list of "rehabilitated" sexual offenders who roamed the streets of Hannover, having been imprisoned for nine months in 1920 for molesting a young boy. Arrested for the crime in 1918, detectives had discovered the pair in Haarmann's bed while searching for another missing child. To their horror, they would learn many years later that the decapitated head of the child they were searching for was in the same dwelling, wrapped in a newspaper and stuffed behind the stove.

After Haarmann was released from jail, he renewed an enamored relationship with a young, handsome male prostitute named Hans Grans, and the pair soon became inseparable and well-known street figures. Despite Haarmann's sketchy past as a homeless vagrant who'd spent time in his late teens in a mental institution, he and his partner developed reputations as well-dressed, respectable gentlemen who earned a decent living selling used clothing and meat on the underground market that had become a vital source for scarce goods to the people of war-ravaged Hannover. Unknown to the public, Haarmann supplemented his income as a paid police informant. Also unknown was that the "respectable" gentlemen were a pairing of unspeakable monstrosity.

Arrested Development

It would be later learned that Haarmann employed his knowledge of the workings of the police by passing himself off as a detective at the Hannover train station, where he would accost homeless runaway boys and frighten them into accompanying him back to his home. Other times, he would offer work or lodging to lure boys to their deaths. But the train station ruse finally proved to be Haarmann's undoing in June of 1924, when he became embroiled in a nasty altercation with a boy of fifteen that attracted the attention of railway police. Panicked by police intervention, Haarmann claimed the boy was traveling with false papers in an effort to have him arrested.

The attempt at diversion failed, and both were dragged to the police station for questioning, where the boy accused Haarmann of sexually harassing him—an accusation that piqued the curiosity of detectives who were working on solving the grim mystery of the sickening discoveries on the riverbank. The detectives searched Haarmann's residence and found piles of clothing and property later identified as having belonged to the growing list of missing youngsters. The spreading news of those discoveries lead to a flood of evidence, with reports of Haarmann being seen leading victims from the train station and the identification of clothing of other victims that Haarmann had sold to unsuspecting buyers.

Fangtastic Folklore

The Hannover Tourist Board created a sensation in 2007 when it issued an advent calendar, that counts down the twenty-four-day period between December 1 and the nativity on December 24. Drawn in cartoon style, the calendar depicted Fritz Haarmann lurking behind a tree with an axe while Santa Claus hands out presents to kids. The uproar escalated with the knowledge that advent calendars are traditionally designed for children. The initial print run of 20,000 was expected to last until Christmas. It sold out before the end of November.

Beware the Butcher

Haarmann broke down under incessant interrogation and confessed to his repulsive crimes, taking the police on a macabre tour of the city to show them stashes of discarded bones and skulls. In horrific detail, Haarmann described the blood-curdling methodology of his psychotic rampage, during which he would persuade boys into his home, overpower and rape them, and then sink his teeth into their windpipes and tear out their throats. Stripped of their clothing, which was later washed and prepared for sale, Haarmann decapitated and butchered the corpses down to the bone, and then coldly and neatly packaged the flesh to pass off as pork. It was revoltingly obvious that the remains and belongings of the victims were the backbone of Haarmann's thriving black market clothing and meat business.

In the sensational trial of the "Hannover Vampire" that captured the attention of the entire country, Haarmann conducted his own defense and tried to implicate his boy toy, Hans Grans, in the murders. The jury convicted Haarmann of the murder of twenty-four boys and found Grans guilty of luring one unfortunate boy into Haarmann's den of depravity. The number of victims that were accounted for, sadly, was a fraction of how many innocents Haarmann had quite literally butchered over a five-year period. Haarmann died for his crimes in April of 1925, on the guillotine of the Hannover Prison—at the hands of an executioner who decapitated him in a last and final irony of justice.

Fangtastic Folklore

As Fritz Haarmann's live-in lover, there's no question that Hans Grans was fully aware of Haarmann's slaughter of scores of victims and undoubtedly helped clean up the mess of butchering them like cattle. After Haarman's execution, Grans went to prison for twelve years for his part in those living nightmares and lived the rest of his life in obscurity. He reportedly passed away with little fanfare in 1980.

THE DÜSSELDORF VAMPIRE

In the documented history of the twentieth century, few pathological sadists with a literal thirst for blood can compete with the gruesome rampages of Germany's Peter Kürten. Only after Kürten's capture and confession in 1930 would an appalled world learn that his personal reign of terror had lasted for seventeen blood-soaked years, beginning with the mysterious murder of little Christine Klein in Köln, Germany, in 1913. Until Kürten's capture, it was only known that ten-year-old Christine had been attacked in her bed by a mysterious predator who'd slashed her throat and then sexually molested her. It was one of the few times that the man who'd killed her would leave behind a calling card—a handkerchief bearing the initials of a vampiric monster: "P.K."

The only suspect in Christine's death was her uncle Otto, who'd had a violent argument with Christine's father, Peter Klein, after being refused a loan. Otto threatened revenge, and it was theorized that he'd stolen Peter's handkerchief and purposely left it with the child's body as a grisly taunt. Years later, Kürten related that just days after the crime, he'd gone to a cafe near the scene and listened gleefully to the outraged conversations of the locals over the dead child and her alleged murderer. Although evidence against Otto was nonexistent, he was taken to trial and quickly acquitted. For Kürten, the excitement of the scandal and Otto's deflection of suspicion served to embolden his sadistic impulses, as did the excitement he gained by drinking little Christine's blood as it spurted from her slashed throat.

SCREEN SCREAM As with all high profile serial killers, Peter Kürten's dysfunction has served as the inspiration for several films, including Fritz Lang's 1931 masterpiece *M*, starring Peter Lorre, and the Robert Hossein's 1965 French film *Le Vampire de Düsseldorf*. Fritz Haarmon's case was the basis for the 1973 German film *Die Zärtlichkeit der Wölfe*, aka *Tenderness of the Wolves*.

The Dogcatcher

Born in 1883, Peter Kürten was raised in poverty in a one-room dwelling where he witnessed his alcoholic and abusive father repeatedly rape and beat his mother and sisters. During that period, Kürten's exposure to abnormality multiplied when he was befriended by a degenerate dogcatcher, who taught him skills that no young mind should ever have been exposed to, namely torturing and killing captured dogs. Through their twisted relationship, the pair formed a mutual bond that would cement Kürten's destiny of depravity.

Solitary Refinement

According to Kürten, his first foray into murdering humans occurred in his early teens while swimming with schoolmates in the Rhine River. Playing on a raft, Kürten held one of the boys under water until he drowned, and when a friend attempted to intervene, Kürten drowned him as well. From there, Kürten moved on to attacking sheep by sodomizing them while he stabbed them with a knife in a frenzy of sexual pleasure and bloody assaults on helpless creatures that ignited his passions to unimaginably horrendous heights. After running away from home at sixteen, Kürten relied on petty thefts to survive and began a mind-boggling string of twenty-seven relatively short prison sentences.

Incredibly, after one of Kürten's prison stints in 1921 he met and married a woman who knew nothing of her husband's perversions. He took a factory job in the city of Altenburg, became active in trade union activities, and kept his sadistic impulses under control for several years. That would change when the couple moved to Düsseldorf, where Kürten recalled that "the sunset was blood-red on my return." Kürten took the image as a signal that Düsseldorf would be the perfect place to fulfill his deadly destiny.

Swan Song

Kürten spent the next four years controlling his atrocious vampiric thirsts, although he committed petty thefts and arsons for which he was never apprehended. In 1929, he finally snapped and went on a rampage of berserk assaults on dozens of women, men, and children, sometimes pouring fuel on their corpses and setting them alight. As the body count continued to rise, the city of Düsseldorf was paralyzed with fearful indignation and disgust. Kürten was finally captured after he lured a young woman named Maria Budlick to his home while his wife was away and asked if he could "have" her. The fortunate woman saved her life by complying—the only woman ever to do so. Astonishingly, Kürten released her. Too frightened to go to authorities, Budlick wrote a letter to a friend detailing the incident, which was misdirected to a woman known as Frau Brückner, who immediately notified the police.

After being questioned, Kürten knew that the worst he could face was a rape charge, but he also knew that deeper investigations would unveil his association as the man the press had labeled "The Düsseldorf Vampire." Although he denied any wrongdoing, Kürten made the startling decision to confess everything to his wife so that she could turn him in to collect the substantial reward. Kürten's wife met with authorities in May of 1930 and he was arrested. He confessed to seventy-nine chilling murders of women, children, and men but was brought to trial for only nine. The extent of Kürten's crazed lust was zealously publicized as he reeled off detail after detail of scores of horrific, bloodthirsty murders that to this day are nearly inconceivable. By his own admission, he often took nighttime strolls along the lake in a city park. In 1930, during one of those forays, he happened upon a swan sleeping on the lakeshore. As evidence of his extreme bloodlust, Kürten, grabbed the swan, cut its throat, and drank from its neck, an action that offered sexual release.

The shell-shocked jury convicted Kürten in less than two hours of deliberation, and he went to the guillotine on July 2, 1932. The Düsseldorf Vampire's last ghastly request in life was to hear the blood gushing from the stump of his neck after his head was lopped off. Just as the monstrosity of Kürten's existence is virtually incomprehensible, the outcome of his final request will forever remain a mystery to the living.

VAMPIRES UNLEASHED

As we've learned in examining both "real" and alleged cases of criminal vampirism throughout history, there's little that a vampiric-oriented mortal won't do to satisfy his or her lust for blood. In the next chapter, we delve into vampiric monsters of a different sort—those born to the imagination of scores of writers who transform the vampire of lore into preternaturals that run the gamut from incredibly frightening to hopelessly romantic to eternally funny.

CHAPTER 13

THE LITERARY VAMPIRE

Just as with film, the literary community has over the decades embraced the vampire in all its preternatural glory. From its earliest inception to the present day, vampire literature has had myriad resurrections, with bloodsuckers taking all types of forms spread across all genres, from serialized novels based on television series to comedies to Westerns to gothic and modern romance and historical horror. Delve into any of these wonderful novels and you'll be quickly transported to another place and time along with some of the most romantic and notorious vampires in history.

SHADOWS AND LIGHT

In Chapter 3, we discuss early vampire literature and the trailblazers—Bram Stoker, John Polidori, James Malcolm Rymer, and Sheridan Le Fanu—who set the standard for all literary and cinematic vampirism to come. Now it's time to take a peek into the modern-day literary realm and all the movers and shakers who have preserved and continue to maintain the evolution of the world's ultimate immortal bad boys and girls. What must be said is that the sheer volume of vampire literature stands in tribute to the fact that no matter what era, what genre, or what type of vampire is imagined or mirrored, audiences *never* lose their taste for bloodsuckers.

LES VAMPIRES DE ANNE RICE

Of the hundreds of thousands of dedicated writers who've put pen to page over the centuries there are but a few who have risen to the level of Anne Rice, who over thirty years ago brought to life the most influential vampire since Stoker's Dracula. During the course of her career, Rice has unleashed upon the world a family of vampires known simply by their singular names: Louis, Pandora, Armand, Marius, Maharet, Merrick, Akasha, and Magnus, to name a few. But it wasn't until the beginning of her literary endeavors in 1976 and the masterpiece *Interview with the Vampire* that we were introduced to the intensely emotional preternatural ebb and flow that *is* the vampire Lestat.

Not since *Dracula* have the collective hearts, minds, and souls of the public been drawn to a vampire whose seductive charm, wicked intellect, philosophical nature, and excruciating thirst to reconcile good and evil make him a true vampire of the ages. Unlike Dracula, Rice instilled in Lestat de Lioncourt—her ultimate hero—a deep and unbridled emotion matched only by the wisdom he so desperately seeks, whether it be in his understanding of his reluctant fledgling Louis de Pointe du Lac, the teachings of Marius and Talamascan David Talbot, the destructive capacities of the ancient Akasha, or his confrontations with God and the alleged devil himself in *Memnoch the Devil*. It is said that Lestat was based on both Rice and her husband, Stan, with the very idea of *Interview with the Vampire* coming to Rice as a result of her five-year-old daughter, Michelle, succumbing to a rare form of leukemia. In life, Lestat was from an aristocratic lineage fallen on hard times during the 1780s. Born as a vampire by Magnus in the latter part of the 1700s, Lestat is, in all his vanity and bold endeavors, the quintessential vampire of the modern era.

Complex and luxuriously rich in their conception, their lineage, and their powers, Rice's *la famille de vampires* are most certainly the most revered in history. Rice has told their tales in what are the renowned Vampire Chronicles including: *Interview with the Vampire, The Vampire Lestat, The Queen of the Damned, The Tale of the Body Thief, Memnoch the Devil, The Vampire Armand, Merrick, Blood and Gold, Blackwood Farm, Blood Canticle*, and additional tales including *Pandora* and *Vittorio the Vampire*. Add to that their crossover into her best-selling series of the Mayfair Witches. Like Stoker, Anne Rice set the standard for all vampire fiction to come, and in her life's work she can, above all, take pride in knowing that she and her beloved vampires are *all* truly immortal.

POPULAR VAMPIRE FICTION

During the mid-1970s, the most popular vampire novels foreshadowed the concept of the vampire epic, with Anne Rice's *Interview with the Vampire* becoming the first of the *Vampire Chronicles*. Beginning in 1978, we were given only a hint of the towering efforts and prodigious talents of Chelsea Quinn Yarbro when she introduced us to what would become the *Saint-Germain* series. Tales of Yarbro's impossibly "human" vampire have been in nonstop evolution for thirty years and there's no sign of Saint-Germain disappearing into that cold dark night.

Welcome to the *Hotel Transylvania*

Chelsea Quinn Yarbro's first effort in the series, *Hotel Transylvania*, is set in the French court of King Louis XIV in the mid-seventeenth century, and features the enduring Count of Saint-Germain, who's been a vampire for hundreds of years and manages, unlike most vampires, to maintain a sense of superior humanity over bloodlust. In sharp counterpoint to Rice's vampires, or to those of virtually any other author, Yarbro's Saint-Germain is suave, sophisticated, and genuinely concerned about other human beings; in effect, he's a vampire with a soul. Both undead and immortal, he's acutely aware of the frailty of human life, and he does his best to respect the living while abhorring the evils that mankind brings upon itself.

To paraphrase Yarbro's personal perspective on the subject of the eternal vampire living in a world of mortals, her unusual approach to the vampire condition is to consider how a rational being would realistically react to the dilemma of being threatened with permanent alienation from mankind. Yarbro's sympathetic approach to the vampiric experience cast a new light on what was previously assumed to be an inherently evil transformation. Unlike Dracula, and in fact unlike most vampires in lore and literature, Saint-Germain "treasures the brevity of human life rather than holding it in contempt." For millions of transfixed readers, the lack of gore and violence in Yarbro's work has hardly been a dull literary experience. In fact, it's instead proven to be life affirming and poetic. Yarbro's twenty-second book in the saga, *A Dangerous Climate*, was published in September of 2008.

The influences of Anne Rice and Chelsea Quinn Yarbro spawned a renewed and unwaning interest in all things dripping crimson. Here are just a few of the notable books and authors who followed in their preternatural steps:

- ☦ *The Vampire Tapestry* by Suzy McKee Charnas (1980)
- ☦ *Fevre Dream* by George R. R. Martin (1982)
- ☦ *Vampire Junction* by S. P. Somtow (1984)
- ☦ *Those Who Hunt the Night* by Barbara Hambly (1988)

✞ *The Golden* by Lucius Shepard (1992)

✞ *Children of the Night* by Dan Simmons (1992)

A Whole *Lot* of Salem

The prodigious and prolific talents of horror-fiction icon Stephen King were put to use in 1975 with his second published novel, *Salem's Lot*. King is said to have begun the novel after pondering what would happen if Dracula re-emerged in twentieth-century America. The result was a truly creepy story set in the sleepy town of Salem's Lot in rural Maine, and it involved a series of disturbing occurrences and missing children that coincides with the arrival of newcomer Kurt Barlow, who now inhabits an old house with a lurid past. Soon the entire community is overrun as townspeople are transformed into vampires one by one. The protagonists in the book are eventually forced to leave Salem's Lot to the vampiric infestation, although they do manage to destroy Barlow before taking flight. *Salem's Lot* has the unusual distinction of having been made into *two* television series; one in 1979, and the second in 2004. Although King originally called the namesake of the book "Jerusalem's Lot," the publishers shortened the title to *Salem's Lot* because they felt the original title carried too many religious connotations.

Feeding *The Hunger*

Taking a fascinating and fresh approach to the vampire novel, Whitley Strieber created one of the most enduring images of the coldly calculating vampire in *The Hunger*, published in 1981. The last of her species of a bloodsucking alien race, vampire Miriam Blaylock has lived for thousands of years and is in the habit of taking human lovers and turning them into lifelong companions—but for only the length of *their* lives (see Chapter 15). Although Miriam has the power to turn humans into vampires, she lacks the capacity to give them everlasting life such as hers and manages to increase their lifespan by only a few centuries—a tragically short time frame from the perspective of a timeless being. After *The Hunger*, Strieber stepped away from the vampire genre and concentrated on speculative fiction and books concerning his own alleged contact with aliens. Twenty years after its publication, however, Strieber returned to the saga of Miriam Blaylock with *The*

Last Vampire in 2001, and again in 2002 with *Lilith's Dream: A Tale of the Vampire's Life.*

SCREEN SCREAM

The Hunger was made into a cult classic film in 1983, starring Catherine Deneuve, David Bowie, and Susan Sarandon. Although there are several variations between the novel and the film, one of the most significant differences is that in Strieber's original story, Miriam Blaylock lives on to continue her hideous legacy (see Chapter 15).

The Historian

It's interesting to note that one of the best-selling books of 2005 was a vampire novel. In *The Historian,* first-time novelist Elizabeth Kostova brought Bram Stoker's *Dracula* into the modern era by excerpting significant chunks of Stoker's novel and working it into her own historical plotline. In the story, a teenage girl living in Amsterdam discovers in her father's library an ancient book that is blank save for a woodcut of a sinister dragon on one page with the word "Drakulya." The discovery leads to a long search for Dracula, and once again Vlad Tepes comes into the picture—this time with truly spine-chilling results. He's not simply the inspiration for the vampire Dracula, but the still-living personification of the father of all bloodsuckers.

THE ROMANTIC VAMPIRE

Perhaps no other character in literary history is better suited—and more destined—to become the subject of pure romantic fiction than the inherently sexy and alluringly charming vampire. It's no surprise that in the field of romance, vampires have taken a huge bite out of the estimated $1 billion in annual sales generated by the romance genre and the 41 million enthralled readers who blissfully bleed for their favorite heroes and heroines whether they be alive or undead. What follows is a list of some the more popular series of romantic vampire novels to capture the imaginations and hearts of a devoted readership:

- ♱ The Riley Jenson Guardian series, by Keri Arthur
- ♱ The Cassandra Palmer series, by Karen Chance
- ♱ The Nightwalker series, by Jacquelyn Frank
- ♱ The Night Huntress series, by Jeaniene Frost
- ♱ The Gardella Vampire Chronicles, by Colleen Gleason
- ♱ The Guardians of Eternity series, by Alexandra Ivy
- ♱ Forever and the Night, For All Eternity, and Time Without End, by Linda Lael Miller
- ♱ The Little Goddess series, by Amy Lane
- ♱ The Brotherhood of Blood series, by Kathryn Smith
- ♱ The Companion series, by Susan Squires
- ♱ The Darkyn series, by Lynn Viehl

PARANORMAL NOSFERATU

Vampire fiction took an inevitable turn into the literary subgenre of paranormal romance in 1986 with the publication of Jayne Ann Krentz's *Sweet Starfire*. The blending of romance, science fiction, and traditional horror created an unforgettable mixture of blood and lust in a far-away galaxy of pure fantasy, and authors who embraced the concept have never looked back. These novels have crossed virtually every line of fantasy and science fiction to tap into an endless supply of mysterious locales and fantastic supernatural abilities that quite literally know no boundaries.

Anita Blake: Vampire Hunter

Beginning in 1993 with *Guilty Pleasures*, Laurell K. Hamilton's Anita Blake: Vampire Hunter series has developed a legion of diehard fans since its inception. In Anita's parallel universe, she reanimates the dead for a *living*, by working for Animators Inc. as a necromancer, raising and healing long-dead zombies, vampires, and werewolves in a series of sixteen hair-raising novels, the latest of which is the 2008 offering *Blood Noir*. During the first five books, Blake remained remarkably celibate, but by book number ten, she was beginning to let it all hang out, and romantically intimate interludes have become a minor, although graphic, element of her adventures.

Dark and Deadly

Since the beginning of this century, novels in the paranormal, romantic, and vampiric veins have exploded both in popularity and in the sheer volume of titles printed. Christine Feehan has virtually owned the paranormal vampire romance genre, beginning in 1999 when the incredibly successful Carpathians (Dark) series captured the imaginations and hearts of millions of spellbound readers. In her first book, *Dark Prince*, Feehan's construction of an ancient race of emotionless shape-shifting vampires, the Carpathians, who can find salvation only through discovering a life mate and true love, set the stage for a string of twenty novels, several of which have been huge bestsellers and have garnered Feehan a clutch of literary awards.

Southern Bites

One of the most well-respected authors of paranormal vampire fiction, Charlaine Harris, developed her writing chops on two standalone novels before considering attacking books in the increasingly popular series approach to character development. Harris' initial foray was with the Aurora Teagarden Mystery series beginning in 1990 that dealt with the sleuthing of a Georgia librarian into mysterious murders. Harris's second series was the creation of the Shakespeare mystery novels in 1996 that again dealt with basic mortal mysteries.

SCREEN SCREAM

The popularity of Charlaine Harris's Southern Vampire novels attracted the attention of Alan Ball, the creator of the television series *Six Feet Under*. After gaining the rights to Harris's books, Ball began developing and producing a takeoff with the new HBO series *True Blood* starring Oscar winner Anna Paquin in the title role of Sookie Stackhouse (see Chapter 18).

Harris hit vampiric paydirt with the introduction of Sookie Stackhouse in the Southern Vampire series, beginning in 2001 with *Dead Until Dark*. The first installment won the prestigious Anthony Award for best paperback mystery the year it was released and paved the way for seven more bestsellers to follow. Harris's depiction of Sookie Stackhouse is that of a young telepathic barmaid in northern Louisiana who's genetically imbued with "faerie" blood, which may explain her telepathic powers and her unfortunate ability to attract the unwanted attentions of unearthly beings, including vampires and werewolves. Much of the series is dedicated to Sookie solving supernatural mysteries, as well as handling the dilemmas of personal relationships with members of the netherworld who've integrated into society with the invention of manufactured synthetic blood. Harris's latest book, *From Dead to Worse*, published in May of 2008, remains a bestseller, and the entire series has developed a loyal following of diehard fans. Here then are the books in Charlaine Harris's popular *Southern Vampire* series:

- ✝ *Dead Until Dark* (2001)
- ✝ *Living Dead in Dallas* (2002)
- ✝ *Club Dead* (2003)
- ✝ *Dead to the World* (2004)
- ✝ *Dead as a Doornail* (2005)
- ✝ *Definitely Dead* (2006)
- ✝ *All Together Dead* (2007)
- ✝ *From Dead to Worse* (2008)

COMEDIC BLOODSUCKERS

It may be difficult to imagine that a mix of vampiric bloodsucking and humor could go hand in hand, but just as the preternatural creatures of the night have crept into science fiction, romance, and historical fiction, they've also made pretty tasty fodder for some bloody fun reading. *Death by the Drop*, by Timothy Massie, is a fairly recent (2008) addition to the relatively small list of vampire novels with distinctly humorous undercurrents that literally drip with sarcastic wit.

The reigning matriarch of wickedly vampiric fun is unquestionably Mary Janice Davidson, whose Undead/Queen Betsy series of hilarious books feature the irrepressible Betsy Taylor as a former model and recently unemployed single woman who finds herself flattened by an SUV and comes back to life a vampiress. Rather than taking to the life of the walking dead, "Queen Betsy" attempts to resume her less-than-normal existence of stocking up on designer shoes and trying to find a job. Of course, Betsy is also sidelined by irritating conflicts with evil vampiric beings who have absolutely no sense of humor. Books in Mary Jane Davidson's Undead series include:

- ♀ *Undead and Unwed* (2004)
- ♀ *Undead and Unemployed* (2004)
- ♀ *Undead and Unappreciated* (2005)
- ♀ *Undead and Unreturnable* (2005)
- ♀ *Undead and Unpopular* (2006)
- ♀ *Undead and Uneasy* (2007)
- ♀ *Undead and Unworthy* (2008)

Young-adults and the Living Dead

Popular literature for young-adults has been a booming element of the publishing world since the early 1800s, and one of the most predominant themes has always been fantasy and horror. Although children's fairytales are generally considered to be fairly mild fare for kids, many of the concepts, such as the story of *Little Red Riding Hood*, were pretty harrowing in their day, especially given that the first versions of the tale simply ended after the wolf had devoured Red Riding Hood and her granny. Even Bram Stoker took a turn in 1881 at writing fairytales in the compilation *Under the Sunset*, which was often considered far too disturbing for impressionable minds (see Chapter 3).

Most modern young-adult literature features teens as the major characters, and fictional forays into the world of the undead are no exception. The book series that followed television's *Buffy the Vampire Slayer* is one case in point, with the ultimate Valley Girl, Buffy Summers, continuing her crusade of monster mayhem against the forces of evil. But in the netherworld of young vampire literature, no one holds a candle—or a crucifix—to Stephenie Meyer and her thoroughly absorbing and heart-pounding Twilight Saga.

Move Over, Harry Potter

Although Anne Rice has developed a literary reputation as the original Queen of the Damned, Stephenie Meyer has achieved her measure of notoriety and success in the young-adult market as more of the Queen of the Darned. In a marked departure from the sexual undertones of much youth-oriented literature, Meyer has sidestepped the hormonal rages of growing up to provide a series of wildly popular books featuring teenaged heroine Bella Swan and her continuing, relatively coy, relationship with the irresistibly considerate and impossibly gorgeous boy vampire, Edward Cullen.

In the original self-titled book of the Twilight Saga, published in 2005 and written when Meyer was twenty-nine years old, Bella Swan moves from sun-soaked Phoenix, Arizona, to the damp and dreary town of Forks, Washington, to live with her father. On her first day in school, Bella notices the ethereally handsome and secretly vampirish Edward Cullen staring at her with a blood-chilling glare while the phrase "if looks could kill" suddenly runs through her mind. As it turns out, Cullen isn't offering a threat—he's just primordially fascinated by her smell. Through the next three novels the pair fall deeply in love and survive painful separations and harrowing scrapes with evil vampires and other creatures of the night.

Innocent Blood

The innocent nature of Meyer's novels is no accident. As a devout Mormon and mother, she insists that much of the sex, drinking, and violence of young-adult literature upsets her, and she directs her work to the vast audience of youngsters—particularly girls—who don't identify with or haven't experienced the darker side of adolescence. For Meyer, her characterization of Bella is that of a nice, normal girl whose boyfriend is attentively and irreproachably respectful. Meyer's unique approach struck a positive chord with an enormous fan base, and the Twilight series is giving the popularity of the Harry Potter series a run for supernatural supremacy. Books in Stephenie Meyer's Twilight series include *Twilight* (2005), *New Moon* (2006), *Eclipse* (2007), and *Breaking Dawn* (2008).

THE ENORMITY OF BUFFYVERSE

In all of vampiredom in the twentieth century, there may be no single phenomenon with a broader sweep than the kick-butt adventures of *Buffy the Vampire Slayer* (see Chapter 18). Resulting from the film of the same name in 1992 and the enormously popular TV series that ran for seven seasons, *Buffy* became one of the most successful vampiric dramas in televised horror, and simultaneously triggered the television spin-off *Angel* and dozens of spin-off original and graphic novels. The list of installments is seemingly endless, and the sheer number of tales told in various Buffy compilations dwarfs those of any other vampiric figure in fiction.

Fangtastic Folklore

One of the first vampire tales for children predates even *The Arabian Nights* in the early 1500s. The Indian compilation of *Twenty-five Tales of Baital,* or *Vikram and the Vampire,* is a series of connected religious fables that pit the wisdom of the fictional King Vikram against the wily vampire Baital in a game of verbal sparring and wit that culminates with the vampire and king becoming allies.

The list of authors who've contributed to Buffy fiction is a virtual who's who of spin-off fantasy writers, including Rebecca Moesta, Mel Odom, Yvonne Navarro, Nancy Holder, and Scott Ciencin, most of whom have contributed to novelizations of well-known cinema classics and media tie-ins such as *Jurassic Park, Charmed, Star Wars, Battlestar Galactica,* and *Godzilla,* along with their own original works. One prolific Buffy contributor, Christopher Golden, has developed a strong following with his Shadow Saga series of vampire novels that follow the trials of modern-day vampire Peter Octavian and his kin, known as the "Defiant Ones," who are forced into bloody conflict with humanity.

THE HEARTBEAT GOES ON

The intensity of interest for the supernatural in the young-adult market has become a publishing phenomenon, and it shows no signs of letting up any time soon. Perhaps part of the charm of many of these supernatural chronicles is that they describe everyday situations and put vampire characters into them. As new and increasingly expanding plotlines begin delving into other areas of preternatural beings, there have been popular spin-offs into fascinating characterizations of zombies, werewolves, faeries, and ghosts. But through it all, there's little doubt that vampires are on the leading edge of the paranormal, perhaps because they're not just inherently sexy, they're *dead* sexy.

There are a number of enduring vampire series in the young-adult market, and each of them has its own throng of avid supporters and fans. Here are a few of the most popular:

- ☥ The Chronicles of Vladimir series, by Heather Brewer
- ☥ The Morganville Vampires series, by Rachel Caine
- ☥ The House of Night series, by P. C. Cast
- ☥ The Blue Bloods series, by Melissa De La Cruz
- ☥ The Vampire Academy series, by Richelle Mead
- ☥ The Vampire Kisses series, by Ellen Schreiber
- ☥ The *Cirque du Freak* series, by Darren Shan
- ☥ The *Night World* series, by Lisa Jane Smith
- ☥ The *Vampire Diaries* series, by Lisa Jane Smith

PRETERNATURAL EXPLOSION

In the next chapter we open the crypt to the incredibly vast arena of the cinematic vampire. In regard to film history, the vampire is as old as the medium itself, having begun in the Silent Era, still continuing to flap, fang, and seduce its way into our hearts and necks to the present day. We begin with the genesis of celluloid suckers, who in no small measure gave us our first solid impression of the vampire and what he or she is capable of. The resulting works have forever changed the vampire genre.

CHAPTER 14

THE GENESIS OF CELLULOID VAMPIRES

Without question, it is the medium of film where Dracula and his kin have achieved their greatest popularity. That success is in part due to the making of the 1922 silent film *Nosferatu*, the 1920s stage adaptation of *Dracula*, and the legacy begun by Hammer Films and their incredible stronghold in classic horror cinema. In this chapter, we open for the first time Dracula's cinematic coffin, and in doing so bring to life one of the silver screen's most charming, virulent, and popular characters in history.

BLOODSUCKING CINEMA

It's no mystery that the filmmaking industry since its inception over a hundred years ago has opened our collective hearts and minds to a seemingly endless array of stories that serve to broaden our horizons, transport us to worlds unknown, and ultimately keep us perpetually entertained. Each movie genre, whether it be drama, romance, western, fantasy, thriller, comedy, action adventure, or science fiction, and every conceivable genre crossover serves to appeal to audiences of all ages who usually find what they're looking for in a film, from a good laugh or cry to a taut thriller, historical epic, or documentary. There is one genre, however, that stands apart from all others in that its presentation throughout the decades has hinged on one single commonality—fear.

Horror films have a rich history featuring a wide range of tales that prey upon the innate human curiosities surrounding all things that shock, creep, scream, howl, bite, vanish, fly, mutate, and generally move to scare the knickers off us. The true creative genius of the horror industry is that audiences of all ages and generations will never cease becoming obsessed with things that go bump in the night. That said, the possibilities for creating and integrating myths and monsters is that like many other genres born of literature and real-life events, a touch of imagination—and in the case of modern films, a dose of computer-enhanced graphics—can become entirely surreal, mesmerizing, and terrifying.

As mentioned in Chapter 1, to understand vampires is to understand their appearance in folklore, the story of Dracula as told by Bram Stoker, and the vampire's evolution in film. As a visual medium reaching widespread audiences beginning in late 1800s, the vampire has endured a host of depictions and genetic propensities. And while there is little dispute such legendary characters, as Frankenstein, the Mummy, the Wolf Man, the creature from the black lagoon, and dozens more monsters have helped build the horror genre, only the vampire has proven throughout each decade that its on-screen presence truly is immortal.

Filmmakers who first brought Dracula to the big screen set in stone the idea that as a cultural medium, the vampire's tale, as with many other genre-specific characters, has the ability to reflect—in all measure of blatant and subliminal methods—what is occurring in society during various eras, while also retaining the mesmerizing stronghold Dracula maintains on its devoted audiences. During the fifties, sixties, and through the mid-seventies, it was England's Hammer films who capitalized on vampirism in all its red-blooded glory.

More importantly, and perhaps not as well known, is the fact that the 1920s stage plays for *Dracula*, written by Hamilton Deane and a later revamp by John L. Balderston, have the distinction of having solidified the trademark characteristics that the majority of cinematic vampires continue to maintain to the present day. With that in mind, we begin our exploration into the vampire's lethal legacy with its earliest introduction to the masses, an irony that Dracula himself would've been proud of given his subtle and sometimes not-so-subtle propensity for wanting to spread his blood plague to the entire world.

SILENT BUT DEADLY

There is little argument that the biggest part of the vampire legacy has been achieved through the medium of film and the growing breadth of vampire literature. The truth of the matter is that no other novel has achieved such acclaim as Bram Stoker's 1897 masterpiece, *Dracula*, which has sold millions of copies throughout the past century and launched a franchise of entertainment on both the literary and theatrical fronts. It is within the film industry, however, that *Dracula* has achieved its greatest popularity, serving as the impetus for more commercially successful films than any other literary work in history. Tragically, that success is an inescapable irony, given the fact that Stoker died in relative poverty never realizing the true cinematic immortality of his legendary creation, whose inspiration began in the Silent Era not long after his death in 1912 (see Chapter 3).

The Silent Era of motion pictures marked not only a groundbreaking period in the evolution of entertainment and technology, but also introduced an entire world of vampiric show and tell, and many of those films prove that silence is indeed golden. While Thomas Edison's 1903 *The Great Train Robbery* is perhaps the best known and earliest of the silent film genre, it's less well known that there are a host of silent vampire flicks that were made, beginning with the short 1896 French film short *Le manoir du diable*, otherwise known as *The Devil's Castle* or *Manor of the Devil*, which is often cited as the first vampire film (see Chapter 16). Many more silent films would follow, but there is one masterpiece in the golden era of silent pictures that stands alone in its popularity among vampire aficionados.

SCREEN SCREAM

Most folks haven't heard the name Alice Guy-Blaché, but her pioneering and innovative work as a filmmaker is legendary. During her over twenty-five-year career beginning in 1894, Guy-Blaché directed, wrote, and produced over 700 films. She is considered by most to be the film industry's first female director. In 1910, together with her husband and another partner, Guy-Blaché founded the Solax Company, one of the largest production companies of the era. In 1915, she directed *The Vampire* with Olga Petrova and William Steele. By 1922, she returned to France and drifted into obscurity. Her works, however, remain a testament to her talent and contributions to moviemaking history.

NOSFERATU: THE SCOURGE OF BREMEN

One of the most well-known and revered vampire movies in history is also one of the few silent films to survive the inevitable ravages of time. Made in Germany and released in 1922, it is *Nosferatu, eine Symphone des Grauens*, the literal translation of which means *Nosferatu: A Symphony of Terror*. But it's better known by a single word: *Nosferatu*. Directed by renowned German director Friedrich Wilhelm (F. W.) Murnau, with a screenplay penned by Henrik Galeen, *Nosferatu* is an expressionist film (meaning its director was given to overuse of special effects), which proved to be engaging and utterly frightening in its time, and remains so to this day.

The film is an unauthorized version of Stoker's *Dracula*, with its characters and geography altered so that the major storyline moves from Transylvania to Bremen, Germany. As is immediately obvious to anyone viewing the film, it wasn't altered enough. Names of the characters were freely (and not very adeptly) altered, for example, Jonathan Harker became William Hutter, Mina Murray was Ellen Hutter, Renfield was known as Knock, and Dracula became Count Graf Orlock (also spelled Orlok). The ploy was used in an effort to avoid copyright infringement, a fact that did nothing to stop the inevitable legal battle that would come at the hands of Stoker's widow, Florence, who with the aid of the British Incorporated Society of Authors would serve the film's producers with an injunction resulting in the 1925 ruling that the negatives and all copies of the film be destroyed. Obviously, a few copies survived as the first American release came around 1929. (In both earlier and later releases of the film, the character names are changed to Stoker's original characters.) After that, the film went into relative obscurity until the early seventies and has since gone on to achieve cult status.

VAMPIRE BITE

The term *nosferatu* is evolved from the word *nosufuratu*, which is Old Slavonic in origin; however, it actually is derived from the Greek word *nosophoros*, which translates to "plague carrier." The confusion that a *nosferatu* is a vampire is often attributed to an 1888 travelogue containing Transylvanian folklore written by Emily Gerard. Called *The Land Beyond the Forest*, it was known to have been used by Bram Stoker in his research for *Dracula* (see Chapter 6). As such, Stoker used the term to also mean vampire, when in fact, "plague carrier" is more accurate as according to lore, vampires were sometimes blamed as the cause of plagues (see Chapter 7).

Fright and Flight

What makes *Nosferatu* so memorable, aside from its silent screen quirks and on-location settings, is by far the character of Count Orlock, played by German actor Max Schreck. (For an added dose of irony, the word *schreck* is the German word for "fright.") Unlike the suave, debonair, tail-coated Draculas we would be treated to in the decades to come, Count Orlock is more in keeping with the heinous vampires of folklore.

Truly ugly in his conception—due in no small part to the film's art director Albin Grau—the unblinking Count has an almost ratlike appearance, with long clawlike fingers, a bald head, hollowed face, pointed ears, exceptionally long rodent-type fangs, and a legion of devoted rats that would give Willard a run for his money. By all accounts, Orlock is positively grotesque and void of the social graces we associate with the classic drawing room vampire. When Orlock's English real estate representative, Thomas Hutter, accidentally cuts his thumb with a knife, for example, Orlock moves to actually lick the blood from Hutter's wound. It's a moment that truly sets up the animalistic reality of Orlock's affliction. With only a few noted exceptions, the silver screen vampire will always be a predator at heart, regardless of his or her beliefs or revulsions, and that is clearly demonstrated in *Nosferatu*.

Death Be Not Proud

Nosferatu is significant on many levels, not the least of which is that its underlying sexuality was represented by the fear villagers had of Orlock and the subversive mechanism of disguising the exchange of bodily fluids with the spread of plague, a concept used by many horror and sci-fi films in later decades and often cited in vampire folklore (see Chapter 2). Count Orlock also represented the scorned of society—a vile creature locked away in a remote run-down Transylvanian castle. Orlock eventually travels to Bremen to take up residence across the street from the traumatized Hutter and his high-strung, somnambulistic wife, Ellen. Behind the entire real estate transaction is Hutter's boss, Knock (aka Renfield), who is under Orlock's spell and spends the film twilling about the village like a caffeinated lunatic who's downed one too many cases of Red Bull.

The choice to forgo film sets in favor of on-location shooting—both outdoors and in authentic interiors—gives *Nosferatu* a distinct aura of both reality and menace; however, it does have the humorous sequences that inevitably come with low production quality. When Orlock arrives in Bremen, the film is unnaturally sped up as he carries his coffin around in almost Keystone Kop fashion searching for his new domicile. What comes to pass at the film's apex is an interesting twist. Reading *The Book of the Vampires*, Ellen learns what she must do to save her beloved husband and destroy Orlock. Willing the vampire to her bedroom, she offers herself to him as a blood sacrifice with the intention of keeping him busy until cock's crow. Naturally, she succeeds, and as the sun rises and beams through the window, Orlock simply dissolves into a wisp of nothingness. Ellen, drained of her blood, has a final embrace with Hutter before dying. Given that most lead female victims of Dracula typically revert to human upon the vampire's death, Ellen's heroic and selfless death is a dandy twist.

ENTER DRACULA, STAGE RIGHT

What most folks may not know is that the first adaptation of Bram Stoker's novel was brought to the stage very quickly after *Dracula's* publication. The playwright was none other than Stoker himself, and sadly, the play was a dismal failure, in part because it was so difficult to present the proper ambience for the Victorian horrorfest. So bad was the production that it was said that even Stoker's close friend Henry Irving couldn't recommend it (see Chapter 3). It wasn't until fellow Irishman, Hamilton Deane, himself a theater producer, playwright, and actor, decided to take on the daunting project that *Dracula* would find its first monetary success.

In 1924, with the permission of Florence Stoker, Deane debuted *Dracula* in Derby, England, at the Grand Theater. The play starred Edmund Blake as the Count and Deane as Dr. Van Helsing. And while critics of the day weren't necessarily kind, it was of little matter. Audiences loved it—and so did Florence Stoker. That first appearance of Dracula on stage is important, as it marks his first transformation as a proper gentleman of royal blood who obviously possesses the mortal grace to interact with his victims, and not the fiend that Stoker professed as described in Jonathan Harker's journal in Chapter Two of *Dracula*:

"His face was a strong, a very strong, aquiline, with high bridge of the thin nose and peculiarly arched nostrils, with lofty domed forehead, and hair growing scantily round the temples but profusely elsewhere. His eyebrows were very massive, almost meeting over the nose, and with bushy hair that seemed to curl in its own profusion. The mouth, so far as I could see it under the heavy moustache, was fixed and rather cruel-looking, with peculiarly sharp white teeth. These protruded over the lips, whose remarkable ruddiness showed astonishing vitality in a man of his years. For the rest, his ears were pale, and at the tops extremely pointed. The chin was broad and strong, and the cheeks firm though thin. The general effect was one of extraordinary pallor."

In 1927, Deane brought his production to London (this time with Raymond Huntley in the lead role) where it again suffered critical disdain but rated high with audiences who kept the play sold out for over five months. It was at that point that Horace Liveright, an American stage producer, purchased the rights to the play in order to bring *Dracula* to Broadway. To further rework and add to Deane's adaptation, American journalist John L. Balderston was hired by Liveright. In his version, Balderston made a number of adjustments, including merging Mina's character into Lucy's and further making Lucy the daughter of Dr. Seward. The play premiered in October of 1927 at New York's Fulton Theater. This time the production starred a relatively unknown Hungarian actor named Bela Lugosi, who would, of course, go on to play Dracula in Tod Browning's 1931 feature-length film.

Fangtastic Folklore

It was said that Bela Lugosi was so obsessed with playing Dracula in the film version that he served as a mediator for Florence Stoker in negotiating the rights with Universal Pictures. Once rights were obtained, Universal tried to hire several other actors, much to Lugosi's dismay. When director Tod Browning was hired, Universal was hoping that Lon Chaney Sr. would accept the role but he passed away in 1930, after which Lugosi agreed to a nominal fee to play the Count, receiving a paltry $500 a week for the seven-week production.

What's so important about the Deane/Balderston renditions of *Dracula* is that their revamping of the Count in regard to physical appearance and also to Stoker's storyline and characters set a precedent for many successful cinematic works to come, beginning with Lugosi's 1931 *Dracula* (see Chapters 15 and 16). The very idea that Dracula was a preternatural malfeasant who could appear as a cultured, domesticated human is in many ways far more frightening than his being a monstrous, bloodthirsty savage. Ultimately, it was Deane and Balderston's creative transformations that helped create the screen-savvy vampire we know today, one that audiences across the decades can relate to.

During the thirties and forties, it was Universal Pictures that dominated the horror front beginning with Lugosi's *Dracula* in 1931 and continuing with films like *Dracula's Daughter, Son of Dracula, House of Frankenstein*, and *House of Dracula*. But by the late 1950s, there came a re-emergence of the vampire film in the form of gothic horror, and on that front there was but one name—Hammer.

HAMMERING OUT HORROR

To fully regale the evolution of horror films and in particular the vampire genre, one must acknowledge the fine works of England's Hammer Films, whose contribution to the world of horror is nothing less than legendary. It all began in 1913 when, in Hammersmith, London, Enrique Carreras purchased his first in a line of cinemas. Three years later, he partnered with William Hind, and together in 1934 they formed Hammer Productions and a year later Exclusive Films Ltd. as a distribution company. They immediately began making films but were halted by the onset of World War II and couldn't continue distributing productions through Exclusive until 1945. Two years later, Hammer was revived and in 1949 became Hammer Film Productions Limited.

What happened in 1957 was Hammer's turning point, when they unleashed director Terence Fisher's *The Curse of Frankenstein* (based on the Mary Shelley novel *Frankenstein*), featuring Peter Cushing as the Baron von Frankenstein and Christopher Lee as the creature. The following year, the same trio teamed up for *Horror of Dracula*, which proved to be just the vehicle Hammer needed to solidify its stronghold as the premiere horror film producer of the day. Both films were incredibly successful and would provide a starting point for a number of sequels and successive films. *Horror of Dracula* in particular is said to have raked in over eight times the cost of the film's production. All the better that *Horror* and the Hammer Films to come were in color, adding to visual appeal of the set designs and, of course, the blood. The film also marked the collaboration of director Fisher, writer Jimmy Sangster, and the duo who are without a doubt the most legendary pair in horror history—Christopher Lee and Peter Cushing (see Chapter 15).

SCREEN SCREAM During the mid- to late 1940s Hammer produced several films, including *Dick Barton Special Agent*, and continued to grow throughout the 1950s. It wasn't until 1955 that *The Quatermass Xperiment* (aka *The Creeping Unknown*) was made as a big-screen feature that played off the immensely popular British sci-fi series of the same name. That film marked Hammer's crossover into the horror realm.

Heart-Pounding Horror

The 1960s would prove to be an interesting decade for Hammer Films. While the 1960 *The Brides of Dracula* was one of Hammer's most popular in their vampire franchise, there's often a mixed cauldron of reviews for the film, which took the bold step of presenting viewers with a young blonde vampire called the Baron Meinster (played by David Peel). No doubt a Dracula flick without the tall, dark, and dangerous presence of Christopher Lee was a risk to be certain, but Peel, despite his youthful good looks, seemed to elicit mixed emotions both with critics and audiences. Folks loved him or hated him.

A trio of other vampire films would follow *Brides*, including *Kiss of the Vampire* (1964), which featured Hammer's first female vampire in Noel Willman, *Dracula: Prince of Darkness* (1966), and *Dracula Has Risen from the Grave* (1968). *Prince of Darkness* marked Christopher Lee's long-awaited return to the role he made famous, having intentionally stayed clear of the renowned fangster with the intent of avoiding being typecast. In what amounted to a nonspeaking, mostly hissing role, Lee again teamed with director Terence Fisher and writer Jimmy Sangster and channeled his inner brute to terrorize two couples who happened upon his castle. Dracula indeed met his inevitable demise at the climax of the film, this time in icy waters.

Employing the intentional plotline succession from the end of one Dracula film to the beginning of the next, Christopher Lee's fiend was unintentionally revived in *Dracula Has Risen from the Grave* by a priest who himself plunged into the water, his blood reawakening the black devil. Without the direction of Terence Fisher, *Risen* lost the distinct romantic aspect so prevalent in the earlier Lee installments, instead favoring more action sequences.

The Nail in the Coffin

Though the subject is often debated, part of Hammer's success in their Dracula productions was not mass producing them. Eight years had passed from the time Christopher Lee first appeared in *Horror of Dracula* until he returned in *Dracula: Prince of Darkness*. By the 1970s, with pressure to create more revenue, the Dracula franchise inevitably suffered with one vampire flick coming after the other. Sadly, that strategy would work to Hammer's detriment and bring an end to their domination in the horror genre.

SCREEN SCREAM

In *Horror of Dracula*, the majority of the story is left to Peter Cushing's Van Helsing. Christopher Lee, as the menacing Dracula, only speaks just over a dozen lines at the beginning of the film to the ultimately doomed Jonathan Harker. In a remarkable turn, the cloak that Lee originally wore during the filming was found in October of 2007 in a London dress shop. Missing for three decades, the cape, which was verified by Lee himself as the original, is valued at upwards of $44,000.

Hammer's first vampiric offering in the seventies was the 1970 film, *Taste the Blood of Dracula*. Starring Christopher Lee, this installment saw his big, bad bloodsucking self yet again resurrected, this time by a Satanist, Lord Courtley, who procured the Count's ring, his cloak, and a vial of blood. Set in Victorian England and focused on Victorian aristocracy, Courtley is hellbent on reviving the dark devil and lures a trio of bored cohorts to help him. His prize for doing do, was, of course, his life. So begins Dracula's insatiable lust for revenge (due to his servant's demise) and the killing of each of the three men's progeny. Later that year, Lee reprised his role in *Scars of Dracula*. Again resurrected with the help of a bat dripping blood on his immortal ashes, a rather sadistic Dracula torments a village until at last being struck by lightning.

Also released in 1970 was Hammer's *The Vampire Lovers*, featuring Ingrid Pitt as a lesbian vampire in a surreal and erotic tale loosely based on Sheridan Le Fanu's "Carmilla" (see Chapter 3). The next year featured *Countess Dracula*, with Pitt basing her character on the evil Countess Erzébet Báthory (see Chapter 11). This was followed by *Lust for a Vampire* (the sequel to *The Vampire Lovers*) directed by Jimmy Sangster. In 1971, Peter Cushing attempted to squash the evils of vampirism in *Twins of Evil*, which again made use of Le Fanu's "Carmilla" characters.

Then in 1972 came *Vampire Circus*, in which a vampire seeks revenge upon a plague-ridden village, and the sixth Christopher Lee performance in *Dracula A.D. 1972*, a more contemporary outing that reunited Lee with Cushing as his interminable foe, Dr. Abraham Van Helsing. Taking place in twentieth-century London, the film also introduced Van Helsing's granddaughter, Jessica, who would also take part in Lee's final Dracula film, *Satanic Rites of Dracula* in 1974, which sadly marked his final vampiric coupling with Cushing.

After *Satanic Rites*, Lee bid adieu to his most famous Hammer alter ego, a true rite of passage to one of the most famous and historic portrayals in vampire cinematic history. Following the release of *Captain Kronos: Vampire Hunter* in 1974 (see Chapter 17), Hammer Films, acquiescing to the realization that gothic horror had run its course, ceased its productions of vampire cinema, ending a legacy and leaving filmmakers of the future to create new and imaginative versions of the vampire of the ages.

GOING BATTY

What would take place from the mid-1970s to the present day, given the precedent set by Hammer Films, was the vampire genre both benefiting and suffering from the inevitable overload that comes with the testing of various plotlines, taking creative license, and making use of technical advancements. With Hammer bowing out of the horror genre, it was as if a Pandora's box was opened, and what arose from the dead, or undead as the case may be, was a virtual cornucopia of vampiric entertainment.

While each decade would contain a host of cinematic vampire gems, they would also feature films that tested the boundaries of the traditional Dracula by crossing over into the comedy, sci-fi, and Western genres, and even a version created for the hearing-impaired community, a 1975 film called *Deafula* (see Chapter 17). The sixties and seventies also marked the beginnings of vampires on television, with the serial *Dark Shadows* and made-for-television versions such as the 1979 *Dracula* starring Jack Palance. Vampires were now slinking their way directly into our living rooms—and audiences loved it.

From there, Dracula and a healthy coven of converts would only serve to fly wherever the film would take them, whether they were transformed into Catherine Deneuve's Egyptian vampire in *The Hunger*, a brood of raucous teens in *The Lost Boys*, a vampire hunter named *Blade*, or continue in the vein of Stoker's revered incarnation of Vlad the Impaler as was retained by Gary Oldman in *Bram Stoker's Dracula*. In the following chapters, we present to you a host of legendary silver screen blood drinkers and a two-part filmography that's certain to have you reaching for your cape and a set of fine-tuned fangs. But first, Dracula and his minions as they are best known for their performances.

CHAPTER 15

LEGENDARY BLOOD DRINKERS

In Chapters 16 and 17 we offer up an extensive vampire filmography and highlight a number of works running the gamut from dramatic to comedic to action-adventure to science fiction, but before exploring the cinematic world of the undead, there are a coffin-full of performances and films worth noting for the characters and storylines they bring to life and the immortality they bring to the horror genre. This includes a host of legendary blood drinkers, like Bela Lugosi and Christopher Lee, who most would readily agree are grade A, or shall we say the type A, of cinematic vampire consumption. Pun intended.

I Vant to Suck Your Blood!

Since the inception of vampiric cinema, dozens of actors and actresses have taken on the challenge of playing the most famous bloodsuckers in history. Some, like Bela Lugosi, Christopher Lee, Frank Langella, and Gary Oldman, to name a few, have left a permanent bite on the genre. Others failed to achieve the same critical acclaim. But it's fair to say that playing a character so embedded in lore, literature, and film is no easy stroll through the cemetary.

For most of us, selecting your favorite Dracula is akin to choosing your favorite James Bond. Some folks prefer the almost balletic and traditional performance of the legendary Bela Lugosi, while others lean toward Christopher Lee's seductive but utterly ruthless Dracula. In the modern era, with the growing sophistication of computer graphics, makeup techniques, and creative camera work, horror fans have the benefit of being treated to more upscale bloodsuckers such as Gary Oldman's seamless vampiric changling from young man to old and then into rats and wolves. Still others would prefer Frank Langella, Willem Dafoe, Stuart Townsend, Jonathan Frid, John Carradine, Kate Beckinsale, Barbara Steele, George Hamilton, or any number of thespians who grabbed a set of sharp canines and took their best shot at proclaiming: "I never drink . . . wine." Or in the case of Gerard Butler in *Dracula 2000*, the very modernized: "I never drink . . . coffee."

For sheer artistry and panache, it must be said that every actor and actress who's portrayed a vampire has brought some measure of charm and idiosyncrasy to his or her undead alter ego, and *all* of their portrayals—the good, the bad, and the ugly—have offered up another crystal to the kaleidoscope of silver screen vampirism. With Max Schreck in his 1922 turn as Count Orlock in *Nosferatu*, a precedent was set for the vampire as both ugly and predatory—a distinct homage to the vampires of folklore. Few would argue that as the film progressed, Orlock, by whatever magic of lighting, makeup, or our own imaginations, became more grotesque and repugnant. For Lugosi, coming at the crossroad of silent film to talkie gave him the added advantage of having been more in tune to his physical movement. What is often termed his intentional almost balletic motion, which with his menacing and arguably exaggerated facial contortions, made him quite an intense Dracula.

For many horror aficionados, Christopher Lee is the quintessential Count Dracula; his statuesque appearance coupled with impeccable British mannerisms and lithe good looks make him the perfect immortal. With a smoldering and undeniable sexuality, and well-portrayed bloodlust, Lee, unlike any other Dracula, showed the world time and time again that his depiction was a force to be reckoned with. Let us focus, then, on some of the most famous of the silver screen players, beginning with Bela Lugosi.

Fangtastic Folklore

The 1931 version of *Dracula* was released on Valentine's Day weekend 1931, which happened to be Friday the thirteenth. Rumor had it that female cinemagoers were fainting in the theater aisles and that men were running from the building! In a final tribute to his legendary portrayal, Lugosi, who died on August 16, 1956, was buried in his Dracula costume.

Bela Lugosi

In 1931, in what many consider to be one of the greatest, if not *the* greatest vampire film of all time, Bela Lugosi introduced the public to Count Dracula in the first official version based on Bram Stoker's novel. For Lugosi, it is arguably the role of a lifetime, one that secured his legacy in the kingdom of silver screen horror and one that was a long time in the making. Given the ferocity with which Stoker's widow, Florence Stoker, fought to have the 1922 "unauthorized" film *Nosferatu* literally destroyed, the rights to Stoker's novel were finally secured when Florence sold them to Universal Pictures.

What resulted was director Tod Browning's interpretation, which was actually based more on the stage production of *Dracula* written by Hamilton Deane and later reworked by John Balderston for the American version (see Chapter 14). While it did draw elements from Stoker's novel, it also took creative license with its characters and progression. For example, in Browning's depiction, it's Renfield who takes center stage rather than the relatively downplayed "John" Harker. Despite it being a low-budget production, *Dracula* went on to become Universal Pictures' highest-grossing film of 1931.

Taking on the first feature-length portrayal of Dracula was for Lugosi a natural progression, as he had in 1927 already performed the part on Broadway in the Deane/Balderston American adaptation of Deane's original hit stage play (see Chapter 14). What many consider to be a crucial point in the evolution of Stoker's original vampire are the changes Deane and Balderston made, taking Stoker's somewhat ghoulish figure to a well-spoken, impeccably dressed, parlor vampire. Ultimately, it was their transformation of the Count and Lugosi's portrayal that set the tone for all Draculas that would follow, that of a preternatural being who could roam among us with few distinctions that would undermine his humanity. Lugosi, with his Hungarian accent and the constant light beaming across his eyes, would set in stone the menace, obsession, charm, and depravity we've come to expect of the most wicked denizen of the night. Many of Dracula's famous lines and powers appeared in the 1931 version and were readily mimicked or slightly altered in many future vampire films.

Christopher Lee

For many vampire aficionados, the bloodsucking buck stops with legendary actor Christopher Lee. With over 260 films to his credit since 1948, Lee is one of this generation's most talented and prolific actors and one of the greatest stars in the history of horror. During his epic career, which shows no signs of slowing, Lee has played Dracula, Frankenstein, the Mummy, Sherlock Holmes, Fu Manchu, and scores of villainous performances from Rasputin to Francisco Scaramanga in *The Man with the Golden Gun*. Most recently, he played Saruman in the *Lord of the Rings* trilogy and Count Dooku in the *Star Wars* episodes *Revenge of the Sith* and *Attack of the Clones*.

Lee ended up playing Dracula over seventeen times in his career, with seven of those portrayals done for Hammer Films including *Horror of Dracula, Dracula: Prince of Darkness, Dracula Has Risen from the Grave, Taste the Blood of Dracula, Scars of Dracula, Dracula A.D. 1972*, and *Satanic Rites of Dracula*. What ultimately makes Lee one of the most—if not *the* most—popular cinematic bloodsucker in history is the amalgam of traits he brought to the character.

At six-foot-five, his tall, dark, and exotically handsome physique, coupled with his trademark intensity, gave Lee the freedom to build his Dracula into not only an animalistic predator, but a shrewd, sexually charged icon. Having played the fiend more than any other actor, Lee, whether he was fighting Van Helsing or securing his latest female conquest, proved to the world that his calculating creature bore the intellect, cunning, and sensual appeal to which all future Draculas could only hope to aspire.

Fangtastic Folklore In addition to being one most prolific actors in history, Christopher Lee is cited in the *Guinness Book of World Records* as holding the record for being the actor who has appeared in the most sword fight scenes in cinematic history. It wasn't until the 2002 film *Star Wars II: Attack of the Clones* that Lee, at the age of eighty, ceased performing his own stunt work.

Peter Cushing

Though he typically played superlative vampire hunter Abraham Van Helsing, it would be woefully inappropriate to exclude Peter Cushing from a discussion of legendary vampire performers, especially given his longstanding screen partnership and lifelong friendship with Christopher Lee. Few acting partnerships are the stuff legends are made of. There's Laurel and Hardy, Bogie and Bacall, Astaire and Rogers, and even Mickey and Minnie. But in the horror realm there is but one duo—Cushing and Lee. They made nineteen films together but are perhaps best known for their vampire cinema.

An impeccably mannered British gent with piercing blue eyes, Cushing—no matter his role—made you feel safe and protected, and in the vampire realm that's a tall order. In truth, more often than not, it was Cushing's Van Helsing who carried the Dracula films, with Lee concentrating his efforts on his bloodthirsty physical intimidation rather than words. Part of what sets Cushing apart from the previous incarnations of Van Helsing, Edward Van Sloan in particular (who played the doctor in both the 1931 *Dracula* and the 1936 sequel *Dracula's Daughter*), is that not only was he the perfect combination of gentle but obsessed intellect, he brought to the character a physical presence. Agile and athletic, Cushing was typically the only voice of reason in the Dracula films, and as such, he was usually the one person who could lay waste to the bloodsucker du jour. In doing so, he would go to great lengths to tussle with the black devil, on many an occasion even being bitten himself. Throughout his distinguished career from 1939 to 1986, Cushing was a consummate pro who played everything from Dr. Frankenstein to Sherlock Holmes to Dr. Who and Grand Moff Tarkin in *Star Wars*. His passing in 1994 is something Christopher Lee still mourns, saying he never felt more open or closer to any of his friends as he did Cushing.

Gary Oldman

In the annals of Dracula legend, Gary Oldman is arguably one of the all-time best portrayers of the Count, if for no other reason that his portrayal of the ancient bloodsucker is a tour de force of emotions one would expect—but are not always entirely shown—from a predator eternally consumed by anger, revenge, lust, love, and power. His brilliant performance in Francis Ford Coppola's 1992 version of *Bram Stoker's Dracula* shows us in no uncertain terms the extent to which the immutable black devil will go to remedy what is at best a tragic tale of love gone horribly wrong. As far as vampire films are concerned, Coppola's version is without question one of the best ever made, from its stylish aura to its stellar cast.

Unfortunately for this film's Jonathan Harker (Keanu Reeves), Dracula has recognized the reincarnation of his wife as Harker's fiancé Mina Murray (Winona Ryder) and is determined to get her back. What makes Oldman's performance so extraordinary in this gothic romantic horrorfest is how seamlessly he shifts from deranged old vampire to handsome young Prince Vlad to various incarnations of wolf and bat and grotesque fanged monster of folklore. Opting to forego CGI technology, Coppola insisted that the cinematography be accomplished using camera trickery, with clever use of camera angles and old-school techniques that proved admirably successful. At its core, the script attempts to retain the best parts of Stoker's original work and greatly benefits not only from Oldman but Sir Anthony Hopkins, who must be duly noted as being one of the best actors to ever take on the daunting role of Abraham Van Helsing.

As did his accomplished vampiric predecessors, Oldman does well to show the core existence of the ultimate nightcrawler, with an accelerated sense of intense charm and intelligence that tautly belies his extreme depravity—the trait of an undeniable predator. Playing off the tale of Transylvania's Vlad the Impaler, Oldman's constant shift from man to animal and killer to lover is absolutely mesmerizing, and his ability to convey the intense loneliness of immortality elicits an empathy rarely captured in vampire cinema. In equal measure, and with wonderful contrast, Hopkins, like Cushing, forgoes the role of the traditional, somewhat boring, scholar of early cinematic Van Helsing's, instead opting for eccentricity and a display of obsession that in its culmination rivals that of Dracula himself. As the hunter, Hopkins's Van Helsing shows a certain respect and empathy for the unholy prince. When Mina mentions to Van Helsing that he admires the vampire, he replies yes, that "he was in life a most remarkable man."

SCREEN SCREAM

Gary Oldman was the final choice to play Dracula in *Bram Stoker's Dracula*, but several other actors did audition for the part, including Viggo Mortensen, Gabriel Byrne, Antonio Banderas, Andy Garcia, and Armand Assante. Steve Buscemi was originally offered the part of crazed Dracula disciple Thomas Renfield, but Buscemi turned down the role. Tom Waits ultimately played the part with delicious zeal.

Another aspect of Oldman's performance worth mentioning is the sexuality he brings to the role. A scene that can be cited as unexpectedly erotic takes place when the young Prince Vlad first meets Mina in London at a viewing of the Cinematograph. After a chaotic crowd dispersal, Mina's confronted by a white wolf, whose attack is quickly halted by the Prince. As she nears the animal, both she and Vlad run their gloved hands over the wolf in intimate strokes, and the stage is immediately set as Vlad states that "there is much to be learned from beasts." Again, those hints of wisdom and compassion interlaced with the Prince's seething ferocity add depth to Oldman's

Dracula, and, in the end, it is that very compassion that makes his demise at the hand of his beloved reincarnated Princess an appropriate conclusion to a long and tumultuous vampiric career.

THE VAMPIRE HALL OF FAME

Since the creation of film, dozens of actors and actresses have played vampires, and while there are a few who stand fang and cape above the rest, there are several other notable performances that must be mentioned, in particular the 1973 American made-for-television production of *Dracula* starring renowned character actor Jack Palance, who with Frank Langella and his 1979 performance triggered a resurgence of Dracula popularity. Well suited to the role with his intimating physique, distinguished guise, and menacing voice, Palance breathed new life into the immortal bad boy, benefiting from a script written by *I Am Legend* author Richard Matheson and *Dark Shadows* director Dan Curtis.

Frank Langella

Starring as Dracula in the 1979 version, Frank Langella is considered by many to be one of the finest actors to play the role. Supremely indulgent in its Edwardian setting and graced with Sir Laurence Olivier as Van Helsing and Donald Pleasence as Dr. Seward, Langella's fiend is the epitome of charm, seduction, and demonic manipulation. Based on the Deane/Balterston stage play (see Chapter 14), it is at times almost campy in its efforts to revive Lugosi's original *Dracula* but with a decidedly modern edge meant to keep female audience members in a hypnotic swoon.

John Carradine

Easily one of history's most prolific actors, the patriarch of the Carradine family played Dracula on numerous occasions (second only to Christopher Lee) on the stage and both big and small screens, most notably during the 1940s in *House of Frankenstein* and *House of Dracula*. In 1956, he had the distinction of playing the first television Dracula in an episode of *Matinee Theatre*. He then went on to portray the bloodsucker in the comedies *Billy the Kid*

Versus Dracula (1966) and *Nocturna*, also known as *Granddaughter of Dracula* (1979), while also appearing in a number of campy vamp flicks. Suffice to say, that in the vampire hall of fame—Carradine is one of the creepiest.

Willem Dafoe

It's a rare occurrence when a horror or sci-fi star receives an Oscar nod, which tells you just how amazing Willem Dafoe's performance was in the 2000 film *Shadow of the Vampire*, which told of the making of the 1922 film *Nosferatu* (see Chapter 14). Portraying actor Max Schreck, Dafoe showed a depth of introspective depravity rarely seen in vampire cinema, one that played well to the film's ultimate twist—that F. W. Murnau's obsession to cast his "perfect" vampire leads to the ominous conclusion that perhaps Schreck so perfectly encapsulated a vampire because he *was* a vampire.

Tom Cruise and Brad Pitt

In 1994, the long-awaited adaptation of Anne Rice's *Interview with the Vampire: The Vampire Chronicles* at last came to fruition (see Chapter 13). It was a lavish period production, but there appears to be little gray area in regard to audience reception—people love it or revile it, with opponents citing Neil Jordan's ultimate casting of Tom Cruise and Brad Pitt as a calculated effort to entice the teenage contingent. Regardless, *Interview*, which ranks third among the all-time grossing vampire films, remains true to the novel and is proficient in relaying the eternal drama of the charming, complex, and magnetic Lestat de Lioncourt and his reluctant fledgling Louis de Pointe du Lac (see chapters 13 and 17).

Stuart Townsend

Based on Anne Rice's Vampire Chronicles (a combination of *The Vampire Lestat* and *The Queen of the Damned*), the 2002 *Queen of the Damned* gave us our second glimpse of the most famous vampire since Stoker's Dracula. Taking on the highly revered Lestat for this adaptation is Stuart Townsend, who on many levels does due justice to the sheer complexity of a vampire whose journey in this installment takes him from his awakening as a rock star to destroyer of Akasha, the ancient mother of all vampires. What Cruise lacks in depth, Townsend finds in his ubergoth arrogance and willingness to irk every vampire on Earth by breaking the code of anonymity.

Richard Roxburgh

As the second-highest-grossing vampire film of all time, the 2004 film *Van Helsing* has much to offer in its action-packed Transylvanian travail, not the least of which is a stellar performance by Aussie actor Richard Roxburgh. Fighting his mortal—or immortal in this case—enemy Gabriel Van Helsing, Roxburgh is arguably one of the best Dracula's we've seen in years. Frightening in his emotional depravity, and utterly manipulative, Roxburgh's evil demon is driven to the point of frenzy in his goal of unleashing his progeny on the world while also playing a wicked hide-and-go-bite with Van Helsing in an epic battle of bat versus werewolf (see Chapter 17).

Wesley Snipes

Born of a mother who was bitten by a vampire just prior to his birth, Wesley Snipes as Blade brings a new dimension to the vampire realm. Not only is he half-human, half-bloodsucker—he's a vampire hunter. Born of Marvel Comics in its 1973 offering *The Tomb of Dracula*, Blade has the distinct advantage of being a "daywalker," meaning he has no aversion to sunlight and relatively few entrapments suffered by the typical vampire (see Chapter 19). Packed with mega-action, the *Blade* trilogy ultimately epitomizes the reluctant vampire to the extreme. Blade doesn't feed on humans or animals, instead using various injectables to quench his thirst.

Gerard Butler

In Wes Craven's *Dracula 2000*, Gerard Butler takes his turn as the black demon. In a very modern tale with a truly inspired plot, Butler's Dracula goes neck-to-neck with both Van Helsing and his unwary daughter, Mary. Unlike the bloodsuckers of old who were typically descended from Stoker's amalgam of Vlad the Impaler and his father Vlad Dracul, Craven chose to link his vampire to a biblical source, namely Judas Iscariot—the betrayer of Christ. With several excellent twists and turns, *Dracula 2000* is one of the better vampire films of the modern era.

Jonathan Frid

In his portrayal of Barnabas Collins in the 1970s gothic soap opera *Dark Shadows*, Jonathan Frid saved the program from imminent cancellation by showing us the multi-dimensional—if not campy—side of a vampire torn apart by reluctance and primal urges (see Chapter 18). The first serious television bloodsucker, Frid's role led to two feature-length films, and many thousands of diehard fans who remain devoted to this day. Frid maintains his own Web site at *www.jonathanfrid.com*, and regularly responds to comments from his adoring fans.

William Marshall

The precursor to Wesley Snipes African-American vampire was a man by the name of Prince Mamuwalde, played by William Marshall, who made the grave mistake of attempting to deal with Dracula during the late 1700s in regard to banishing slave trade. Bad idea. Mamuwalde wakes up in 1972 only to realize he's become Blacula. A classic blaxploitation film, it's no mystery that *Blacula* came on the tails of the Civil Rights movement, but Marshall deserves props for playing the somewhat campy vamp with dignity, panache, and a rugged charm that led to the sequel *Scream Blacula Scream* in 1973.

Anders Hove

Though it's often classified as a B movie for its direct-to-video releases, the *Subspecies* series is unique in its willingness to forgo the traditional debonair Dracula in favor of one more typical of folkloric vampires and *Nosferatu's* heinous Count Orlock. Anders Hove's portrayal of the ghoulish Romanian vampire Radu Vladislaus, with his huge fangs, drippy drool, mutant features, and raspy voice, is *truly* the stuff nightmares are made of.

HERE COME THE BRIDES

Until the onset of the modern era of vampire cinema, most females were often relegated to portraying Dracula's "brides," typically chosen from a contingent of barmaids, peasants, travelers, or various amalgams of Stoker's Lucy Westenra or Mina Murray (see Chapter 4). In the usual Dracula format, one or more of these women perish either due to having been bitten or at the hands of a vampire hunter, with the last bride's vampiric condition often reversed with Dracula's demise. But over the years, a small brood of leading actresses crept from their coffins to begin the evolution of the female vampire as a legitimate dyed-in-the-cape threat.

Over the decades, it was common for lead actresses to make their vampiric debut playing roles adapted from the legendary exploits of the bloodthirsty Countess Erzébet Bathóry (see Chapter 11) or as Carmilla, the notorious lesbian vampire made famous by author Sheridan Le Fanu (see Chapter 3). Not until the 1970s did the female vampire begin to fly onto the big screen with regularity, a fact partially attributed to filmmakers featuring more nudity and branching out into mixing the traditional female vampire with other genres.

THE EARLY VIXENS OF VAMPIRISM

One of the first of the silver screen vamps was Gloria Holden, who captured the lead in the 1936 *Dracula's Daughter*, a sequel to Lugosi's *Dracula* (see Chapter 14). As Countess Marya Zaleska, Holden gave an icy and hypnotic portrayal that was not without its manipulative charms. Contrary to the action-oriented female vampires of the modern era, the Countess was a reluctant vampire longing to find a cure for her evil affliction. At its core, Holden's portrayal put the cinematic world on notice that female vampires—with their own seductive ploys and predatory capacities—were on the hunt.

Maria Menado

During the 1950s, several more female vampires surfaced from their coffins. Rarely mentioned as a leading lady vampire, most likely due to the fact the film wasn't widely released in the States, is Maria Menado, who in 1957 played the vampire antagonist in a pair of Malaysian films called *Pontianak* (*The Vampire*) and *Dendam Pontianak* (*Revenge of the Vampire*) based on the Malaysian revenant of folklore (see Chapter 2). Given the fact that vengeful bloodsuckers are tricky to kill and fast to reanimate, Menado arose from the dead again in 1958 in *Sumpah Pontianak* (*The Vampire's Curse*), and *Pontianak Kembali* (*The Vampire Returns*) in 1963.

SCREEN SCREAM

One of the more prominent female bloodsuckers of the sixties was Annette Vadim, the star of husband Roger Vadim's French film *Et mourir de plaisir*. Popularly known as *Blood and Roses*, the film is one of the first adaptations of Sheridan Le Fanu's *Carmilla*. Other female vampires appeared in *Queen of Blood*, *Draculita*, and *The Devil's Mistress*.

Barbara Steele

During the 1960s, Italian director Mario Bava produced a number of classic horror films including *Black Sabbath*, *Planet of the Vampires*, and *Hercules vs. the Vampires*, but it was his 1960 cult classic *La Maschera del demonio*, commonly known as *Black Sunday*, that turned the tide of Italian vampire cinema. It was on the set of the 1956 film *I Vampiri* (aka *The Devil's Commandment*) that cinematographer-turned-director Mario Bava realized the horror potential of a strikingly beautiful brunette actress named Barbara Steele.

Playing the dual role of Princess Asa Vajda and Katia Vajda, Steele gives a spectacular performance as a seventeenth-century vampiric witch and the virgin Katia in what is a stylish, romantic, and sexually charged feast of chilling vampiric squander. Steele would go on to star in one of Roger Corman's Edgar Allen Poe classics *The Pit and the Pendulum*, as well as *The Spectre*, *The Long Hair of Death*, and *Castle of Blood*.

Ingrid Pitt

During the 1970s, Hammer Films came out with a trilogy of highly successful and boldly erotic films based on *Carmilla*, including *The Vampire Lovers*, *Lust for a Vampire*, and *Twins of Evil*. Managing to escape censors with a measurable amount of intentional nudity and titillation, the films have become cult classics. The first of the three also launched the horror career of Polish-born beauty Ingrid Pitt. As the vampire Mircalla/Carmilla in *Vampire Lovers*, Pitt proved herself to be a sexually charged bloodsucker who turns a trio of her own brides in the ultimate female power play. As one would expect, it's left to Peter Cushing's character, General von Spielsdorf, to finally cause Mircalla to literally lose her head.

Pitt continued padding her vampiric acting resume by playing the lead in the 1971 film *Countess Dracula*, based on the story of Erzébet Bathóry as told in the book *The Bloody Countess* by Valentine Penrose. That same year, she once again fanged up for *The House that Dripped Blood*, a somewhat comedic horror anthology in which she starred in an episode entitled *The Cloak*.

Bloodthirsty Babes Gone Berserk

After the exotic, erotic vampires of the seventies, the next two decades introduced us to a number of naughty vampiric vixens that ran the gamut from dramatic to comedic to otherworldly. Among them were Louise Fletcher in *Mama Dracula* (1980), an entirely nude Mathilda May in *Lifeforce* (1985), Lauren Hutton in *Once Bitten* (1985), Grace Jones in *Vamp* (1986), Britt Ekland in *Beverly Hills Vamp* (1989), Sylvia Kristel in *Dracula's Widow* (1989), Anna

Parillaud in *Innocent Blood* (1992), Talisa Soto in *Vampirella* (1996), and Denice Duff in the *Subspecies* series.

All of these hypnotic hellcats brought to the genre a new breed of female fiend that would set in motion the idea that women *could* carry a vampire film, perhaps even without the trappings of Carmilla's lesbian tendencies or Countess Bathóry's slaughter of innocents for the evil purposes of retaining her youthful good looks. Of all the films of that era, however, there are a few female vampires who put on a bloody good show, in particular, one of vampire cinema's most renowned immortals— Catherine Deneuve.

Catherine Deneuve

Legendary French ingénue Catherine Deneuve is arguably one of the best actresses of her time, beginning with her one of her earliest major roles in Roman Polanski's 1965 *Repulsion* to the 1967 tour de force role as a frigid housewife moonlighting prostitute in the 1967 *Belle de jour* to her 1992 Oscar-nominated Best Actress performance in *Indochine*. But in 1983, Deneuve transformed into a sensuous creature of a different kind when she became Miriam Blaylock, the several millennia-old vampire in *The Hunger*, adapted from the 1981 Whitley Strieber novel (see Chapter 13).

As with all novel-to-film adaptations, there are noted differences in plot (especially the film's ending), but what sets *The Hunger* apart from other film's of the genre is the stylish upper-crust look created by director Tony Scott (who went on to direct *Top Gun* and *Days of Thunder* among others). The film was largely criticized for its primary focus on visual appeal, but ultimately there's little to dislike about Deneuve's icy vampiric portrayal. With a torrid mix of decadence and predatorial ferocity, Miriam is a classy but subliminally terrifying vampire whose preternatural *je ne sais quoi* combined with her intimidating bisexuality offer a glimpse into the ruthless psyche of an ancient immortal. Also starring David Bowie as her "dying" lover and Susan Sarandon as Miriam's chosen replacement, the cult classic is most commonly noted for its erotic yet tasteful lesbian scenes between Deneuve and Sarandon.

Kate Beckinsale

Starting in the late seventies, a handful of elite actresses like Sigourney Weaver in the *Alien* franchise and Linda Hamilton in the *Terminator* series set the stage for strong female action heroes in the horror and sci-fi genres. Those performances, which in the case of Sigourney Weaver and Linda Hamilton in *Terminator* and *Aliens* garnered Oscar nods for Best Actress. Those two pioneers of feminine protagonists breathed life into the concept that chicks could make successful action flicks, an idea that also took hold in the vampire realm. With the onset of successful literary adaptations, including Coppola's *Bram Stoker's Dracula* in 1992 followed by Anne Rice's *Interview with the Vampire* and *Queen of the Damned* and the ongoing *Blade* series, the world of vampire cinema was searching for fresh female blood. What they found was Kate Beckinsale, cast in the lead role of Selene in the 2003 film *Underworld* and its sequel, *Underworld: Evolution* in 2006 (see Chapter 17).

More than just your average run-of-the-mill bloodsucking vixen, who's traditionally cast as Dracula's midnight snack and object of his obsession, Selene epitomizes a new-age girl power, casting herself smack in the middle of a deadly war being fought for the better part of a millennium between vampires and lycans (arguably the best werewolves you'll *ever* see transform on the big screen). Selene's smoldering immortal sexuality plays in brilliant contrast to her extreme survival instinct as a "death dealer" and the tumultuous risks she takes in the name of revenge, regardless of the laws of her coven. Also intermingled in the bloody savoir faire is the introduction of a male protagonist, Michael, who in his fight against becoming a hybrid, stirs in Selene the memories of what it was once like to be human. While the sequel, which takes off where its predecessor ends, doesn't quite hold the same serum as the original, it does serve to further establish that there's nothing sexier than a female predator in skintight leather—especially one who knows right from wrong and can play the undead game from hilt to blade.

The action-oriented vampirism of *Underworld* proved successful enough to bring viewers to the 2006 film *Ultraviolet*, where a seriously pumped-up vampiric plague sufferer, brilliantly played by Milla Jovovich, wreaks major havoc in a futuristic society hellbent on eliminating her "kind" (see Chapter 17). Using those films as inspiration, many other action-oriented vampires have burst from their coffins, including Kristanna Loken as the hybrid human/dhampir in the 2005 film *BloodRayne*, and Lucy Liu in *Rise* (2007).

FUN WITH VAMPIRISM

As with all movie genres, there exist films that, while the intent was to provide serious drama and suspense, the ultimate product proved to be unintentionally humorous. Vampire films, as with many other horror and science fiction films, fall victim to that rule on many occasions. Movies such as *Plan Nine from Outer Space* and the bizarre *Atom Age Vampire* don't just lose something in the translation of time—they never had it to begin with. Thankfully, there are a few vampire comedies, spoofs and otherwise, made for the express purpose of being funny, and they serve to lighten the mood of the terminally dark creatures of the night.

SCREEN SCREAM

Many genre-related spoofs have become box office successes that spawned sequels or entered the realm of cult classics. The writing and directing team of Jim Abrahams and brothers David and Jerry Zucker began their spoof onslaught with the 1980 classic air disaster extravaganza *Airplane!*, followed by the 1984 film *Top Secret*, the first of three *Naked Gun* films in 1988, and a pair of *Hot Shots!* in 1991 and 1993. Also very popular and financially successful is the *Scary Movie* franchise, which plays off the horror and sci-fi genres.

Over the decades, many filmmakers have made attempts at vampire comedy, some, perhaps unintentional in their comedic results. Several of the more well-known send-ups are *Tempi duri per i vampiri* aka *Hard Times for Dracula* (1959), *The Fearless Vampire Killers* (1967), *Andy Warhol's Dracula* (1974), *Vampira* (1974), *Dracula, Father and Son* (1976, based on the Claude

Klotz novel *Paris Vampire*), *Once Bitten* (1985), *Mr. Vampire* (1986), *I Married a Vampire* (1987), *My Grandfather is a Vampire* (1991), *Innocent Blood* (1992), *Vampire in Brooklyn* (1995), *Karmina* (1996), and *Bordello of Blood* (1996).

Arguably the most successful of the vampire comedy-spoofs in terms of longevity is the 1992 film *Buffy the Vampire Slayer*, which follows the exploits of a cheerleader turned vampire hunter (see Chapters 13 and 18). Destined to become a television series, Buffy ran for seven seasons, beginning in 1997. Comedy and spoof filmmakers of the modern vampire genre take on a major challenge, because in truth, they are held up to the high standard set by what's considered by many to be the ultimate horror spoof—the 1974 classic, *Young Frankenstein*. With its stellar cast, unforgettable script, and perfect comedic panache, the Mel Brooks film set the bar high.

Love at First Bite

In the subjective world of comedy, it's a known fact that it's tough to please everyone. What one individual thinks is funny may not remotely incite giggles in another moviegoer. But as far as vampire parodies go, there's one that many consider to be the definitive classic of the vampire spoof genre, and that vampire came in the form of immortally tanned actor George Hamilton. The film is *Love at First Bite*, and as a spoof, the 1979 offering really was tailor-made for the likes of the tall, dashing, debonair Hamilton who posed little threat to classic Draculas by giving an over-the-top performance as an ages-old nosferatu attempting to meld into modern-day New York City.

Coming five years after the release of *Young Frankenstein*, *Love at First Bite* made a strong attempt at regaling the vampire films of old with a distinctly modern edge. For example, when Dracula is told that he can spend the rest of his life in an efficiency apartment with seven dissidents and a single toilet, he asks Renfield: "What is an efficiency apartment?" To which Renfield (played by comedian Arte Johnson) replies: "What's a toilet?"

It's moments like those that give the vampire spoof its best showing. After all, with a lead character who's that old and that tan, there's much opportunity for comedy. As far as legendary Dracula dialog, it's likely few fans of the vampire genre will forget Hamilton retiring to his coffin, which is equipped with a nightlight, or his heavily accented classic lines, including

"Children of the night . . . shut up!" or "How would you like to be dressed as a head waiter for the last 700 years?"

Dead and Loving It

In 1995, over two decades after *Young Frankenstein* hit the silver screen, director Mel Brooks again delved into the world of horror, giving it a shot in the arm with *Dracula: Dead and Loving It*. Still enjoying his resurgence as the ultimate spoof comedian in *Airplane!*, the *Naked Gun* series, and a pair of *Scary Movie* sequels, Leslie Nielsen bares his fangs as the goofball Count, flanked by an admirable group of comedians, including Harvey Korman (Dr. Seward), Steven Weber (Jonathan Harker), Amy Yasbeck (Mina), and Mel Brooks himself as Van Helsing.

SCREEN SCREAM

For the hilarious scene of Lucy's staking, it's said that Mel Brooks didn't let on to Steven Weber that when Weber staked Lucy he would be covered in 200 gallons of fake blood. What resulted was a classic reaction from Weber and hysterical dialog when, after two stakings, Brooks informs Weber that "she's almost dead," with a completely blood-soaked Weber replying "she's dead enough."

Though it draws off a host of vampire classics, *Dead and Loving It* focuses primarily on Tod Browning's 1931 version of *Dracula* and Coppola's *Bram Stoker's Dracula*. It must be said, of course, that *Young Frankenstein* is a nearly impossible film to follow up given its cult status and the fact that to this day it remains terminally funny. But *Dead* has its moments, many of which are absolutely stolen by Peter MacNicol, who as Renfield pays perfect comedic homage to Dwight Frye's demented portrayal in the 1931 film. From his inability to move through the infamous spider web on Dracula's staircase to his maniacal bug swallowing and classic happy face drawn in the Count's ashes, MacNicol is a scream. Which is not to say that Nielsen doesn't do well by the immortal Count. His "hat," which mimics Gary Oldman's outrageous wig, and his uttering "Children of the night . . . what a mess they make!" before slipping down the staircase courtesy of a pile of bat droppings makes for some hearty giggles.

From Here to Eternity

In the next two chapters you will find the ultimate graveyard of vampire cinema in a two-part filmography that's certain to send you online or flying to the nearest video store. As a cinematic genre, the vampire realm is incredibly vast but well worth the effort for vampire aficionados who appreciate the attempts filmmakers have made over the years to release all sorts of vamps out of their respective coffins and into our living rooms. Dracula and his kin are never more at their best than when they're flying across the silver screen, flashing their toothy chompers of death, and dissolving into our minds like so much mist in an abandoned crypt.

CHAPTER 16

REEL-TIME VAMPIRISM: THE SILENT ERA THROUGH THE SWINGING SIXTIES

For over a century, the moviemaking industry has produced all measure of films in the horror genre, and a large and historically significant part of that body of work are films focused on vampires and vampirism. From the Silent Era to the present day, we've been treated to a variety of bloodsuckers, from the dramatic to the frightening to the downright comedic. No matter the decade, each of these films has made a contribution to vampirism, paying homage to both the literary works they're based on and the creative minds who've conjured up some of the most terrifying and engaging creatures the world has ever seen.

SILVER SCREEN SUCKERS

Vampires and the subject of vampirism in its various incarnations have played an important role in horror history since the Silent Era, and the power of bloodsuckers shows no sign of fizzling into the sunrise any time in the fore-seeable future. While the horror genre has most certainly seen its share of B movies and requisite blood, guts, and gore, there are plenty of early classics that in their simplicity make vampires convincingly real and utterly frighten-ing. In truth, many of the vampire films of the mid-twentieth century have withstood the test of time, with a host of additional films becoming cult clas-sics many years later. Even more compelling are the vampires of the modern-era, where new breeds of bloodsuckers have emerged with stylish aplomb.

In perusing this two-part vampire filmography, you may be surprised by how many films exist and the wide range of storylines they follow, from those building off Bram Stoker's *Dracula* to artistic spin-offs, action-adven-ture extravaganzas, foreign interpretations, and even a few prized spoofs for good measure. It must be said that for the purposes of this book, we've cho-sen films that show the full range of creative efforts filmmakers have worked hard to present, from short silent films to formidable full-blown big-budget epics. No matter your vampiric cinematic preference, if you're a vampire lover, then *all* of these films are worth sinking your teeth into.

An important aspect of vampire films worth mentioning is that many films over the decades are equally well-known by several different titles. Oftentimes, this is attributed to their country of origin with later theatrical release around the world, but that isn't always the case. For this filmogra-phy, we've listed each film by its most commonly recognized title, its year, and the principle actors. In this chapter, we focus on films from the Silent Era through the 1960s, while in Chapter 17 we discuss films from the 1970s through the new millennium. That said, we now introduce you to the vampyr through the ages as seen through the eyes of filmmakers the world over.

THE SILENT ERA

Silent films by their very nature are classics, and those in the horror genre are no exception. While the most recognizable of the silent vampire films is

F. W. Murnau's 1922 film *Nosferatu* (see Chapter 14), there are dozens more that give audiences a glimpse into the true evolutionary beginnings of the cinematic vampire as well as the underpinnings of the political and societal constrictions and conflicts of the era. Sadly, a fair number of these silent gems did not survive the ravages of time, so their legacy, like so many Draculas, is turned to dust. Regardless, we pay homage to the insight and creative efforts of those early filmmakers, their actors, and their contributions to the vampiric realm.

The first glimpse of vampirism saw the light of day in 1896 in a two-minute French film called *Le Manoir du diable*, or *Manor of the Devil*. Short but horrifyingly sweet, *Manoir* starred a bat that transformed itself into Mephistopheles. Despite it being a short piece, the film is considered by many to be the first vampire film. Several dozen more vampire films would follow over the next two decades, and their creation would reveal an interesting contrast between European and American filmmakers of the era, the Europeans choosing to focus more on artistic and expressionist moviemaking, and the Americans beginning a trend of producing more action-oriented films.

The international contingent of silent vampire films included a variety of storylines from Sweden (*The Vampire*), France (*Manor of the Devil* and *The Vampire*), Germany (*Nosferatu*, *A Night of Horror*, and two versions of *Alraune*), Hungary (*Alraune* and *Drakula*), Austria (*Lilith und Ly*), Russia (*Dracula*), India (*Wife and the Vampire*), and Poland (*Vampires of Warsaw*). These early foreign films set the stage for many more international endeavors that would see Mexico and especially Italy delve into the vampiric cinematic crypt.

One of the most noteworthy films of the Silent Era is director Tod Browning's 1927 horror mystery *London After Midnight*. Browning was one of the directors who crossed over from the silent to talkie films and is often considered to be one of America's premiere silent film directors. Part of his success was his association with Lon Chaney Sr., who achieved acclaim for his 1923 portrayal of Quasimodo in *The Hunchback of Notre Dame* and a number of other silent films that earned him the nickname the "Man of a Thousand Faces." As the star of *London After Midnight*, replete with a mouthful of sharp vampire teeth, bulging eyes and droopy eyelids, and stovepipe hat and vampire cloak, Chaney certainly lived up to his nickname.

Based on an original story written by Browning, *London After Midnight* is a Scotland Yard mystery, one that many experts playfully consider to be the first "fake" vampire film, given that Chaney serves double duty as both Inspector Burke and a mysterious vampiric character created as part of an elaborate deception to uncover a murderer. The film was remade by Browning in 1935 as *Mark of the Vampire* starring Lionel Barrymore and Bela Lugosi.

SCREEN SCREAM

With the onset of talking film, Tod Browning went on to direct the pièce de résistance of vampire films, the 1931 version of *Dracula*. Interestingly, it was Lon Chaney Sr. who was Browning's choice to play the infamous Count, but Chaney passed away in 1930, and the part eventually went to Hungarian actor Bela Lugosi.

Despite the vampiric cinematic efforts of the first two decades of the twentieth century, it wasn't until 1922 that what most consider to be the first full-fledged legitimate vampire made its entrancing appearance. The film is *Nosferatu, eine Symphone des Grauens*, which as a classic representation of the vampire in folklore, rather than the suave debonair vampires to come, is a mainstay in any vampire lover's film collection (see Chapter 14). *Nosferatu's* significance to the world of vampire cinema cannot be understated. Despite its crude production values, its vampire was, for its time, and shall forever remain, a shocking amalgam of preternatural predator and subversive sexual deviant. Max Schreck as Count Orlock is, quite simply, a terrifying monster by all accounts.

Silent films featuring vampires and vampirism include:

- ✝ *Manor of the Devil* aka *The Devil's Castle* aka *Le Manoir du diable* (1896, France) Jeanne d'Alcy, Georges Méliès
- ✝ *Vampire of the Coast* (1909)
- ✝ *The Vampire* (1910) Charles Clary, Margarita Fischer. (Based on a Rudyard Kipling poem)
- ✝ *The Vampire's Trail* (1910)

- ✝ *In the Grip of the Vampire* (1913)
- ✝ *The Vampire* (1913) Harry F. Millarde, Marguerite Courtot, Alice Hollister
- ✝ *The Vampire* aka *Vampyren* (1913, Sweden) Lili Bech, Nils Elffors, Victor Sjöström
- ✝ *Vampire of the Desert* (1913) Helen Gardner, Tefft Johnson, Harry T. Morey
- ✝ *The Vampire's Tower* aka *La Torre dei vampiri* (1913, Italy) Alfredo Bertone, Giulietta De Riso, Oreste Grandi
- ✝ *The Forest Vampires* (1914) Walter Edwards, J. Barney Sherry, Clara Williams
- ✝ *The Vampire's Trail* (1914) Alice Joyce, Alice Hollister, Harry F. Millarde
- ✝ *A Fool There Was* (1915) Theda Bara, Edward José, Mabel Frenyear
- ✝ *The Devil's Daughter* (1915) Theda Bara, Paul Doucet, Victor Benoit

VAMPIRE BITE

The term *vamp* didn't always apply to a typical cinematic bloodsucker—at least not in the Silent Era. Actress Theodosia Goodman, otherwise known as Theda Bara, was one of the film industry's first sex goddesses. So popular were her femme fatale alter egos that she's credited with immortalizing the silver screen "vamp," which in this case had more to do with her characters draining cash or affection from her targeted paramours!

- ✝ *Saved from the Vampire* (1915) Clarence Barr, Madge Kirby, Florence Lee
- ✝ *The Vampires* aka *Les Vampires* (1915, France) Musidora, Édouard Mathé, Marcel Lévesque
- ✝ *The Vampire* (1915) Olga Petrova, Vernon Steele, William A. Morse
- ✝ *Was She A Vampire?* (1915) Edna Maison
- ✝ *A Night of Horror* aka *A Night of Terror* aka *Nächte des Grauens* (1916) Emil Jannings, Laurence Köhler, Werner Krauss
- ✝ *A Vampire Out of Work* (1916) Josephine Earle

- ✟ *An Innocent Vampire* (1916) Arthur Albertson, Rose Melville, Henry Murdock
- ✟ *The Kiss of a Vampire* (1916) Kenneth Hunter, Virginia Pearson
- ✟ *The Latest in Vampires* (1916) Harry Myers, Rosemary Theby, Sidney Bracey
- ✟ *Mr. Vampire* (1916) Francis Ford, Roberta Wilson, Jack Holt
- ✟ *The Mysteries of Myra* (1916) Jean Sothern, Howard Estabrook, Allan Murnane
- ✟ *She Was Some Vampire* (1916) Billy Franey, Gale Henry, Milburn Morante
- ✟ *The Village Vampire* (1916) Fred Mace, Anna Luther, Earle Rodney
- ✟ *Jerry and the Vampire* (1917) George Ovey, Goldie Colwell, Janet Sully
- ✟ *To Oblige a Vampire* (1917) Eddie Lyons, Lee Moran, Edith Roberts
- ✟ *Alraune* (1918, Hungary) Karoly Arnyai, Géza Erdélyi, Gyula Gál
- ✟ *Alraune* aka *Sacrifice* (1918, Germany) Gustav Adolf Semler, Hilde Wolter
- ✟ *Mutt and Jeff Visit the Vampire* (1918) Theda Bara, Bud Fisher
- ✟ *Lilith und Ly* (1919, Austria) Elga Beck, Ernst Escherich, Franz Kammauf

SCREEN SCREAM

The 1919 Austrian film *Lilith und Ly* presented an intriguing twist when its male protagonist falls in love with a statue of Lilith that he animates with a ruby. Lilith, as it turns out, is a vampire and proceeds to drain the life out of her savior and his female companion, Ly.

- ✟ *Dracula* (1920, Russia)
- ✟ *Drakula* (1921, Hungary)
- ✟ *The Blonde Vampire* (1922) De Sacia Mooers, Joseph W. Smiley, Charles Craig
- ✟ *Nosferatu* aka *Nosferatu, eine Symphone des Grauens* (1922, Germany) Max Schreck, Gustav von Wangenheim, Greta Schröder

- ♱ *The Last Man on Earth* (1924) Earle Foxe, Grace Cunard, Gladys Tennyson
- ♱ *Vampires of Warsaw* (1925, Poland) Oktawian Kaczanowski, Halina Labedzka
- ♱ *Wife and the Vampire* aka *Prem Ane Vaasna* (1925, India)
- ♱ *London After Midnight* aka *The Hypnotist* (1927) Lon Chaney, Marceline Day, Henry B. Walthall
- ♱ *Unholy Love* aka *Alraune* (1928, Germany) Brigitte Helm, Paul Wegener, Iván Petrovich

Fangtastic Folklore

Though the plot bears a similarity to Richard Matheson's 1954 novel *I Am Legend*, the 1924 film *The Last Man on Earth* is unrelated. In this film, an aptly named plague called "man-itis" has wiped out all maledom save for a fertile Ozark hillbilly named Elmer Smith who's at the mercy of the entire female population. A 1933 Spanish remake of the film was plagued by "masculitis" and the same evil physician—Dr. Prodwell—who sounds like something out of a James Bond flick!

THE 1930S: THE DAWN OF DRACULA

While it's often debated as to which vampire film marks the actual "birth" of vampiric cinema, with many noting that *Nosferatu* is the first to follow—albeit without permission—Bram Stoker's *Dracula*, there really should be little dispute. The first official portrayal of the classic Count and his torrid Transylvanian tale falls to Bela Lugosi, who in 1931 brought the traditional Dracula to the screen with every ounce of panache he could muster (see Chapter 15). Though many versions would follow over the decades, Lugosi's portrayal of Dracula is significant on many levels. It was indeed this film that introduced many of the bloodsucker's characteristics, including his ability to transform into bats, wolves, mist, and dust, his aversion to mirrors, and the utterances of what have become trademark dialog for Dracula. No vampire fan will *ever* forget Lugosi's heavily accented and diabolical: "I never drink . . . wine."

The 1930s also saw the emergence of one of the most notable and some-what underrated female vampires of the genre, Gloria Holden, who in 1936 flew onto the big screen in *Dracula's Daughter*. Picking up the story pre-cisely where Lugosi's version ends, Holden, as the Countess Marya Zaleska, is one of the first in a long line of what would come to be known as *reluctant vampires*—those who seek to break the curse of immortality. Allegedly based on Bram Stoker's story *Dracula's Guest* (many experts cite the script as having actually been the original work of Garrett Fort, who also wrote the 1931 *Dracula*), this sequel is often overlooked. Despite its obvious low budget, however, it remains a stylish example that would only serve to help further the brood of female vampires to come (see Chapter 15).

Fangtastic Folklore

Though the 1931 *Dracula* suffered from what many early films main-tained—low production values—there are a number of reasons that Lugosi's version of *Dracula* was so successful, not the least of which was the tremendous reception the stage versions of *Dracula* received during the 1920s (see Chapter 14).

Several other films of the thirties are worthy of note, the first of which is director Carl Theodor Dreyer's 1932 German offering *Vampyr*, a somewhat bizarre and cryptic tale based on Sheridan Le Fanu's *Carmilla* (see Chapter 3). A year later, audiences were treated to *The Vampire Bat*, featuring Lionel Atwill, Fay Wray, a young Melvyn Douglas, and Dwight Frye, who gave a truly lunatic performance as Bela Lugosi's slave, Renfield, in the 1931 *Dracula*. And in 1935, came *Mark of the Vampire*, the remake of Tod Browning's *London After Midnight*. Films of the 1930s include:

- † *Daughter of Evil* aka *Alraune* (1930) Brigitte Helm, Albert Basser-mann, Harald Paulsen
- † *Vampiresas* (1930) Antonio Ozores, Lina Morgan, Yves Massard
- † *Dracula* (1931) Bela Lugosi, Helen Chandler, David Manners, Edward Van Sloan

- ✝ *Drácula* (1931, Mexico) Carlos Villarías, Pablo Álvarez Rubio, Barry Norton, Lupita Tovar
- ✝ *Vampyr* aka *Castle of Doom* aka *Vampyr—Der Traum des Allan Grey* aka *The Strange Adventure of David Gray* (1932, Germany) Julian West, Maurice Schutz, Rena Mandel
- ✝ *The Last Man on Earth* aka *El Ultimo varon sobre la Tierra* (1933, Mexico) Raul Roulien, Rosita Moreno, Mimi Aguglia
- ✝ *The Vampire Bat* (1933) Lionel Atwill, Fay Wray, Melvyn Douglas
- ✝ *Condemned to Live* (1935) Ralph Morgan, Maxine Doyle, Pedro de Cordoba
- ✝ *Mark of the Vampire* (1935) Lionel Barrymore, Elizabeth Allan, Bela Lugosi, Lionel Atwill
- ✝ *Dracula's Daughter* (1936) Gloria Holden, Otto Kruger, Marguerite Churchill
- ✝ *The Macabre Trunk* aka *El Baúl macabro* (1936, Mexico) Ramón Pereda, René Cardona, Manuel Noriega
- ✝ *The Return of Dr. X* (1939) Humphrey Bogart, Rosemary Lane, Wayne Morris

SCREEN SCREAM

If you're a fan of *Casablanca* and *The Maltese Falcon*, hold on to your capes, because believe it or not, even Humphrey Bogart took his turn as a vampire/zombie in the 1939 flick *The Return of Dr. X*. Yep. Complete with white streak in his hair, Bogie portrays an executed murderer who's reanimated with the added benefits of vampirism. As a matter of curiosity, the role was originally meant for Boris Karloff.

THE 1940S: THE COMEDY OF HORROR

The onset of the 1940s saw the vampire genre endure a few wicked and amusing escapades (some not intentionally comedic), while also highlighting a few horror heavyweights who took their turn playing Dracula. Lugosi returned to the role in several films including *The Devil Bat, Spooks Run*

Wild, The Return of the Vampire, and even played the bloodsucker in *Abbott and Costello Meet Frankenstein.* Of these films, only *Return* gives Lugosi a role he can chomp into, playing Armand Tesla a vampire who's initially destroyed during the London blitz in 1918, but is uncovered and reanimated during World War II. Significantly, the film marks the first time a vampire meets the Wolf Man.

Also joining the crypt of the distinguished vampyr is Lon Chaney, as the mustached Count Alucard (palindrome anyone?) in *Son of Dracula.* Chaney had a busy decade, pulling triple monster duty as famed Wolf Man Lawrence Talbot in *Abbott and Costello Meet Frankenstein, House of Frankenstein,* and *House of Dracula.* It was, in fact, the latter two romps that introduced us to yet another legendary cinematic bloodsucker—John Carradine, who is arguably one of the creepiest of the classic Draculas (see Chapter 15). The dramas and comedy of horrors from the forties include:

- ✝ *The Devil Bat* (1940) Bela Lugosi, Suzanne Kaaren, Dave O'Brien, Hal Price
- ✝ *Spooks Run Wild* (1941) Bela Lugosi, Leo Gorcey, Dennis Moore
- ✝ *Dead Men Walk* aka *Creatures of the Devil* (1943) George Zucco, Mary Carlisle, Nedrick Young
- ✝ *Dr. Terror's House of Horrors* (1943) Henriette Gérard, Murdock Mac-Quarrie, Paul Wegener
- ✝ *Son of Dracula* (1943) Lon Chaney Jr., Robert Paige, Louise Allbritton, Evelyn Ankers
- ✝ *House of Frankenstein* (1944) John Carradine, Boris Karloff, Lon Chaney Jr., Lionel Atwill
- ✝ *The Return of the Vampire* (1944) Bela Lugosi, Matt Willis, Frieda Inescort, Nina Foch
- ✝ *House of Dracula* (1945) Lon Chaney Jr., John Carradine, Lionel Atwill
- ✝ *Isle of the Dead* (1945) Boris Karloff, Ellen Drew, Marc Cramer
- ✝ *Memorias de una Vampiresa* (1945, Mexico) Manuel Noriega, Clifford Carr, Adriana Lamar
- ✝ *The Vampire's Ghost* (1945) John Abbott, Roy Barcroft, Peggy Stewart

- ☦ *Devil Bat's Daughter* (1946) Rosemary La Planche, John James, Michael Hale
- ☦ *The Face of Marble* (1946) John Carradine, Claudia Drake, Robert Shayne
- ☦ *The Spider Woman Strikes Back* (1946) Brenda Joyce, Gale Sondergaard, Kirby Grant, Rondo Hatton
- ☦ *Valley of the Zombies* (1946) Robert Livingston, Adrian Booth, Ian Keith
- ☦ *Abbott and Costello Meet Frankenstein* (1948) Bud Abbott, Lou Costello, Lon Chaney Jr., Bela Lugosi

VAMPIRE BITE

A version of the Greek *vrykolakas* made its cinematic debut in the 1945 Boris Karloff film *Isle of the Dead*, which was set during the First Balkan War of 1912. In the film, Karloff plays a fictional Greek general who's killed during his misguided attempts to protect the inhabitants of a tiny Greek island from the spread of a plague that was suspected to have been brought on by the actions of a beautiful—but ultimately innocent—personification of the *vrykolakas* (see Chapter 2).

THE 1950S: BAT OUT OF HELL

Coming off a decade of classically eccentric vamp flicks, the 1950s started out with the bang and just kept going. A large contingent of foreign films made their mark on the vampire legacy, and with them began a new renaissance of the vampire film as a cinematic stronghold. Films including Riccardo Freda's 1956 *I Vampiri*, which follows the legend of the evil Countess Erzébet Bathóry (see Chapter 11), mark the emergence of an Italian legacy of vampiric filmmaking. The 1958 film *Blood of the Vampire* would also serve as an introduction to the striking Barbara Steele, who would later become one of horror's most recognizable scream queens and a consummate vampire witch in Mario Bava's 1960 cult classic *Black Sunday* (see Chapter 15).

While there were many classic films to emerge from the fifties, there is one that arguably stands fang and cape above the rest and it can be summed up in two words: Christopher Lee. In 1958, Lee rose from the grave and made his vampiric debut in the Hammer film *Horror of Dracula* (also called *Dracula*). Fresh off a stint playing the monster to Peter Cushing's Baron Victor Frankenstein in the 1957 *The Curse of Frankenstein*, Lee was again partnered with Cushing in *Horror*. The result was a one of the best Dracula movies to date and the birth of what many assert is the most epic partnership in horror history (see Chapter 15). The film was also a turning point for Hammer, marking the beginnings of its dominance in the horror genre for over a decade.

Unlike Bela Lugosi's Count in the 1931 version, Lee, with his graying locks, red eyes, and bloodthirsty hypnotics, proved to be a stunning Dracula whose athleticism, bold sexual underpinnings, and raw animal instincts brought new life to the character while also proving to be an admirable foe to Cushing's equally provocative, action-oriented Van Helsing. Audiences were enamored by director Terence Fisher's interpretation and the social subtext of the demise of the aristocracy of the nineteenth century. Films of the fabulous fifties include the following:

- ✝ *The Thing From Another World* (1951) Kenneth Tobey, Margaret Sheridan, James Arness
- ✝ *Batula* aka *Fearless Fosdick meets Dracula* (1952) Puppet flick written by Al Capp
- ✝ *Old Mother Riley Meets the Vampire* (1952) Arthur Lucan, Bela Lugosi, Dora Bryan
- ✝ *The Black Vampire* aka *El Vampiro negro* (1953, Argentina) Olga Zubarry, Roberto Escalada, Georges Rivière
- ✝ *Dracula in Istanbul* aka *Drakula Istanbul'da* (1953, Turkey) Atif Kaptan, Annie Ball, Bülent Oran
- ✝ *I Vampiri* aka *The Devil's Commandment* (1956, Italy) Gianna Maria Canale, Carlo D'Angelo, Dario Michaelis
- ✝ *Pity For the Vamps* aka *Pitié pour les vamps* (1956, France) Viviane Romance, Giselle Pascal
- ✝ *The Vampire Moth* aka *Kyuketsuki-ga* (1956, Japan) Ryo Ikebe, Asami Kuji, Akio Kobori
- ✝ *Blood of Dracula* (1957) Sandra Harrison, Louise Lewis, Gail Ganley

- *Daughter of Dr. Jekyll* (1957) Gloria Talbott, John Agar, Arthur Shields
- *Not of This Earth* (1957) Paul Birch, Beverly Garland, Morgan Jones
- *Revenge of the Vampire* aka *Dendam Pontianak* (1957, Singapore) Maria Menado, Puteh Lawak, S.M. Wahid
- *Space Ship Sappy* (1957) Moe Howard, Larry Fine, Joe Besser
- *The Vampire* aka *El Vampiro* (1957, Mexico) Germán Robles, Abel Salazar, Ariadna Welter
- *The Vampire* aka *Mark of the Vampire* (1957) John Beal, Coleen Gray, Kenneth Tobey

Fangtastic Folklore

What must be duly noted in this decade is the acclaim of the 1951 Howard Hawks film *The Thing From Another World*, which crosses the boundaries of the traditional vampire and brings into play the melding of the horror and sci-fi genre and its broad use of vampirism often used in plagues and other sordid bloodsucking monsters. Remade in 1982 by director John Carpenter, the sequel, while also featuring a bloodthirsty alien, is often classified as mainstream sci-fi. Its predecessor, however, toes the line. A classic to be certain, *The Thing From Another World* is a blood-craving vegetative creature (played by an unspeaking James Arness) who's reanimated from the Arctic grave of his alien spaceship.

- *The Vampire* aka *Pontianak* (1957, Singapore) Maria Menado, M. Amin, Salmah Ahmad
- *Son of the Vampire* aka *Anak Pontianak* (1958, Singapore) Kemat Bin Hassan, Hasimah, Haj Sattar
- *The Vampire's Coffin* aka *El Ataúd del Vampiro* (1958, Mexico) Germán Robles, Abel Salazar, Ariadna Welter
- *Blood of the Vampire* (1958) Donald Wolfit, Vincent Ball, Barbara Shelley
- *Castle of the Monsters* aka *El Castillo de los monstruos* (1958, Mexico) Germán Robles, Antonio Espino, Evangelina Elizondo

- *Horror of Dracula* aka *Dracula* (1958) Christopher Lee, Peter Cushing, Michael Gough, Melissa Stribling
- *It! The Vampire From Beyond Space* (1958) Marshall Thompson, Shawn Smith, Ray Corrigan
- *The Return of Dracula* aka *The Curse of Dracula* (1958) Francis Lederer, Norma Eberhardt, Ray Stricklyn
- *The Vampire's Curse* aka *Sumpah Pontianak* (1958) Maria Menado, Mustaffa Maarof, Salmah Ahmad
- *Curse of the Undead* (1959) Eric Fleming, Michael Pate, Kathleen Crowley
- *First Man Into Space* (1959) Marshall Thompson, Marla Landi, Robert Ayres
- *Plan Nine From Outer Space* (1959) Gregory Walcott, Mona McKinnon, Duke Moore
- *The Woman Vampire* aka *Onna kyuketsuki* (1959, Japan) Shigeru Amachi, Keinosuke Wada, Junko Ikeuchi
- *Hard Times for Dracula* aka *Uncle Was a Vampire* aka *Tempi duri per i vampiri* (1959, Italian satire) Christopher Lee, Renato Rascel, Sylva Koscina

THE 1960S: REVIVAL OF THE FITTEST

The success of Christopher Lee's portrayal of Dracula breathed new life into the vampire genre, and for the next two decades, vamps, scamps, and various ghoulish creatures would grace the silver screen with style, humor, and plenty of creative license. The silver screen vampire continued its onslaught throughout the sixties, with a variety of filmmakers from around the world staking claim to the Dracula legend.

In 1960, Peter Cushing reprised his role of Abraham Van Helsing in the classic Hammer film *The Brides of Dracula*, only this time the immortal fiend took on a different look, which to this day is debated as to whether or not it proved effective. David Peel's appearance as the wicked Baron Meinster stands in direct contrast to Lee's tall, dark, and deadly Dracula. Peel was blonde, blue-eyed, and to the viewing audience, decidedly *not*

Christopher Lee. *Brides* remains a cult favorite, however, if for no other reason that Cushing continues his legacy as Van Helsing with the class and active instinctiveness of a true vampire hunter (see Chapter 15). Lee, who spent his time becoming the leading horror star of his era, returned to his Transylvanian roots in 1966 again teaming up with director Terence Fisher for *Dracula: Prince of Darkness*, and he also appeared in a handful of additional films including *The Castle of the Living Dead, Dr. Terror's House of Horrors, Theatre of Death, The Blood Demon*, and *Dracula Has Risen From the Grave*. For a true dose of classic Swinging Sixies vampirism, be sure to check out the following:

- ✞ *Atom Age Vampire* aka *l'erede di Santana Seddok* (1960, Italy) Alberto Lupo, Susanne Loret, Sergio Fantoni
- ✞ *Black Sunday* aka *La Maschera del demonio* aka *Mask of the Demon* (1961, Italy) Barbara Steele, John Richardson, Ivo Garrani
- ✞ *Blood and Roses* aka *To Die with Pleasure* aka *Et mourir de plaisir* (1960, France) Mel Ferrer, Elsa Martinelli, Annette Vadim
- ✞ *The Brides of Dracula* (1960) Peter Cushing, Yvonne Monlaur, David Peel
- ✞ *L'Amante del vampiro* aka *The Vampire's Lover* (1960, Italy) Hélène Rémy, Maria Luísa Rolado, Tina Gloriani
- ✞ *The Bad Flower* aka *Akui ggot* (1961, South Korea) Ye-chun Lee, Geum-bong Do, Seon-ae Ko
- ✞ *Goliath and the Vampires* aka *Maciste contro il Vampiro* (1961, Italy) Gordon Scott, Guido Celano, Gianna Maria Canale

SCREEN SCREAM

Rumor has it that Christopher Lee was displeased with the script for *Dracula: Prince of Darkness* and insisting the dialog was atrocious, he refused to speak any of the lines. If the tale is to be believed, then that could account for the fact that Lee indeed never uttered a word throughout the entire film, only hissing and conveying his performance with his trademark stares and immortal bad boy antics.

- ✝ *The World of the Vampires* aka *El Mundo de los vampiros* (1961, Mexico) Mauricio Garcés, Erna Martha Bauman, Silvia Fournier
- ✝ *The Bloody Vampire* aka *El Vampiro sagriento* (1962, Mexico) Carlos Agostí, Begoña Palacios, Erna Martha Bauman
- ✝ *Sampson vs. the Vampire Women* aka *Santo vs. las mujeres vampiro* (1962, Mexico) Santo, Lorena Velázquez, María Duval
- ✝ *Bring Me the Vampire* aka *Échenme al vampiro* (1963, Mexico) Pompín Iglesias, Joaquín García Vargas, Fernando Soto
- ✝ *House of Frights* aka *La Casa de los espantos* (1963, Mexico) Pompín Iglesias, Joaquín García Vargas, Fernando Soto
- ✝ *The Horror of It All* (1963) Pat Boone, Erica Rogers, Dennis Price
- ✝ *Kiss of the Vampire* (1963) Clifford Evans, Edward de Souza, Noel Willman, Jennifer Daniel
- ✝ *The Vampire Returns* aka *Pontianak Kembali* (1963, Singapore) Maria Menado, Malik Selamat
- ✝ *Blood and Black Lace* (1964) Cameron Mitchell, Eva Bartok, Thomas Reiner
- ✝ *The Blood Drinkers* aka *Kulay dugo ang gabi* (1964, Philippines) Ronald Remy, Amalia Fuentes, Eddie Fernandez
- ✝ *Castle of Blood* aka *Danza macabra* (1964, Italy) Barbara Steele, Georges Rivière, Margarete Robsahm
- ✝ *The Castle of the Living Dead* aka *Il Castello dei morti vivi* (1964, Italy) Christopher Lee, Gaia Germani, Philippe Leroy
- ✝ *The Curse of the Green Eyes* aka *Der Fluch der grünen Augen* (1964, Germany) Adrian Hoven, Erika Remberg, Carl Möhner
- ✝ *The Last Man on Earth* (1964) Vincent Price, Franca Bettoia, Emma Danieli
- ✝ *Terror in the Crypt* (1964) Adriana Ambesi, Christopher Lee, Ursula Davis
- ✝ *The Vampire of the Opera* aka *Il Vampiro dell'opera* (1964, Italy) Marco Mariani, Giuseppe Addobbati, Barbara Howard
- ✝ *The Bloodless Vampire* (1965, Philippines) Charles McCauley, Helen Thompson

- *Devils of Darkness* (1965) William Sylvester, Hubert Noël, Carole Gray, Tracy Reed
- *Dr. Terror's House of Horrors* (1965) Peter Cushing, Christopher Lee, Donald Sutherland
- *Planet of the Vampires* aka *Terror in Space* aka *Terrore nello spazio* (1965, Italy) Barry Sullivan, Norma Bengell, Angel Aranda
- *The Vampire of Düsseldorf* aka *Le Vampire de Düsseldorf* (1965, France) Robert Hossein, Marie-France Pisier, Roger Dutoit
- *Billy the Kid versus Dracula* (1966) John Carradine, Chuck Courtney, Melinda Plowman

Fangtastic Folklore

In 1964, legendary horror master Vincent Price starred in *The Last Man on Earth*, a film based on Richard Matheson's novel *I Am Legend*. Matheson himself was a cowriter of the script for the 1964 outing. Fighting against vampire zombies, Price's turn as Robert Neville would be reprised in 1971 by Charleton Heston in *The Omega Man* and again by Will Smith in the 2007 blockbuster *I Am Legend*.

- *Carry On Screaming* (1966) Harry H. Corbett, Kenneth Williams, Jim Dale
- *The Devil's Mistress* (1966) Joan Stapleton, Robert Gregory, Arthur Resley
- *Dracula: Prince of Darkness* (1966) Christopher Lee, Barbara Shelley, Andrew Keir
- *The Hand of Night* aka *Beast of Morocco* (1966) William Sylvester, Diane Clare, Aliza Gur
- *Queen of Blood* aka *Planet of Blood* (1966) John Saxon, Basil Rathbone, Judi Meredith
- *Satan's Sister* aka *La Sorella di Satana* (1966, Italy) Barbara Steele, John Karlsen, Ian Ogilvy
- *Theatre of Death* aka *Blood Fiend* (1966) Christopher Lee, Julian Glover, Lelia Goldoni

- ☩ *Track of the Vampire* aka *Blood Bath* (1966) William Campbell, Lori Saunders, Marissa Mathes
- ☩ *The Blood Demon* aka *The Snake Pit and the Pendulum* aka *Die Schlangengrube und das Pendel* (1967, Germany) Christopher Lee, Lex Barker, Karin Dor
- ☩ *A Taste of Blood* (1967) Bill Rogers, Elizabeth Wilkinson, Otto Schlessinger
- ☩ *Dr. Terror's Gallery of Horrors* (1967) Lon Chaney Jr., John Carradine
- ☩ *The Empire of Dracula* aka *El Imperio de Drácula* (1967, Mexico) Lucha Villa César del Campo, Eric del Castillo
- ☩ *The Fearless Vampire Killers* aka *Pardon Me, But Your Teeth Are in My Neck* (1967) Jack McGowran, Roman Polanski, Sharon Tate
- ☩ *The Blood Beast Terror* (1968) Peter Cushing, Robert Flemying, Wanda Ventham
- ☩ *Carmilla* (1968, Sweden) Monica Nordquist, Birger Malmsten
- ☩ *Dracula Has Risen From the Grave* (1968) Christopher Lee, Rupert Davies, Veronica Carlson
- ☩ *Queen of the Vampires* aka *Le Viol du vampire* (1968, France) Solange Pradel, Bernard Letrou, Catherine Deville
- ☩ *Blood of Dracula's Castle* (1969) Alexander D'Arcy, John Carradine, Paula Raymond

SCREEN SCREAM

Can you guess which famous British comedian played Van Helsing's daughter in one of the last Hammer films Christopher Lee made? Believe it or not, Joanna Lumley portrays Peter Cushing's daughter, Jessica Van Helsing, in the 1973 film *The Satanic Rites of Dracula*, in which Dracula's dastardly plan is to release upon the world a biological plague. Lumley is best known for playing the sex-crazed, nicotine-addicted, drunk Patsy on the hit series *Absolutely Fabulous*.

FROM DAMNED TO DECADENT

From its inception during the Silent Era through the Swinging Sixties, the cinematic vampire has benefited by its distinct evolution as a prime time protagonist. In the next chapter, that evolution continues so fast that Darwin himself would be spinning in his grave. From the 1970s to the present day, a Pandora's box of vampires and vampirism is opened—and there's no closing the lid.

CHAPTER 17

REEL-TIME VAMPIRISM: THE SEVENTIES THROUGH THE NEW MILLENNIVM

As we learned in Chapter 16, the cinematic vampire realm is historically vast and varied. Now we move on to the more modern era, from the seventies to the present day, and an amazing preternatural explosion of vampires sucking their way through everything from horror to comedy. What is perhaps most impressive about the films of the past three decades—aside from their sheer numbers—is how truly immortal the vampire has become, serving up guile, gore, and wiley wit to generations of truly mesmerized fans.

THE VAMPIRE IN MODERN CINEMA

The vampire genre of films is immortal in regard to moviemaking history, having begun with the Silent Era in 1896. From the 1930s through the 1960s, the genre grew stronger, in part as a result of both international and domestic filmmakers casting a wide net over Bram Stoker's historical character and also with the emergence of Hammer Films and their churning out one horror flick after another (see Chapter 15). Beginning in the seventies, despite the fact that Hammer productions began to slide, that trend continued and moved on throughout the following decades in a natural progression that would see vampires and vampirism brought to new levels of intrigue, violence, comedy, and otherworldly proportions.

THE 1970s: LOVE, LUST, AND THE LUDICROUS

As with all things seventies, the vampire genre contains an enormous mixed bag of cinema that provides all measure of horrific entertainment. In truth, the seventies are absolutely jam-packed with vamp flicks featuring everything from traditional Draculas to a postapocalyptic blood scourge to epic battles between Frankenstein and the Wolf Man to campy vamps, kung fu vampirism, blaxploitation, a vampire musical, and even a Dracula adaptation geared toward the hearing impaired. The wide variety of films speaks to the fact that so many vampire flicks were being made that filmmakers were in danger of beating the genre into an early grave.

For starters, the 1970s introduced us to another of the Hammer Films's brood—the ineffable Polish actress Ingrid Pitt, who first bared her fangs in the 1970 film *The Vampire Lovers* and again in 1971 in one of the four tales comprising *The House That Dripped Blood*. That same year, Pitt took yet another bite out of the genre, playing the lead in *Countess Dracula* (see Chapter 15). Christopher Lee, Peter Cushing, and John Carradine figured prominently throughout the decade as did several others who made their first appearance as Dracula, including Klaus Kinski in a 1979 remake of *Nosferatu*.

Also leading a tour de force of the prestigious mix of actors lending their talents to world of the undead are Jonathan Frid as Barnabas Collins (in the 1970 spin-off *House of Dark Shadows*), Robert Quarry (as *Count Yorga, Vampire* in 1970 and in *The Return of Count Yorga* the following year), Jack Palance (in the 1973 television premiere of *Bram Stoker's Dracula*), Udo Kier (in the bizarre 1974 virgin-hunting outing *Andy Warhol's Dracula*), David Niven (as the hysterical "Old Dracula" in the 1974 film *Vampira*), and Louis Jourdan (*Count Dracula* as part of Great Performances in 1977).

SCREEN SCREAM

In 1972, the first substantial African-American bloodsucker bared his fangs in the classic blaxploitation film *Blacula* and again a year later in the sequel *Scream Blacula Scream*. In both installments, Blacula was played by William Marshall with a cast of African-American actors who used the films as a springboard to bigger future endeavors (see Chapter 15).

Worthy of special note in this explosion of bloodthirsty ghouls are two actors who are often singled out for their 1979 performances. The first is George Hamilton for his over-the-top Count in *Love at First Bite*, the tenth-highest-grossing vampire film of all time. A cult classic in its own right, Hamilton's take on the famous Dracula line in reference to the "children of the night" won't soon be forgotten. "Children of the night," he says in perfect accent. "Shut up!" (see Chapter 15). The second performance of that year is that of Frank Langella in *Dracula*, which ranks at number eighteen on the all-time list. This film is widely considered to be one of the best in the vampire genre, with Langella giving a smoldering portrayal in a remake of Lugosi's 1931 *Dracula* that played off the Hamilton Deane and John L. Balderston stage play (see Chapter 14).

Yet another cult favorite graced the big screen in this decade, offering up a new take on the vampire hunter and setting a standard for those who would follow. The 1974 film *Captain Kronos: Vampire Hunter* features dashing German actor Horst Janson as the suave and debonair Kronos and John Cater as his hunchbacked sidekick Professor Grost. What makes this outing so fun and memorable is director Brian Clemens's melding of several film genres, most notably a type of Western with hints of traditional mystery, romance, science fiction, and Count of Monte Cristo swordplay all interwoven amid a steady dose of drama and cliché.

Chasing a vampire who has the ability to literally meld into society by virtue of being unaffected by sunlight leaves Kronos to suss out who could be wiping out local villagers. It should be noted that Clemens was the primary writer and associate producer for the 1960s smash series *The Avengers*, a fact that plays heavily into the playful plotline and humorous tongue-in-cheek detail *Kronos* offers. For true vampire aficionados, *Captain Kronos* is a must see. So if you're up for a few good shivers, a bit of gore, and some big laughs, you don't want to miss the vampy campy artistic and fantastic films of the seventies, including:

- ✝ *Bloodsuckers* aka *Incense for the Damned* (1970) Peter Cushing, Patrick McNee, Patrick Mower
- ✝ *Count Dracula* aka *Nachts, wenn Dracula erwacht* (1970, Germany) Christopher Lee, Klaus Kinski, Herbert Lom
- ✝ *Count Yorga, Vampire* (1970) Robert Quarry, Roger Perry, Michael Murphy
- ✝ *Countess Dracula* (1970) Ingrid Pitt, Nigel Green, Sandor Elès
- ✝ *Guess What Happened to Count Dracula?* (1970) Des Roberts, Claudia Barron, John Landon
- ✝ *Horror of the Blood Monsters* (1970) John Carradine, Robert Dix, Vicki Volante
- ✝ *House of Dark Shadows* (1970) Jonathan Frid, Grayson Hall, Kathryn Leigh Scott
- ✝ *Jonathan* aka *Vampire sterben nicht* (1970, Germany) Jürgen Jung, Hans-Dieter Jendreyko, Paul Albert Krumm
- ✝ *Scars of Dracula* (1970) Christopher Lee, Dennis Waterman, Jenny Hanley
- ✝ *Taste the Blood of Dracula* (1970) Christopher Lee, Geoffrey Keen, Gwen Watford
- ✝ *The Vampire Lovers* (1970) Ingrid Pitt, George Cole, Peter Cushing, Kate O'Mara
- ✝ *Blood Thirst* (1971) Robert Winston, Yvonne Nielson, Judy Dennis

- ☩ *Dracula vs. Frankenstein* (1971) J. Carrol Naish, Lon Chaney Jr., Zandor Vorkov
- ☩ *The House That Dripped Blood* (1971, England) Christopher Lee, Peter Cushing, Denholm Elliott, John Bennett
- ☩ *Lust for a Vampire* (1971) Ralph Bates, Barbara Jefford, Suzanna Leigh
- ☩ *Night of Dark Shadows* (1971) Jonathan Frid, Grayson Hall, David Selby
- ☩ *The Omega Man* (1971) Charleton Heston, Anthony Zerbe, Rosalind Cash
- ☩ *The Return of Count Yorga* (1971) Robert Quarry, Mariette Hartley, Roger Perry
- ☩ *Twins of Evil* (1971) Peter Cushing, Damien Thomas, Madeleine and Mary Collinson
- ☩ *The Werewolf versus the Vampire Women* aka *La Noche de Walpurgis* (1971, Spain) Paul Naschy, Gaby Fuchs, Barbara Capell
- ☩ *Blacula* (1972) William Marshall, Vonetta McGee, Denise Nicholas
- ☩ *The Daughter of Dracula* aka *La Fille de Dracula* (1972, Mexico) Britt Nichols, Anne Libert, Howard Vernon

SCREEN SCREAM

Despite the fact that the 1974 comedy *Vampira* (also known as *Old Dracula*) isn't of critical acclaim, it's a must for David Niven fans. As "Old Dracula," Niven is on the hunt for a rare blood type in an effort to reanimate his beloved vampire bride (Teresa Graves). Of course, after an "abby-normal" mix-up courtesy his daft assistant, his immortal squeeze wakes up, only to find that due to the transfusion she's now become an African-American vampire!

- ☩ *Deathmaster* (1972) Robert Quarry, John Fiedler, Bill Ewing
- ☩ *Dracula A.D. 1972* (1972) Christopher Lee, Peter Cushing, Stephanie Beacham, Christopher Neame

- † *Dracula vs. Dr. Frankenstein* aka *Drácula contra Frankenstein* (1972, Mexico) Dennis Price, Howard Vernon, Britt Nichols
- † *Dracula's Great Love* aka *El Gran Amor del conde Drácula* (1972, Mexico) Paul Naschy, Haydée Politoff, Rosanna Yanni
- † *Night of the Devils* aka *La Notte dei diavoli* (1972, Italy) Gianni Garko, Agostina Belli, Maria Monti
- † *The Night Stalker* (1972) Darren McGavin, Simon Oakland, Carol Lynley
- † *Saga of the Draculas* aka *La Saga de los Drácula* (1972) Tina Sáinz, Tony Isbert, Helga Liné
- † *Bram Stoker's Dracula* (1973) Jack Palance, Simon Ward, Nigel Davenport

SCREEN SCREAM

It's not often that filmmakers can break entirely new barriers in mainstream industry, but the 1975 film *Deafula* did just that. *Deafula* is the brainchild of its director, writer, and star Peter Wolf Wechsberg (cited under the name Peter Wolf), who is himself deaf. Unchallenged in its unique approach to filmmaking, *Deafula* is the first-ever feature film conveyed entirely in sign language. The character of Deafula, played by Wechsberg, is a theology student who slowly becomes a vampire, realizing that he was in his youth bitten by the real bloodsucker.

- † *The Devil's Wedding Night* aka *Full Moon of the Virgins* aka *Il Plenilunio delle vergini* (1973, Italy) Sara Bay, Mark Damon, Esmeralda Barros
- † *Hannah, Queen of the Vampires* aka *La Tumba de la isla maldita* (1973, Spain) Andrew Prine, Patty Shepard, Mark Damon
- † *The Legend of Blood Castle* aka *Ceremonia sangrienta* (1973, Spain) Lucia Bosé, Espartaco Santoni, Ewa Aulin
- † *Lemora: A Child's Tale of the Supernatural* (1973) Lesley Gilb, Cheryl Smith, William Whitton

✝ *The Satanic Rites of Dracula* (1973) Christopher Lee, Peter Cushing, Michael Coles, Joanna Lumley

✝ *Scream, Blacula, Scream* (1973) William Marshall, Don Mitchell, Pam Grier

✝ *Allen and Rossi Meet Dracula and Frankenstein* (1974) Marty Allen, Steve Rossi

✝ *Barry McKenzie Holds His Own* (1974, Australia) Barry Crocker, Barry Humphries, Donald Pleasence

✝ *Blood* (1974) Allan Berendt, Hope Stansbury, Patricia Gaul

✝ *Blood for Dracula* aka *Andy Warhol's Dracula* (1974) Joe Dallesandro, Udo Kier, Arno Juerging

✝ *Captain Kronos: Vampire Hunter* (1974) Horst Janson, John Cater, Shane Briant

✝ *Chosen Survivors* (1974) Jackie Cooper, Alex Cord, Bradford Dillman, Diana Muldaur

✝ *The Evil of Dracula* aka *Chi o suu bara* (1974, Japan) Toshio Kurosawa, Kunie Tanaka, Katsuhiko Sasaki

✝ *Grave of the Vampire* (1974) William Smith, Michael Pataki, Lyn Peters

✝ *The Legend of the Seven Golden Vampires* (1974, kung fu vampirism!) Peter Cushing, David Chiang, Julie Ege

✝ *Son of Dracula* aka *Count Downe* aka *Son of Dracula* (1974 musical) Harry Nilsson, Ringo Starr, Dennis Price, Peter Frampton, Keith Moon

✝ *Vampira* aka *Old Dracula* (1974) David Niven, Teresa Graves, Peter Bayliss

✝ *Vampyres* (1974) Marianne Morris, Anulka Dziubinska, Murray Brown

✝ *Deafula* (1975) Peter Wolf, Gary R. Holstrom, Lee Darel

✝ *Dracula, Father and Son* aka *Dracula père et fils* (1976, France) Christopher Lee, Bernard Menez, Marie-Hélène Breillat

✝ *Count Dracula* (1977) Louis Jourdan, Frank Finlay, Susan Penhaligon

✝ *Martin* (1977) John Amplas, Lincoln, Maazel, Christine Forrest

- ✝ *Doctor Dracula* (1978) John Carradine, Don "Red" Barry, Larry Hankin
- ✝ *Dracula's Dog* aka *Zoltan, Hound of Dracula* (1978) Michael Pataki, Jan Shutan, Libby Chase, José Ferrer
- ✝ *Dracula* (1979) Frank Langella, Laurence Olivier, Donald Pleasence, Kate Nelligan
- ✝ *Dracula Bites the Big Apple* (1979) Peter Loewy, Barry Gomolka
- ✝ *Love at First Bite* (1979) George Hamilton, Susan Saint James, Richard Benjamin
- ✝ *Nocturna* aka *Granddaughter of Dracula* (1979) Yvonne De Carlo, John Carradine, Nai Bonet
- ✝ *Nosferatu the Vampyre* aka *Nosferatu: Phantom der Nacht* (1979, Germany) Klaus Kinski, Isabelle Adjani, Bruno Ganz
- ✝ *Salem's Lot* (1979) David Soul, James Mason, Lance Kerwin
- ✝ *Vlad Tepes* aka *Vlad the Impaler: The True Life of Dracula* (1979, Romania) Ferenc Fábián, Emanoil Petrut, Alexandru Repan

THE 1980S: HORROR HEAVEN

While the horror genre continued to accelerate during the 1980s with a new breed of evil ghouls and mutants, like Michael Myers, Freddy Krueger, and Jason Vorhees, making their first or repeat performances, the vampire realm offered up a distinct melting pot of bloodsuckers from this and other worlds. Lacking the classic charm of their predecessors of the fifties, sixties, and seventies, the vamps of the eighties, like so many disco songs, are often left to obscurity. (If you actually own a copy of *Transylvania 6-5000*, then you likely still have platform shoes in your repertoire.)

But as with all film genres of the time, there are a few gems hidden in the shadows, several of which are cult classics. One of these is the 1983 film *The Hunger*, an artistic and overly sumptuous tale based on Whitley Strieber's 1981 novel of the same name (see Chapter 13). It stars the timeless Catherine Deneuve as Miriam Blaylock, a cold-blooded alien vampire of ancient Egyptian origin now residing in New York. Her lover, John, played by David Bowie, is one of many she's had over the centuries—partners to whom she's promised eternal life but who end up rapidly aging but unable to die. Deneuve makes for a spectacular vampire—arguably one of the best females to ever take on a bloodsucker (see Chapter 15).

Of the vamp films of the eighties, a handful still maintain rankings on the all-time list, including Jim Carrey's 1985 comedy *Once Bitten*, the Jeff Goldblum vampire spoof *Transylvania 6-5000* also in 1985, and the frightening brood of Southern bloodsuckers featured in Kathryn Bigelow's 1987 offering *Near Dark*. What did prove to be a box office success in 1987 was director Joel Schumacher's *The Lost Boys*, a vamp flick with decidedly more comedy than drama that pits teen vampires against teen vampire hunters in a small coastal community dubbed the "murder capital of the world." A cult fave to be certain, the film grossed over $32 million. Here are the films of the eighties:

- ♱ *Dracula's Last Rites* (1980) Patricia Hammond, Gerald Fielding, Victor Jorge
- ♱ *Mama Dracula* (1980) Louise Fletcher, Maria Schneider, Marc-Henri Wajnberg
- ♱ *The Monster Club* (1980) Vincent Price, John Carradine, Donald Pleasence
- ♱ *Desire, the Vampire* (1982) Dorian Harewood, David Naughton, Marilyn Jones
- ♱ *The Hunger* (1983) Catherine Deneuve, David Bowie, Susan Sarandon.
- ♱ *Blood Suckers from Outer Space* (1984) Pat Paulsen, Thom Meyer, Laura Ellis
- ♱ *A Polish Vampire in Burbank* (1985) Mark Pirro, Lori Sutton, Bobbi Dorsch
- ♱ *Evils of the Night* (1985) Neville Brand, Aldo Ray, John Carradine, Tina Louise, Julie Newmar
- ♱ *Fright Night* (1985) Roddy McDowall, Chris Sarandon, William Ragsdale
- ♱ *Lifeforce* (1985) Steve Railsback, Peter Firth, Mathilda May
- ♱ *Once Bitten* (1985) Lauren Hutton, Jim Carrey, Cleavon Little
- ♱ *Transylvania 6-5000* (1985) Jeff Goldblum, Geena Davis, Joseph Bologna, Carol Kane

- *Vampire Hunter D* aka *Banpaia hanta* (1985, Japanese anime) Kaneto Shiozawa, Michael McConnohie
- *Demon Queen* (1986) Mary Fanaro, Clifton Dance
- *Mr. Vampire* aka *Geung si sin sang* (1986, Hong Kong) Ching-Ying Lam, Siu-hou Chin, Ricky Hui
- *The Seven Vampires* aka *As Sete Vampiras* (1986, Brazil) Alvamar Taddei, Andréa Beltrão, Ariel Coelho

SCREEN SCREAM

In 1985 came the campy horrorfest known as *Fright Night*, featuring Roddy McDowall as a former horror star, William Ragsdale as a teenage horror fan, and Susan Sarandon's former husband, Chris Sarandon, as the "real" vampire they must conquer. *Fright Night* was a commercial success, raking in close to $25 million and ranking sixteenth on the all-time vampire movie list. Its 1989 sequel didn't fare quite as well but remains in the top fifty.

- *Vamp* (1986) Grace Jones, Chris Makepeace, Dedee Pfeiffer, Billy Drago
- *Graveyard Shift* (1987) Silvio Oliviero, Helen Papas, Cliff Stoker
- *I Married a Vampire* (1987) Rachel Gordon, Brendan Hickey, Ted Zalewski
- *The Lost Boys* (1987) Jason Patric, Corey Haim, Kiefer Sutherland, Dianne Weist
- *The Monster Squad* (1987) André Gower, Robby Kiger, Stephen Macht
- *Near Dark* (1987) Adrian Pasdar, Lance Henriksen, Bill Paxton
- *Nightmare Sisters* (1987) Linnea Quigley, Brinke Stevens, Michelle Bauer
- *A Return to Salem's Lot* (1987) Michael Moriarty, Ricky Addison Reed, Samuel Fuller
- *Dance of the Damned* (1988) Starr Andreeff, Cyril O'Reilly, Debbie Nassar

- ✞ *Dinner with a Vampire* aka *A cena col il vampiro* (1988, Italy) George Hilton, Patrizia Pellegrino, Riccardo Rossi
- ✞ *Fright Night Part 2* (1988) Roddy McDowall, William Ragsdale, Julie Carmen
- ✞ *My Best Friend Is a Vampire* (1988) Robert Sean Leonard, Rene Auberjonois, Cheryl Pollack
- ✞ *Not of This Earth* (1988) Traci Lords, Arthur Roberts, Lenny Juliano
- ✞ *Teen Vamp* (1988) Clu Gulager, Karen Carlson, Beau Bishop
- ✞ *The Understudy: The Graveyard Shift II* (1988) Wendy Gazelle, Mark Soper, Silvio Oliviero
- ✞ *Vampire at Midnight* (1988) Jason Williams, Gustav Vintas, Lesley Milne
- ✞ *The Vampire Princess Miyu* aka *Kyūketsuki Miyu* (1988, Japan) Naoko Watanabe, Annemarie Zola, Marie Louise Thompson, Ian Mackinnon
- ✞ *Beverly Hills Vamp* (1989) Britt Ekland, Eddie Deezen, Tim Conway Jr.
- ✞ *Dracula's Widow* (1989) Sylvia Kristel, Josef Sommer, Lenny von Dohlen
- ✞ *To Die For* (1989) Brendan Hughes, Sydney Walsh, Amanda Wyss
- ✞ *Vampire's Kiss* (1989) Nicolas Cage, Maria Conchita Alonso, Jennifer Beals

THE 1990s: FROM RAGE TO RICHES

Coming off a decade of decidedly chaotic vampire cinema, the nineties were primed and ready for a resurgence of a nosferatu that could bring the world of the undead back to its roots. Fortunately, we received just that. If there's one film of the nineties that fits the bill, it's Francis Ford Coppola's 1992 version of Bram Stoker's *Dracula*, a stylish and taut retelling of Stoker's masterpiece with an exceptional cast and stellar performance by Gary Oldman, who as Prince Vlad is arguably one of the best vampires ever to grace the silver screen (see Chapter 15).

In its telling, Dracula begins in 1462 in Transylvania with Vlad the Impaler's tragedy and transformation before moving to the late 1800s to imprison

Jonathan Harker (Keanu Reeves) and embark to London to pursue Harker's fiancé Mina, the reincarnation of Vlad's beloved wife Elisabeta. Along the way, Vlad must deal with the traditional Stoker characters and match wits with Abraham Van Helsing, a role that would've suited no other actor than the brilliant Anthony Hopkins. It should also be noted that Tom Waits's performance as Renfield is perhaps one of the most underrated of the film. With its stunning visual appeal, tense storyline and action sequences, and strong sexual undercurrent, this rendition is a must for all vampire aficionados.

Two years later, in 1994, yet another blockbuster bloodsucker arrived in the long-awaited film adaptation of Anne Rice's best-selling novel *Interview with the Vampire: The Vampire Chronicles*. Much ado was publicly made by Rice herself when the final casting was announced, but she later recanted her comments after viewing the film. Whether one agrees with the casting of Tom Cruise and Brad Pitt or not, it must be said that what resulted was a lush if not accurate portrayal of Lestat, who aside from Stoker's Dracula, is the best-known vampire in this and other worlds (see Chapters 13 and 15). Coming in third on the all-time box office vampire gross with a take of over $105 million, as compared to Coppola's fourth-place ranking at over $82 million, *Interview* is faithful to the novel and rife with the interplay of Lestat's arrogance matched up against Louis's pensiveness and the wicked countenance of their daughter Claudia, played by Kirsten Dunst.

Fangtastic Folklore

The casting of Anne Rice's *Interview with the Vampire* was a matter of speculation since its publication in 1976. During the late seventies it was John Travolta who was said to have been slated as the film's star. Rice herself over the years made mention of Rutger Hauer, Jeremy Irons, and Daniel Day-Lewis taking part. It's also said that for the big-screen version, Johnny Depp was also offered the part.

The nineties also gave us our first glimpse of the popular franchise that would become *Buffy the Vampire Slayer*. A feature film in 1992, it stars Kristy Swanson, Donald Sutherland, and Rutger Hauer. In the top twenty all-time grossing vamp flicks, the film launched the popular television franchise and star Sarah Michelle Gellar (see Chapters 13 and 18). Yet another trio of vamp flicks hit the big screen in the nineties, with the original and both sequels produced in rapid succession. Robert Rodriguez's 1996 flick *From Dusk Till Dawn* gave new meaning to the term "blood bar," as an unsuspecting Harvey Keitel, George Clooney, and Quentin Tarantino attempt to fight their way out of a Mexican boondocks watering hole. Both sequels followed in 1999.

The year 1998 marks the arrival of one of the more innovative and popular vampire/human hybrids, who kicks some serious bloodsucker booty. As with most vampires, he's known by a single name—Blade—and he's a force to be reckoned with (see Chapters 15). Starring Wesley Snipes, *Blade* is adapted from the character who first appeared in Marvel Comics in July of 1973 in *Tomb of Dracula* (see Chapter 19). In *Blade*, his fight against an evil underground network of hard-core vampires casts him as somewhat of a necessary but reluctant hero that carries through both sequels, *Blade II* in 2002 and *Blade: Trinity* in 2004. That said, we now introduce you to the films of the nineties:

- ☦ *Carmilla* (1990) Roy Dotrice, Meg Tilly, Ione Skye, Roddy McDowell
- ☦ *Daughter of Darkness* (1990) Mia Sara, Anthony Perkins, Robert Reynolds
- ☦ *Nightlife* (1990) Ben Cross, Maryam D'Abo, Keith Szarabajka
- ☦ *Pale Blood* (1990) George Chakiris, Wings Hauser, Pamela Ludwig
- ☦ *Rockula* (1990) Dean Cameron, Toni Basil, Bo Diddley, Thomas Dolby
- ☦ *Sundown: The Vampire in Retreat* (1990) David Carradine, Morgan Brittany, Bruce Campbell, Maxwell Caulfield
- ☦ *Transylvania Twist* (1990) Robert Vaughn, Teri Copley, Steve Altman
- ☦ *Children of the Night* (1991) Karen Black, Peter DeLuise, Ami Dolenz
- ☦ *Kingdom of the Vampire* (1991) Matthew Jason Walsh, Cherie Petry, Shannon Doyle
- ☦ *My Grandfather Is a Vampire* (1991, New Zealand) Al Lewis, Justin Gocke, Milan Borich
- ☦ *Son of Darkness: To Die for II* (1991) Michael Praed, Jay Underwood, Scott Jacoby

- ☦ *Subspecies* (1991) Anders Hove, Angus Scrimm, Laura Mae Tate
- ☦ *Bram Stroker's Dracula* (1992) Gary Oldman, Anthony Hopkins, Winona Ryder
- ☦ *Buffy the Vampire Slayer* (1992) Kristy Swanson, Donald Sutherland, Rutger Hauer

VAMPIRE BITE

The term *Buffyverse* is commonly used today to encompass the amazing franchise spawned by the 1992 film *Buffy the Vampire Slayer,* which served to inspire the long-running television series. The Buffyverse is huge in its offerings of fan sites, clubs, all conceivable paraphernalia, and scores of serialized novels showcasing the beloved Valley Girl vampire hunter (see Chapters 13 and 18).

- ☦ *Innocent Blood* (1992) Anne Parillaud, Chazz Palminteri, Anthony LaPaglia, Robert Loggia
- ☦ *Tale of a Vampire* (1992) Julian Sands, Suzanna Hamilton, Kenneth Cranham
- ☦ *Blood in the Night* (1993) Reggie Athnos, Mark Moyer, David Laird Scott
- ☦ *Bloodstone: Subspecies II* (1993) Anders Hove, Denice Duff, Kevin Blair
- ☦ *City of the Vampires* (1993) Matthew Jason Walsh, Anne-Marie O'Keefe
- ☦ *Cronos* (1993) Federico Luppi, Ron Perlman, Claudio Brook
- ☦ *Darkness* (1993) Gary Miller, Michael Gisick, Randall Aviks
- ☦ *Dracula Rising* (1993) Christopher Atkins, Stacey Travis, Doug Wert
- ☦ *Love Bites* aka *The Reluctant Vampire* (1993) Adam Ant, Kimberly Foster, Roger Rose
- ☦ *Project Vampire* (1993) Myron Natwick, Brian Knudson, Mary Louise Gemmil
- ☦ *To Sleep With a Vampire* (1993) Scott Valentine, Charlie Spradling
- ☦ *Bloodlust: Subspecies III* (1994) Anders Hove, Denice Duff, Kevin Blair

- ✟ *Interview with the Vampire: The Vampire Chronicles* (1994) Tom Cruise, Brad Pitt, Kirsten Dunst
- ✟ *Addicted to Murder* (1995) Mick McCleery, Laura McLauchlin, Sasha Graham
- ✟ *Dracula: Dead and Loving It* (1995) Leslie Nielsen, Peter MacNicol, Harvey Korman, Amy Yasbeck
- ✟ *Embrace of the Vampire* (1995) Alyssa Milano, Martin Kemp
- ✟ *Vampire in Brooklyn* (1995) Eddie Murphy, Angela Bassett, Allen Payne
- ✟ *Bordello of Blood* (1996) John Kassir, Dennis Miller, Erika Eleniak
- ✟ *Karmina* (1996) Isabelle Cyr, Robert Brouillette, Yves Pelletier
- ✟ *From Dusk Till Dawn* (1996) Harvey Keitel, George Clooney, Quentin Tarantino
- ✟ *Vampirella* (1996) Talisa Soto, Roger Daltrey, Richard Joseph Paul
- ✟ *An American Vampire Story* (1997) Trevor Lissauer, Johnny Venokur, Adam West
- ✟ *The Vampire Journals* (1997) David Gunn, Kirsten Cerre, Starr Andreeff
- ✟ *Addicted to Murder: Tainted Blood* (1998) Sasha Graham, Mick McCleery, Sarah K. Lippmann
- ✟ *Blade* (1998) Wesley Snipes, Stephen Dorff, Kris Kristofferson
- ✟ *John Carpenter's Vampires* (1998) James Woods, Daniel Baldwin, Sheryl Lee
- ✟ *Modern Vampires* (1998) Casper Van Dien, Rod Steiger, Kim Cattrall, Udo Kier
- ✟ *Subspecies 4: Bloodstorm* (1998) Anders Hove, Denice Duff, Jonathon Morris
- ✟ *Teenage Space Vampires* (1998) Robin Dunne, Mac Fyfe, James Kee
- ✟ *The Wisdom of Crocodiles* (1998) Jude Law, Elina Löwensohn, Timothy Spall
- ✟ *Bats* (1999) Lou Diamond Phillips, Dina Meyer, Bob Gunton
- ✟ *Cold Hearts* (1999) Marisa Ryan, Robert Floyd, Amy Jo Johnson
- ✟ *From Dusk Till Dawn 2: Texas Blood Money* (1999) Robert Patrick, Bo Hopkins, Duane Whitaker

- *From Dusk Till Dawn 3: The Hangman's Daughter* (1999) Marco Leonardi, Michael Parks, Temuera Morrison
- *Carmilla* aka *J. Sheridan Le Fanu's Carmilla* (1999) Stacia Crawford, Marina Morgan, Bootsie Cairns

SCREEN SCREAM

John Carpenter's 1998 film *Vampires* (usually cited as *John Carpenter's Vampires*) provides an intriguing twist to the typical vampire hunter's conundrum. As a hunter hellbent on revenge for the death of his parents at the hand of a vampire, Jack Crow (James Woods), working for the Vatican, must race to find a crucifix before a wicked fourteenth-century vampire can secure it and be granted the power to walk by daylight.

THE NEW MILLENNIUM: PRETERNATURAL REVOLUTION

The turn of the century brought about a new strain of vampire cinema, and while many films and filmmakers paid homage to their distinguished predecessors by retaining some portion of the Dracula legend, many encompassed within this new breed of cinema came with a few decidedly welcome twists, including bigger and better monsters courtesy innovative CGI techniques, slick Japanese anime, and a few kick-butt female action heroes.

In 2000, vampire aficionados were treated to *Shadow of the Vampire*, a film that paid its respects to the 1922 silent film classic, *Nosferatu*. In *Shadow*, Willem Defoe takes on the role of Max Schreck, the actor who played Count Orlock in *Nosferatu*, and the purported real-life turmoil that came with his relationship to *Nosferatu's* director F. W. Murnau (played by the appropriately creepy John Malkovich) during the silent film's production. So compelling was Dafoe's performance that he garnered an Oscar nomination for Best Actor. Hardly the standard for a vampire flick (see Chapter 15).

Though it was panned by critics when it hit the big screen in 2004, the film *Van Helsing* proved to be no slouch at the box office, garnering over $120 million and becoming the second-highest-grossing vampire film of all time. Taking very little from the Van Helsing legacy of Peter Cushing or Edward Van Sloan, Aussie heartthrob Hugh Jackman transformed himself into an action superhero of supernatural proportion. For pure fun and a visual CGI feast, *Van Helsing* is a fangtastic preternatural romp.

SCREEN SCREAM

Reminiscent of the 1940s films *House of Dracula* and *House of Frankenstein*, *Van Helsing* features the somewhat campy trifecta of the Wolf Man, Frankenstein, and Count Dracula, each on a mission to find a cure for what ails them, which in Dracula's case is procreation.

Action oriented in its base conception, this fast and furious horrorfest shows Van Helsing in the secret employ of the Vatican during the late 1800s as a somewhat conflicted troubadour of the underworld. As a hired gun, Gabriel Van Helsing has the unenviable job of hunting down the crème de la crème of paranormal perpetrators, including a rather hulked-up Mr. Hyde, a sympathetic Frankenstein, and, of course, Dracula. In what would prove to be an epic battle of werewolf versus vampire, and with the help of Anna Valerious, a gypsy princess played by Kate Beckinsale, Van Helsing ventures to Transylvania to take on Count Vladislaus Dracula, played to the hilt by Richard Roxburgh (see Chapter 15). What makes Jackman's interpretation of Van Helsing intriguing is the plot twist, whereby Dracula, through his taunting, helps Van Helsing regain his lost memories of how he came to be—a revelation with, shall we say, eternally angelic consequences. Despite its lack of critical acclaim, *Van Helsing* proves yet again that Bram Stoker's legendary conception continues to provide inspiration while also keeping vampire fans firmly seated at the edge of their coffins.

In the 2000s, we were also introduced to a new kind of female vampire in Kate Beckinsale, who for a pair of installments transformed herself into Selene, the rebellious "death dealer" and star of 2003's *Underworld* and its 2006 sequel, *Underworld: Evolution*, both of which are ranked ninth and seventh respectively on the all-time top-grossing vamp flicks (see Chapter 15). Along those same lines, only with a distinctly futuristic sci-fi bend, is

Milla Jovovich's turn in the 2006 tour de force *Ultraviolet*. In the film, Violet stands alone amid a raging war between a totalitarian late-twenty-first-century government and a subfaction of individuals at the bad end of a biological warfare experimentation that resulted in a vampirelike disease. With its graphic novel style, primary colors, and *Matrix/Aeon Flux*-type aura, *Ultraviolet* is hands-down one of the most succulent and mind-blowing films to date. As one of the infected "Hemophages," Violet's sole purpose is protecting a young boy and seeking revenge for her kind. Vampire fans should hunt down the uncut version of *Ultraviolet*, which more fully draws on the vampiric aspect of the plot.

Yet another crossover of the vampiric horror and sci-fi genre is the third remake of Richard Matheson's 1954 novel *I Am Legend*. For Matheson's concept, the third time was the charm. Will Smith's 2007 portrayal as military virologist Robert Neville in *I Am Legend* was a blockbuster, amassing over $256 million at the box office and making it the highest-grossing vampire film in history.

Fangtastic Folklore

I Am Legend isn't the only one of Matheson's novels to be adapted for the big screen. *The Shrinking Man, Stir of Echoes, Comedy of Terrors, Hell House, What Dreams May Come, Bid Time Return* (released as *Somewhere in Time*), and *Duel* have all been made into major motion pictures. Several of his short stories have also been adapted for *The Twilight Zone*, including *Third from the Sun, The Doll*, and the classic *Nightmare at 20,000 Feet*, which was part of the series and the feature-length film.

Eagerly anticipated is the 2008 winter release of the screen adaptation of the Stephenie Meyer's novel *Twilight*, a modern-day twist on *Romeo and Juliet*, featuring Bella, a young high school girl in love with Edward, a stunning young lad who, as luck would have it, happens to be a vampire. That said, let's take a look at some of the bloodsucking cinema the new millennium has offered up thus far:

- ✝ *Addicted to Murder 3: Blood Lust* (2000) Mick McCleery, Nick Kostopoulos, Cloud Michaels
- ✝ *Blood: The Last Vampire* (2000, anime) Youki Kudoh, Saemi Nakamura, Joe Romersa
- ✝ *Blood* (2000) Adrian Rawlins, Lee Blakemore, Phil Cornwell
- ✝ *Dark Prince: The True Story of Dracula* (2000) Rudolf Martin, Jane March, Christopher Brand
- ✝ *Dracula 2000* (2000) Gerard Butler, Christopher Plummer, Jonny Lee Miller, Justine Waddell
- ✝ *The Little Vampire* (2000) Jonathan Lipnicki, Richard E. Grant, Alice Krige

Fangtastic Folklore

The 2003 film *Underworld* and its 2006 sequel *Underworld: Evolution* feature Kate Beckinsale as vampiric heroine Selene. In Greek mythology, Selene is the goddess of the moon in all its phases, representing the fullness of life. Selene was also the name of the vampire in *La Ville Vampire*, written by French novelist and dramatist Paul Féval in 1867, which featured a band of vampire hunters led by renowned gothic novelist Ann Radcliffe.

- ✝ *Mom's Got a Date with a Vampire* (2000) Matt O'Leary, Laura Vandervoort, Myles Jeffrey
- ✝ *Shadow of the Vampire* (2000) Willem Dafoe, John Malkovich, Udo Kier, Cary Elwes
- ✝ *Vampire Hunter D: Bloodlust* (2000, Japanese anime) Hideyuki Tanaka, Ichirô Nagai, Kôichi Yamadera
- ✝ *Fangs* (2001) Corbin Bernsen, Tracy Nelson, Whip Hubley
- ✝ *The Forsaken* (2001) Kerr Smith, Brendan Fehr, Izabella Miko
- ✝ *Hellsing* aka *Herushingu* (2001, Japanese anime) Jôji Nakata, Yoshiko Sakakibara, Fumiko Orikasa

- ✞ *Jesus Christ Vampire Hunter* (2001) Phil Caracas, Murielle Varhelyi, Ian Driscoll
- ✞ *Blade II* (2002) Wesley Snipes, Kris Kristofferson, Leonor Varela
- ✞ *Queen of the Damned* (2002) Stuart Townsend, Lena Olin, Marguerite Moreau, Vincent Perez
- ✞ *Vampire Clan* (2002) Drew Fuller, Alexandra Breckenridge, Timothy Lee DePriest
- ✞ *Vampires: Los Muertos* (2002) Jon Bon Jovi, Cristián de la Fuente, Natasha Wagner
- ✞ *Dracula II: Ascension* (2003) Jennifer Kroll, Jason Scott Lee, Craig Sheffer
- ✞ *The Twins Effect* aka *Chin gei bin* (2003, China) Ekin Cheng, Charlene Choi, Jackie Chan
- ✞ *Vampires Anonymous* (2003) Paul Popowich, Michael Madsen, Judith Scott
- ✞ *Vlad* (2003) Billy Zane, Paul Popowich, Francesco Quinn
- ✞ *Underworld* (2003) Kate Beckinsale, Scott Speedman, Michael Sheen, Bill Nighy
- ✞ *Blade: Trinity* (2004) Wesley Snipes, Kris Kristofferson, Dominic Purcell, Jessica Biel
- ✞ *Dracula 3000* (2004) Casper Van Dien, Erika Eleniak, Coolio
- ✞ *Thralls* aka *Blood Angels* (2004, Canada) Lorenzo Lamas, Leah Cairns, Siri Baruc
- ✞ *Vampires: Out for Blood* (2004) Kevin Dillon, Vanessa Angel, Lance Henriksen
- ✞ *Vampires vs. Zombies* (2004) Bonny Giroux, C.S. Munro, Maritama Carlson
- ✞ *Van Helsing* (2004) Hugh Jackman, Kate Beckinsale, Richard Roxburgh
- ✞ *BloodRayne* (2005) Kristanna Loken, Michael Madsen, Matt Davis, Udo Kier
- ✞ *Vampires: The Turning* (2005) Colin Egglesfield, Stephanie Chao, Roger Yuan

- ✝ *Bram Stoker's Way of the Vampire* (2005) Rhett Giles, Paul Logan, Andreas Beckett
- ✝ *Trinity Blood* (2005, Japanese anime series) Hiroki Touchi, Mamiko Noto, Takako Honda
- ✝ *Day Watch* aka *Dnevnoy dozor* (2006, Russia) Konstantin Khaben-sky, Mariya Poroshina, Vladimir Menshov
- ✝ *Frostbiten* (2006, Sweden) Petra Nielsen, Carl-Åke Eriksson, Grete Havnesköld
- ✝ *Hellsing Ultimate OVA Series* (2006, Japanese anime series) Jôji Nakata, Yoshiko Sakakibara, Fumiko Orikasa
- ✝ *Ultraviolet* (2006) Milla Jovovich, Cameron Bright, Nick Chinlund
- ✝ *Underworld: Evolution* (2006) Kate Beckinsale, Scott Speedman, Tony Curran

SCREEN SCREAM

Based on a three-issue graphic novel, the 2007 film *30 Days of Night* follows an interesting premise. What would happen to an Arctic town that during the winter stays dark for thirty days? The answer is sheer mayhem, especially when a band of ruthless bloodsuckers show up with the express purpose of wiping out the entire population.

- ✝ *BloodRayne II: Deliverance* (2007) Natassia Malthe, Zack Ward, Michael Paré
- ✝ *I Am Legend* (2007) Will Smith, Alice Braga, Abby (as Sam the dog)
- ✝ *The Irish Vampire Goes West* (2007) Ken Baker, Paul A. Hardiman, James Coughlan
- ✝ *Rise* (2007) Lucy Liu, Robert Forster, Cameron Richardson
- ✝ *30 Days of Night* (2007) Josh Hartnett, Melissa George, Danny Huston
- ✝ *Blood: The Last Vampire* (2008) Gianna Jun, Allison Miller, Masiela Lusha

- ✝ *Dracula's Guest* (2008) Wes Ramsey, Andrew Bryniarski, Kelsey McCann
- ✝ *The Thirst: Blood War* (2008) Tony Todd, A.J. Draven, Jason Connery
- ✝ *Let the Right One In* (2008, Sweden) Kåre Kedebrant, Lina Leandersson, Per Ragnar
- ✝ *The Lost Boys: The Tribe* (2008) Tad Hilgenbrink, Angus Sutherland, Autumn Reeser
- ✝ *Twilight* (2008) Kristen Stewart, Robert Pattinson, Taylor Lautner

FROM BIG SCREEN TO SMALL SCREEN

Given the rich history of vampires in film, it would only be a matter of time before Dracula and his kind would show up in our living rooms. In the next chapter, we examine the evolution of television vampires, from made-for-tv movies and miniseries to kiddie nosferatu and some of the most beloved television series in history.

CHAPTER 18

SMALL-SCREEN BLOODSUCKERS

As is obvious by the incredibly rich history of vampiric cinema, there's little public interest in sending silver screen vampires to an early grave. The same also applies to the television medium, where scores of bloodsucking bad boys and bombshells have clawed their way out of their crypts and into our homes. And while made-for-tv vamps have always been around, it wasn't until the last two decades that they've begun to gain an immortal following. In this chapter we take a closer look at prime time preternaturals and the bitingly good small-screen vampires who keep us mesmerized on a weekly basis.

EARLY TELEVISION VAMPIRES

As we've learned in the previous chapters, the vampire has left more than a few prominent bite marks on the silver screen, with a film legacy beginning in the Silent Era. Because of that, it's easy to see why, with the onset of television, vampires gained even more exposure as those classic films finally made it into our collective living rooms. As more and more people became exposed to vampires, so too did the course of television programmers, who staked a claim in several vampiric characters and series that served to set the stage for public acceptance of the vampire taking part in everything from cartoons to made-for-tv movies to weekly serials and even a legendary gothic soap opera. It was indeed that soap opera that got the public's hemoglobin churning and gave television watchers their first shadowed glimpse of how truly mesmerizing a television vamp could be. But audiences got their first official taste of television vampires in the form of comedy and a wacky family known simply as the Munsters.

THE MUNSTERS

The year 1964 marks the arrival of two of the most unique and legendary families to ever show up on the small screen—the eccentric and macabre Addams Family and the lovable, wacky bunch known as the Munsters. Paying homage to the horror genre by spoofing some of its most delicious characters and concepts, both families gave audiences two years of solid laughs and a new appreciation for the humor of what most individuals conceive as horrifying. Without a doubt, *The Munsters* provided a brilliant way of easing the public into accepting vampires as leading characters. Fred Gwynne, Yvonne De Carlo, Al Lewis, Butch Patrick, and Pat Priest were respectively transformed into Frankenstein, father/daughter vampires, a werewolf progeny, and a perfectly human niece.

Housed together in their spooky abode at 1313 Mockingbird Lane, the Munsters had everything a monster could hope for: a Grandpa who hung from the rafters like a bat, a pet bat named Igor, a dragon named Spot, and even a car nicknamed "Drag-u-la," likely an homage to Grandpa's last name and Lily's maiden name—Dracula. Even legendary Dracula portrayer John

Carradine made a few guest appearances as one of Herman's bosses at the funeral parlor he worked for. Even funnier was the opening segment to the show, which featured Lily parodying the opener to the Donna Reed show, giving light to the notion that the Munster's were just like any other red-blooded American family. Though the series, like *The Addams Family*, only lasted two seasons, both left an indelible mark on television history with reruns still playing daily. Even more spectacular is the fact that Herman Munster was ranked nineteenth in *TV Guide's* June 2004 issue of "The 50 Greatest TV Dads of All Time."

DARK SHADOWS

In 1966, television audiences were treated to a new kind of vampire, a more dark and dramatic breed whose sinister past eventually turns him into the characteristic reluctant vampire. That bloodsucker is Barnabas Collins, and he was the star of the gothic television soap opera *Dark Shadows*. Now, it's no mystery that soap operas have unbelievably huge followings, with fans hinging on every actor's word, action, interview, and convention appearance. *Dark Shadows* almost missed that fanfare, when after six months it was faced with cancellation. It was at that point that the supernatural element was introduced, with Barnabas's arrival in Collinwood. Running every weekday afternoon on ABC from June of 1966 through April of 1971, *Dark Shadows* became a cult classic that to this day retains its immortality through major Internet fan sites, fan clubs, societies, conventions, CD audio dramas, DVDs, reruns, and a pair of feature-length films: *House of Dark Shadows* in 1970 and *Night of Dark Shadows* in 1971. The series also spawned a short-lived television remake in 1991, comic books, and a slew of serialized novels.

What's unique about *Dark Shadows*, among many aspects, is its telenovela-style and live-to-tape format with complex overlapping character arcs, time travel, séances, a parallel universe, ghosts, witches, werewolves, and dream and fantasy sequences that took the story from present-day Collinsport, Maine, to its late 1700s colonial roots and beyond. Throughout all of the plotlines spread amongst over 1,200 episodes, the repertoire of actors involved played multiple roles—typically their own ancestors—squeezing every ounce of melodrama they could muster. So groundbreaking was the series, that even Robert Cobert's eerie soundtrack ranked on Billboard's Top 20 charts in 1969, with one of the tracks earning Cobert a Grammy nomination.

The Collinwood Phenomena

The series begins when governess Victoria Winters arrives at the Collinwood estate to care for a young boy named David Collins. Surrounded by a rather eccentric and secretive family, strange occurrences begin almost immediately, setting the stage for all the dark drama to follow. After six months and sagging ratings, *Dark Shadows* creator Dan Curtis took the bold step of introducing a 200-year-old vampire into the mix, which though radical at the time, turned the entire series rightside up. Actor Jonathan Frid—who has built an entire career off his fiend—made his first appearance in episode 211 as Barnabas Collins, a vampire released from his slumber who arises to wreak havoc upon a new generation. A tortured soul, Barnabas reintegrates himself into the wealthy Collins family by claiming to be a long lost relative, and from there his story takes more twists and turns than a Swiss mountain road.

Cursed by the evil witch Angelique in the late 1700s, Barnabas bears many of the traditional trappings of the drawing room bloodsucker, namely sleeping in a coffin, casting no reflection in mirrors, and the ability to transform into a bat. Naturally, the public became enamored with Barnabas and all the melodramatic characters and situations one would expect of a daytime soap. What may seem campy now was actually for its time a clever use of sets, costuming, makeup, and special effects that for a tape-and-go serial drama made up for the occasional appearance of a cameraman or microphone interrupting a scene.

Dark Shadows Redux

Dark Shadows was cancelled in 1971, but its cult following relentlessly clamored for more. The show was partially syndicated in 1975 and aired in syndication through 1990. For the next three years, all of the episodes were released to and aired by the Sci Fi Channel. In 1991, twenty years after its cancellation, NBC ran a short-lived remake of the series in prime time. Again directed by Dan Curtis, and starring Ben Cross as Barnabas, Jean Simmons, Lysette Anthony, and 1960s scream queen Barbara Steele (see Chapter 15), the revival was a weekly series with a big budget. Timing in this case proved its undoing, as Gulf War coverage caused the show's pre-empting and odd scheduling contributing to its inevitable demise after only a dozen episodes. The fact that the series ended with a whopper of a cliffhanger, of course, resulted in viewer outrage. With any luck, their incantations will be answered by actor Johnny Depp, who so loved *Dark Shadows* that as a child he claimed he wanted to *be* Barnabas Collins. Depp's wish may come to fruition, as he recently announced he would play Jonathan Frid's legendary role in a *Dark Shadows* feature-length film that Depp's production company purchased the rights to in July of 2008.

SCREEN SCREAM

Did you know that one of the original *Charlie's Angels* played in *Dark Shadows*? Indeed, it was Kate Jackson who from 1970 to 1971 portrayed Daphne Harridge in seventy episodes. Also appearing on the series as Sheriff Patterson was Dana Elcar, best known for his character of Pete Thornton who appeared in seven seasons of the popular series *MacGyver*, beginning in 1985.

MADE-FOR-TELEVISION VAMPS

Over the decades, there have been dozens of made-for-television vampire movies that crossed all genres ranging from the 1996 comedy *Munster, Go Home!* to *Mom's Got a Date With a Vampire* (2000). The truth is that never a week goes by without some vampire flick being shown on the tube. How good they are when measured against the classics is a subject that's always up for debate. As with all genres, however, there are always a few gems hidden in a mountain of cubic zirconia.

The Night Stalker

In the television vampire realm, that first gem was an unlikely 1972 television movie that spun off into a wildly popular late-night television series. The movie was *The Night Stalker,* and it starred legendary actor Darren McGavin as Carl Kolchak, the intrepid, bumbling, and relentlessly persistent reporter who attracts evil supernatural critters like a vryokolas to a rotting corpse (see Chapter 2). With a teleplay written by *I Am Legend* author Richard Matheson based on a novel by Jeff Rice, and directed by *Dark Shadows* creator Dan Curtis, the aptly titled *The Night Stalker* (no doubt referring to both the protagonist and antagonist) was enormously successful for ABC. In the film, Kolchak finds himself up against ancient Romanian vampire Janos Skorzeny who's prowling Vegas and sucking dry a score of young women until Kolchak himself stakes him.

The following year, in 1973, McGavin, along with Curtis, Matheson, and Rice, once again teamed up for another Kolchak foray, *The Night Strangler.* The year 1974 marked the premiere of the television series *Kolchak: The Night Stalker,* with its third episode, entitled "The Vampire," paying homage to Kolchak's vampiric skills by featuring a prostitute-turned-bloodsucker running amok in Las Vegas. In September of 2005, a remake of *Night Stalker* briefly appeared featuring *Queen of the Damned* star Stuart Townsend, but it was sadly pulled after only six episodes. No doubt, Kolchak himself would've attested that *some* things are better left untold.

Drac Is Back!

Another shining gem in the television vampiric realm is Jack Palance, who in 1973 donned cape and fangs to play Dracula in a winning version of Bram Stoker's novel, pulled together by the same duo who gave us *Night Stalker,* director Dan Curtis and author Richard Matheson. As the legendary bloodsucker, Palance is by many accounts one of the best to ever play the role, his smoky voice coupled with his overpowering physical presence allowing him a command and confidence that only a select few Dracula portrayers have been able to channel (see Chapter 15).

In 1977, another television vampire of note took to the small screen in the form of renowned French actor Louis Jourdan, who starred in *Count*

Dracula, a version produced by the BBC for its Great Performances series. Closely following Bram Stoker's legendary novel—more so than most adaptations—Jourdan brought many of the same subtleties to his Count as Frank Langella did to his 1979 portrayal (see Chapter 15).

SCREEN SCREAM

Over the years, many of television's most highly rated prime time shows have featured vampires in their repertoire. *Alfred Hitchcock Presents, Night Gallery, Tales of the Crypt, Tales of the Darkside, The Twilight Zone, The Man from U.N.C.L.E., Starsky and Hutch, The Hardy Boys/Nancy Drew Mysteries, Buck Rogers in the 25th Century, CSI: Crime Scene Investigation, Sabrina, the Teenage Witch, The X-Files,* and *Crossing Jordan* have all embraced the immortal undead.

Lots of Luck

Also premiering in prime time in 1979 was the adaptation of Stephen King's vampire extravaganza *Salem's Lot*, which focuses on a writer who returns to his hometown to find that something's not quite right with the haunted house on the hill. Starring David Soul, James Mason, and Lance Kerwin, *Salem's Lot*, like many of King's horror adaptations, has become a cult favorite in the vampire realm (see Chapter 13). In 1990, Ben Cross took yet another turn in his coffin, playing Vlad to Maryam D'Abo's vampiric Angelique in the dark comedy *Nightlife*. Written by *Saturday Night Live* Emmy-winning writer Anne Beatts, the amusing romp finds Angelique ditching Vlad and awakening in Mexico City after a 100-year nap only to find that vampires are merely considered "diseased individuals." Of course, falling in love with her doctor creates a love triangle that makes for a bloody good time.

Prime Time Bloodsuckers

Given the very nature of vampires, specifically their propensities of bloodlust, eroticism, and murder, it's easy to see why creatures of the night have a tough time getting past television mucky-mucks and particularly television censors. In regard to long-term vampiric success, there's no arguing that *Dark Shadows* has thus far had the longest run. A few other series attempted a rise from the grave with short-lived success, including *Dracula: The Series* (1990), *Kindred: The Embraced* (based on the role-playing game *Vampire: The Embraced*), and more recently, a single season of the 2007 drama *Moonlight* featuring a vampire private investigator.

But along the way, there have been a few highly "sucksessful" vampire-based series whose characters have television immortality that, for shows like *Forever Knight, Angel,* and *Buffy the Vampire Slayer,* resulted in serialized novels, comic books, companion books, hugely popular Internet fan sites, fan clubs, societies, and have launched franchises complete with bobbleheads, action figures, magazines, video games, conventions, and all measure of paraphernalia (see Chapter 19).

Forever Knight

One of the more successful television vampire series ranks high under the endearment category. In 1989, the CBS made-for-tv movie *Nick Knight* gave us our first glimpse of one of the more tortured reluctant vampires ever conceived. The film starred musician and former *General Hospital* heart-throb Rick Springfield as a four-centuries-old vampire working in Los Angeles as a detective solving a host of grisly murders involving victims being drained of blood. In 1992, the pilot was remade into the late-night series *Forever Knight,* with the affable Welsh-Canadian actor Geraint Wynn Davies assuming the lead role of homicide detective Nicholas Knight. Primarily a Canadian production, the plot differs from the pilot on several accounts in that it was based in Toronto and Nicholas is now 800 years old, a fact that only adds to his extreme derision and angst in attempting to make restitution for his evil past and ultimately rid himself of his vampirism. He's helped in his quest by pathologist and close mortal confidant Natalie Lambert (Catherine Disher), who stands in contrast to Nick's vampiric confidant and former lover Janette (Deborah Duchene).

Complicating matters throughout *Forever Knight's* three-season run is Nick's maker, the intensely philosophical and wickedly sinister Lucien LaCroix, brilliantly played by Nigel Bennett. A 2,000-year-old former

Roman army general made in Pompeii during the eruption of Mt. Vesuvius, LaCroix's obvious distain for Nick's quest for absolution and humanity beautifully portrays the misuse of vampiric power and its alternate usefulness as a tool for creating a better society. Like many traditional vampires, those in *Forever Knight* have superhuman strength, hypnotic powers, heightened senses, and the typical aversion to sunlight and staking. They also possess the capacity for flight, moving at great speeds, and tissue regeneration.

SCREEN SCREAM

It can be said that fans of *Forever Knight* are as dedicated and fervent as they come. On more than one occasion, it was the show's intense fan base that saved it from cancellation. In 1995, a lobbyist group called the *Friends of Forever Knight* pushed their case all the way to the National Association of Television Programming Executives, who were utterly astonished and impressed by their professionalism and efforts to save the series.

What has arguably endeared *Forever Knight* to the hearts of all vampire aficionados, aside from the various love/hate triangles and vampiric antagonists, is the constant interplay between Nick and LaCroix, whose toying with mortals leads him to moonlight as "The Nightcrawler," a late-night radio host, in which his broadcasts invariably shed light on Nick's all-consuming pathos and fight to control his bloodlust and rage. Indoctrinated into the undead by LaCroix in 1228, Nicholas de Brabant remains one of the more high-profile vampires ever to grace the small screen.

Buffy the Vampire Slayer

When it comes to Valley Girls turned vampire hunters there's only one name that comes to mind: Buffy. In 1992, writer Joss Whedon introduced us to the self-obsessed, flitty shopaholic cheerleader Buffy Summers in the feature-length film *Buffy the Vampire Slayer.* Cute and campy, the film stars Kristy Swanson, Donald Sutherland, and Rutger Hauer as the evil Lothos.

Though Buffy proved successful at the box office, it was decidedly a flop in Whedon's mind, as his intent was not to create a high school horror romp but an extraordinary character of staunch female embodiment.

Five years later, in 1997, Whedon got his chance as executive producer of the series *Buffy the Vampire Slayer*, which premiered on the small WB Network. For seven seasons, the Emmy-winning series gave us an empowered Buffy (played by Sarah Michelle Gellar), who kicked all kinds of demonic and vampiric butt in her hometown of Sunnydale, California, and beyond, focusing primarily on the "Hellmouth," a demonic gateway below Sunnydale High. At its most base metaphor, one can't help but be amused by the dichotomy of high school being equated to hell.

Amid all the campy comedy, drama, paranormal terror, and martial arts wrapped around scores of vampires and other malfeasants, Buffy came to know Angel, played by the ever-charming David Boreanaz, whose badass vampire rears its ugly head when he and Buffy engage in a night of passion. Tragic and metaphorical in its subtext, this meeting of vampire and vampire slayer proved so successful that it launched a spin-off, simply titled *Angel* (see Chapter 13).

Angel

Premiering in 1999 on the WB, *Angel* highlights the triumphs and extremely tortured soul of the 200-year-old vampire Angelus, who spends his first millennia killing with reckless abandon but who, courtesy a band of revenge-minded gypsies, has his human soul firmly restored to his vampiric body. An exceptional twist on vampire lore, Angel is tormented by the zeitgeist of his murderous ways and driven to help others as a private investigator in a quest to alleviate his eternal angst and remorse. With *Buffy* creator Joss Whedon at the helm, David Boreanaz truly shines as a tortured creature, whose somber reckonings, memories, and killings offer up the dichotomy of a reluctant vampire and alternately a vampire unwilling to forfeit his immortality so that he can continue making restitution to humanity.

Darker in its conception than *Buffy*, *Angel* has the added benefit of crossover characters including Buffy herself. Told in a serial format like most serial dramas, with self-contained tales that add to a more powerful long-term storyline, Angel in many ways is held to the same standard as other television vampires such as Nick Knight and *Moonlight's* Mick St. John in that despite being a creature based in evil, his intent is to accomplish good. In the vampire realm, that puts Boreanaz and his angelic alter ego in a class of their own. Running for five seasons, *Angel*, like *Buffy*, has achieved television immortality. Upon its cancellation, and prompted by fan outrage, Angel's ambiguous farewell resulted in a 2007 comic book series called *Angel: After the Fall*.

VAMPIRE BITE

Though it's not officially listed in Webster's, the word *Elvira* is by definition a raven-haired, ultracampy cult classic beauty clad in skimpy, tight-fitting, cleavage-enhancing black dresses, who since 1981 has been pushing her vampire schtick with unbelievable fun and immortal aplomb. To Elvira, aka actress Cassandra Peterson, we say this: Honey, you *are* the prime time vampiric hostess with the mostess and you will in the vampire realm forever remain immortalized as the ultimate Mistress of the Dark!

True Blood

Though it's only just begun, HBO has high hemoglobic hopes for its new vampire series, *True Blood*, based on the Sookie Stackhouse series written by author Charlaine Harris (see Chapter 13). With its September 2008 premiere, *True Blood* introduced the world to the inhabitants of Bon Temps, a fictional town in Louisiana that is home to eccentric, reluctantly telepathic waitress Sookie Stackhouse, played by Oscar winner Anna Paquin, and the man she falls in love with, Bill Compton (played by Stephen Moyer), who just happens to be a 173-year-old vampire. Of course, the fact that Bill is 148 years older than Sookie matters little, considering vampires, courtesy the invention of synthetic blood by Japanese scientists, have now become accepted among society. After the airing of the first two episodes, it was announced that *True Blood* would return for a second season.

KIDDIE NOSFERATU

While the majority of traditional literary and cinematic vampires are considered too frightening for small children, there have been a number of programs that introduced vampiric characters through cartoons such as *Scooby Doo* and even on *Sesame Street*, where the lovable purple muppet Count von Count has been teaching kiddies how to count since the early 1970s. Modeled somewhat after Bela Lugosi's Dracula, the Count sports a pair of fangs, a monocle, a nifty goatee, and the ever-present black cape. The Count's obsessive need to count—intentional or not—harkens back to a popular folkloric practice of using seeds to keep a vampire at bay (see Chapter 9).

Count Duckula

One of the more innovative twists on the Dracula legend is the animated British cartoon *Count Duckula*, a spin-off of the popular 1981—1992 cartoon *Danger Mouse*. A clear parody of Dracula reworked for the kiddies, Duckula is an obsessive stage-struck vegetarian vampire duck who resides, naturally, in Castle Duckula with his bumbling vulture manservant Igor and equally inept hen nursemaid called Nanny. How Duckula came to be a vegetarian is that during the ritual for his resurrection, Nanny provided Igor with ketchup instead of blood, thereby rendering the daffy vampire more inclined to consume vegan rather than red-blooded victims. In hot pursuit of Duckula during his fame-seeking escapades is German goose and vampire hunter Dr. Von Goosewing. From 1988 to 1993, sixty-five episodes of *Count Duckula* were created, as well as a Marvel Comics version of the wacky vampiric quacker.

The Groovie Goolies

Only in the seventies would you find a show with the word "groovy" in the title, which in this case refers to a band of animated monsters who constitute the *Groovy Goolies*. Spun off of the very popular *The Archie Show* and then combined with *Sabrina, the Teenage Witch* before branching out on their own, the Goolies are a motley crew who room together at Horrible Hall. This includes Bella LaGhostly, Drac, Mummy, Hagatha, Franklin "Frankie" Frankenstein, Wolfgang "Wolfie" Wolfman, the two-headed Doctor Jeckyll and Hyde, and animated skeleton Boneapart among others. Based primarily on classic Universal horror films, the show aired in 1971, with several other specials presented over the years. Of course, being a literal band of monsters, each of its sixteen episodes ends with an original Groovie Goolies rock song.

FANGED AND FLAMBOYANT

While literature and lore give us the ability to picture in our minds the most romantic and heinous vampires in fictional history, it's ultimately film and television that put a name to a face. In this instance . . . a fanged face. As we've learned through our discussion of film and TV vamps, the fiends run the gamut of interpretation in physical, spiritual, and emotional realms, but the bottom line is that no matter how frightening these interpretations are—they aren't real. Or are they?

In the next chapter we examine vampires of the modern day, and as far as the current vampiric subculture is concerned, these folks do indeed believe they are the real deal, right down to their goth garb and fancy dental work.

CHAPTER 19

MODERN-DAY VAMPIRISM

Though most folks likely subscribe to the belief that vampires don't exist, there is a growing contingent of individuals who believe they do, and who subscribe to a vampiric lifestyle including blood fetishism, or aspects of magnetic, astral, or psychic vampirism. In this chapter, we also examine various types of vampires and an immense range of vampiric practices, commerce, Internet interaction, games, comic books, and every conceivable item of paraphernalia, from fangs to Bela Lugosi capes.

TYPES OF VAMPIRES

When discussing vampires in casual conversation, it's safe to say that the majority of the population equates the vampire to Dracula and alternately to the drawing room Dracula portrayed by Bela Lugosi in 1931. This obviously begs the question: "Aren't all bloodsuckers alike?" In a word—no. They aren't. While the majority do possess basic characteristics such as bloodlust, a combination of varying powers, and certain weaknesses inherited from the vampires of lore and early literature and film, each vampire, as do humans, has its own cross to bear and its own methods of madness. With that in mind, let's take a look at some of the more prevalent types of vampires other than the traditional we've covered throughout the book.

THE EXOTIC, EROTIC BLOODSUCKER

By their very nature, vampires are insufferably erotic creatures who with the help of their hypnotic powers can bend just about everyone to do their bidding, sexual or otherwise. After all, the act of simply biting someone on the neck is itself a highly erotic, personal, and sexual act. What gives the vampire its "romantic" edge are several things. First, if the participant is willing, the romantic notion of immortality acts as an enticement. Then there's the bad boy/bad girl syndrome that caters to humanity's wild rebellious side and the knowledge that what's good for you must be assured by testing out what you perceptibly know is bad for you. Unwilling participants, its often argued, are in a sense being raped—sexually approached and forced to engage in something against their will. This places the vampire firmly in the sexual deviant category, which goes neck in neck with his obsessive stalker personality when pursing a victim—especially a bride or long-term companion.

Homoerotic Tendencies

The topic of vampire sexuality is one that remains a hotly debated subject. Are they straight, homosexual, lesbian, or bisexual? The safe answer is all of the above. While the majority of vampires are indiscreet about their sexual preference when killing, many do tend to obsess over one sex or the other. Their choice of companions in many instances of fiction and film, however, can tend toward same-sex companionship. This is clearly evident, for example, in many of the protagonists of Anne Rice's Vampire Chronicles. Magnus chooses Marius. Marius chooses Lestat. Lestat indoctrinates Louis. While none of them has issue taking the lives of either sex, they often choose as their companions, or "children" as they are often termed, a member of their own sex. Is it a love relationship? Of course. Does it involve sex? Sometimes. Whereas the typical vampire romance tends to focus on a male/female relationship, or other offshoots such as vampire/vampire hunter, the concept of a homoerotic companionship, though typically not sexual, provides a seething and unmistakable undertone.

Lesbian Vampires

In 1872, the aspect of not only the female vampire but the lesbian vampire was born in Sheridan Le Fanu's novella, "Carmilla" (see Chapter 3). In this case, the vampire Carmilla, masquerading as the evil Countess Mircalla Karnstein, imbued fervent readers to the notion that seductive evil wasn't just for the so-called stronger sex. Carmilla *is* the mother of all female vampires and the standard by which all future models adhere. Not only does she possess the necessary vampire characteristics, but Le Fanu's bold seductive interplay between Carmilla and Laura, the object of her obsession, is slow and smoldering to the point of titillating frenzy:

> "It was like the ardour of a lover; it embarrassed me; it was hateful and yet over-powering; and with gloating eyes she drew me to her, and her hot lips travelled along my cheek in kisses; and she would whisper, almost in sobs, "You are mine, you shall be mine, you and I are one for ever."

Many would argue that the prospect of lesbian vampire seduction is the product of male fantasy—a probability that holds true to the present day throughout vampiric fiction and film. Psychologists would no doubt breathlessly theorize for hours on the subject, but fanciful male daydreaming about lesbian encounters between two beautiful women is a common staple of the male psyche, which adds immeasurably to the interest in the tension of such scenes in fiction and film. Even with the certainty that one of the women is intent on taking away her partner's essence and existence, there are many who would wish that they were part of the encounter. In every sense, the depictions of such scenes invite vampiric voyeurism.

PSYCHE IT TO ME

Several complex theories created during the early 1900s have evolved until the present day and offer arguments defending the existence of vampires, and explanations for how they could come to be. The plausibility of many of these obscure concepts have leaked into modern culture and have undoubtedly added fuel to our avid interest and suspension of disbelief in such exotic and highly disturbing entities. For the relatively sane mind, the very idea of revenants leaving the grave to walk among us unnoticed is inherently absurd, but arguments that suggest that the universe is much more complicated than we could possibly imagine are difficult to dispute. The universe *is* complicated, and many of us *do* believe in some form of life after death through our religious or spiritual convictions. That combination of basic truths in the human condition can open the door just a tiny bit to the frightening idea that maybe—just maybe—there are spiritual phenomena afoot that we can't explain. Theorists of psychic vampirism are only too happy to fill in the gaps.

The Flight of the Astral Body

An early proponent of psychic vampirism, Dion Fortune was a noted writer and occultist during the early to mid-1900s in England. As did many occult theorists of the era, Fortune believed that humans are a combination of two very separate entities—the physical body and the spiritual, or *astral body*. Upon normal death, both entities perish. In her book *Psychic Self-Defense*, Fortune cites a case during World War I in which several eastern European troops had been killed in combat. Among them were practitioners of black magic who could avoid going to the "Second Death," as she refers to the death of the astral body, and "maintained themselves in the etheric double by vampirising the wounded . . . systematically drawing its etheric nutriment from him." Regarding the fate of the victims of vampires, Fortune goes on to say: "the person who is vampirised, being depleted of vitality, is a psychic vacuum, himself absorbing from anyone he comes across in order to refill his depleted sources of vitality."

Much of Dion Fortune's writings imply that there are those who purposely become vampires by practicing black magic and vampires who become so only because they are victims. She was of the firm belief that actual vampirism was rare in western Europe and believed that eastern Europe was the seat of "Black Magic" and thus the natural homeland of the true vampire.

Fangtastic Folklore

From fangs to theatrical contact lenses, and capes to white hairspray, the market for vampire paraphernalia is booming with blood-curdling special effects gear. Going hunting? You can find vampire slaying kits that include crucifixes, stakes and mallets, special potions to ward off pesky nightstalkers, and even garlicky perfumes for anointing yourself with nature's own bloodsucker repellent.

Undead and Unbled

One of the most common concepts in the variety of theories of psychic vampirism is that people with questionable intentions can purposely drain the energy of their victims without killing them, or without their knowledge or consent. Variously known as *pranic vampires, empathic vampires, energy parasites,* and *psy-vamps* (also spelled *psi-vamps*), these practitioners often describe their activities in self-congratulatory terms, claiming that they are merely returning to an innocent and traditionally spiritual relationship with other humans.

Part of the argument centers on the idea that modern people have been turned into soulless zombies by an industrialized and heavily controlled world of technology and science, and that the natural human exchange of spiritual energy has been quashed. To achieve a more natural balance in the universe, these psychic vampires believe that the "normal" human condition is for some to yield energy and others to thrive on it. If you ever get the creepy feeling that someone is staring at you and trying to read your mind, beware, a psy-vamp might just be trying to psychically suck you dry instead.

WHAT'S YOUR TYPE?

In the world of gritty psychological oddities, the concept of the *blood fetish* sounds like a figment of a demented mind. For those who consume blood either as part of a lifestyle or by obsession, there are variations on the theme triggered by separate desires and needs. *Sanguinarians* are people who have a psychological desire to consume blood to maintain their health, and usually do so in a fashion that does not harm others. Those who suffer from *clinical vampirism* are utterly convinced that they require blood to survive and will procure it at any cost, even so far as committing murder. Clinical vampirism is usually associated with far more complex and serious psychological issues such as schizophrenia and is seldom a single diagnosis.

SCREEN SCREAM

One of the casual observations about the vampire lifestyle is in reference to "blood bars," where wannabe vampires can get a little nip. Since the introduction of the HBO series *True Blood*, about vampires in the Deep South, a real bar is doing a booming business in Shreveport, Louisiana. Called "Fangtasia," the bar is rife with vampire-related themes, and the owners insist that they really are vampires. What they *really* are is clever at marketing!

For those who have sunk their teeth into the vampire lifestyle, and often refer to themselves—at least in print—as *vampyres*, the wish to behave like, or become, vampires can be satiated by interacting with those of a similar propensity. As with most groups of like-minded individuals, the Internet is the medium of choice for searching out companions. Active vampirism is practiced by members taking on the roles of vampires and donors, with various forms of bloodletting that seldom includes actual biting. Donors usually makes a small cut in their own skin with a razor blade, and the "vampire" sucks the blood from the wound. Many members of vampire social communities are involved only to act as donors. Donors are sometimes classified as *swans* and fall into several categories:

- ✝ **Black swans:** Encompass families and friends of members who have little to do with vampire activities
- ✝ **Crimson swans:** Donors who participate in bloodletting
- ✝ **Crystal swans:** Members who donate only psychic or spiritual energy
- ✝ **Amber swans:** The jack of all trades, the amber swan donates in every way

FANGS FOR THE CHAT!

For those interested in vampires in general, and those intrigued by the modern vampire culture, that incredible piece of technology sitting on your desk is a gateway to the dark side. Go ahead—type "vampires" into your favorite search engine and you'll get over twenty-four million Web pages at your disposal. The Internet is a goldmine for research into lore, research, fiction, film, and vampire enthusiasts seeking companionship. In the chat room arena, you can find plenty of online friends to share your interests with, but we implore you—please—be very wary of Internet relationships. By its very nature, interest in vampires involves delving into the dark side, and there *are* genuine nut cases who lurk in chat rooms and forums, and they can be, in every sense of the word, preda-tory. Make sure you explore and learn from the many websites concern-ing Internet safety. One Internet Web safety site specific to vampires is: *www.drinkdeeplyanddream.com/realvampire/internet-safety.html.*

MUSIC FOR NIGHTCRAWLERS

Maybe real vampires have failed to infiltrate society, but there's no question that interest in them has touched virtually every element of the entertain-ment world including the musical realm. For the classically minded, origi-nal scores to the soundtracks of several vampire films contain absolutely stunning orchestrations. Among the best are the tracks to *Bram Stoker's Dracula, The Hunger, Interview with the Vampire*, and *Blade.* In the edgier music scene that combines goth rock with fangs, there are several bands who direct their energies directly at vampirism, including Cradle of Filth, Blood Lust, and Dead by Dawn. There's also a compilation CD called "Drac-ula: King of Vampires" that features over a dozen active goth bands with songs that pay homage to our favorite bloodsucker and his kin.

SCREEN SCREAM

The 1983 film *The Hunger* made amusing use of current vampire music in its opening credits and first scenes as vampire Miriam and her lover John prowl about a goth club looking for their dinner. Throughout the seduction and killing scenes, the 1979 gothic rock song "Bela Lugosi's Dead" is performed by its creators, the band Bauhaus.

THE VAMPIRE GAMER

Vampire video games have crept into the cyberworld to offer an amaz-ing array of blood-chills and thrills. Video games can offer one of the closest encounters you'll ever have with creatures of the night, and with role-playing shooters, you can take on—and take out—the personifications of evil as one of the walking dead yourself. Some of the most popular vampire games include:

- ♰ *Buffy the Vampire Slayer*
- ♰ *Buffy the Vampire Slayer: Chaos Bleeds*
- ♰ *Dark Watch*
- ♰ *Lunar Knights: Vampire Hunters*
- ♰ *Vampire Hunter D*
- ♰ *Vampire Rain: Altered Species*
- ♰ *Vampire Night*
- ♰ *Vampire: The Masquerade—Bloodlines*
- ♰ *Vampire: The Masquerade–Redempton*

Fangtastic Folklore

Not surprisingly, the vast interest in all things vampiric in the past few years has also generated an incredible output of vampire art by some extremely talented artistes of the undead. Of course, richly illustrated calendars are *de rigueur* for the lair of any self-respecting vampire or aficionado, and poster art of the walking dead will remind your "day-walking" friends that you're no novice of the dark side.

THE DARK SIDE OF COMIC BOOKS

Forget *Superman, Batman,* and the *Fantastic Four,* and heaven forbid you should pick up a copy of *Archie* and the cheerful gang at Riverdale High. Vampire comics have hit the mainstream market with a bloody bang, and they make for toothsome entertainment for any bloodthirsty enthusiast to flip through under the covers with a flashlight. Among the most enduring vampire comic book heroes is Blade, which was adapted for a trilogy of highly successful films beginning in 1998 (see Chapter 15). The comic book character began in 1973 in a supporting role in the Marvel comic *Tomb of Dracula*, went on to star and costar in several series, and was most recently a feature of the comic book *Captain Britain and MI: 13* in September of 2008.

One of the best-known comic book characters is Vampirella, who began her career in 1969 and continued through 112 issues. The character originated as an alien who flees destruction on her home planet and comes to earth to do good deeds. Other well-known vampires and series in comics are *Dracula, Midnight Sons, Morbius, Spider,* and *Baron Blood,* along with dozens upon dozens of vampire characters who are featured in the prolific "Marvel Universe" of Marvel Comics.

Forever and the Night

While literature and lore give us the ability to picture in our minds the most romantic and heinous vampires in fictional history, it's ultimately film and television that put a name to a face. In this instance . . . a fanged face. As you've likely learned throughout this tome, immortal nightcrawlers run the gamut of interpretation in the physical, spiritual, emotional, and metaphorical realms. But the bottom line is that no matter how frightening these interpretations are—they aren't real.

Or are they?

With all that you've now gleaned about immortals, it's time to examine the ups and downs of being part of the undead. Would you really want to be a vampire? What are the limitations and benefits? How can you tell if your neighbor is a nosferatu? All this and more in the next chapter.

CHAPTER 20

So You Want to Be a Vampire?

With a range of superhuman abilities and a lifestyle that has such unearthly appeal, the vampire cuts a dramatic figure that some—especially vampire aficionados—would love to emulate if only for a day. For mere mortals, the lure of immortality is intoxicating, and is perhaps the best reason for wanting to become *le vampyre*. In this chapter, you'll learn the ups and downs of what it would be like being the ultimate vampire, along with a handy list of how you can identify one. We begin, however, with the perils of eternal life.

THE DOWNSIDE OF IMMORTALITY

If you were given the option to live forever in exchange for becoming a bloodthirsty creature of the night, would you do it? Being posed that question in a stable state of mind evokes serious thought about the pros and cons of immortality. Yes, you could roam the planet, decade after decade, century after century, watching humanity evolve right before your very acute preternatural eyes. You could travel the world, indulge in the arts, live a sumptuous lifestyle, and partake and likely abuse all the superhuman powers you've been granted. So where's the downside?

Like any addiction, one tends to hit rock bottom. Is there such a thing as too much of a good thing? You bet. No matter how old a vampire you'd become, you'd have to struggle with the inevitable loneliness that comes with being an immortal, coupled with the reality that you must live with the fact that you're using the human race—the same race you were once an intrinsic part of—as food. That said, would you become one of the walking undead, or would you choose to live out your natural life to its predestined conclusion, whatever that may be? Lets take a closer look at what you're up against.

One Is a Lonely Number

Both in literature and film, the aspect of vampires as lonely creatures is often emphasized, usually playing upon the fact that century upon century of stalking and hiding in the shadows slowly breeds a measure of insanity. As some vampires do, Anne Rice's preternaturals have the ability to disappear for centuries at a time, burying themselves for a prolonged rest until which time they reawaken and reassert their immortality. In the *Underworld* films, the vampire elders "leapfrog through time," one ruling their coven a century at a time while the others sleep in a mummified state until reanimated via blood transfusions. There's a strong logic in those clever processes, as not only are the vampires re-energized by their extended nap, but once oriented to their current era, they're able to function—in most cases—with few hints of psychological impairment.

For the vampire who chooses to go solo or one with only a few fledglings as companions, the aspect of being alone can weigh heavily on one's psyche.

Take, for example Miriam Blaylock, the protagonist of Whitley Strieber's 1981 novel *The Hunger*. Miriam is of ancient Egyptian times and has lived for thousands of years. During that time, she's had many lovers, only her companions aren't immortal as she promises when turning them. They have an expiration date. They live only for a few short centuries before nature takes a cruel turn and they begin rapidly aging—but not dying. They must endure a living death locked away in a coffin by Miriam, fully aware but unable to function. Being a vampire of an allegedly alien species, Miriam simply chooses another lover and moves on. But roiling under the surface is the knowledge and fear that comes with realizing that it's only a matter of time before she will lose her current love and spend eternity grieving for him (or her). That's quite a conundrum—even for a bloodsucker.

The bottom line for most vampires is that at one time or another most succumb to depression or madness as a result of realizing that as an undead predatorial species they are truly alone. Now that's not to say that there aren't contingents of blood fiends who have no remorse and no earthly qualms about wreaking havoc on humanity. Most certainly these monsters are prevalent throughout fiction, film, and especially folklore, but the fact remains that no matter a vampire's level of aggression, the so-called dark gift of immortality is more often a curse that manifests itself in myriad ways, through violence, madness, depression, psychosis, or bloodthirsty revenge. All of that must be considered by those considering a vampiric lifestyle.

Do or Die

Here again is another point of consideration. If a vampire is to remain a vampire, it has little choice in its survival. Kill to survive or be killed for others' survival. This comes down to one basic factor—blood (see Chapter 8). The majority of vampires in folklore, fiction, and film feast on human blood, with a contingent of reluctant vamps choosing animal blood or synthetic blood for sustenance. Still others, like Blade (see Chapters 15 and 19) use injectables in order to control the thirst and forgo killing anything for the sole purpose of food. Yeah, it's cool. But it's also a movie.

Something else to ponder. In the television series *Forever Knight*, Nicholas de Brabant, otherwise known as homicide detective Nick Knight, drinks animal blood in an effort to make restitution for all the lives he's taken over eight centuries (see Chapter 18). That's not to say he doesn't occasionally succumb to his vampiric urges, because he does. That issue plagues even the most hardcore reluctant vamps. They long to be human again and be rid of the madness that comes with stalking and killing humans. Of course in the meantime, they have no choice but to obtain blood by any means possible, be it a rat, a junkie, an heiress, or in some cases, another vampire or otherworldly creature such as a werewolf. So if you're considering vampirism, bear in mind that the happy little picnic that is immortality comes with torrents of fire ants determined to stake a claim in your demise.

Fangtastic Folklore

For those who are part of a coven or clutch of vampires, the loneliness factor may not prove as overwhelming, depending of course on the social hierarchy of the group's system and whether they've acquired wealth and security or are merely running amok on the streets.

TALES FROM THE CRYPT

Let's face it. Vampires are nothing if not resourceful creatures, whether it comes to ensnaring their prey, creating a coven, or just blending into society while at the same bleeding it dry without being detected. In Chapter 8 we discuss the origins of the vampire's coffin and the trappings of resting on native soil. If you're interested in living the lifestyle of the vampire, we now expand on the notion of how you would go about procuring and securing an abode fit for the undead.

Finding New Digs

Let's assume for a moment that you're a bloodsucker. Last night, one of Van Helsing's pesky descendents found your lair and set fire to it. You managed to save your ash, but now you need a new place to shack up. What do you do? Well, the most logical and efficient means of securing a new domicile is to bite the hand that feeds you—literally—and then take over their residence. For the literary and celluloid vampire this is a common practice and a rather ingenious way of acquiring not only homeland security but building up financial resources. That is, assuming it's done correctly. Making Paris Hilton your Saturday night sushi combo and then moving into her pad would obviously draw too much attention. No, the best avenue to take is hunt down some reclusive billionaire whose holdings you can acquire by means of hypnosis, pose as a family member, and build your assets from there.

VAMPIRE BITE

Night of the Living Dead Syndrome is, well, something you won't find listed in CDC info, but it's still an affliction. Bear in mind that folkloric revenants are hideously ugly, stinky, mangled, reanimated corpses. They do not in *any* way resemble Christopher Lee, Kate Beckinsale, or George Hamilton. Depending on how you're created, you stand a good chance of looking like Freddy Krueger after a fist fight with Michael Meyers.

For the majority of vampires, their lifestyle is derived from a number of elements from Bram Stoker's *Dracula*, whether it be the ability to become mist or shape shift into other creatures, sport fangs or long fingernails, or live in a remote outpost. Other vampiric lifestyles in fiction and film are an amalgam of creative minds playing off Stoker's original concepts while also setting vampires off in an entirely new direction. In the gothic soap opera *Dark Shadows*, for example, Barnabus Collins hides away in the basement of Collinwood mansion (see Chapter 18). In the 1979 comedy *Love at First Bite*, George Hamilton sets himself up in a New York hotel after being booted from his Romanian castle, and in the 2007 film *I Am Legend* the vampiric plague sufferers have an extreme aversion to sunlight but bear no interest in luxury surroundings, instead awaiting daylight in dark, dank buildings.

Flight Plan

Here's yet another thing to ponder. The most successful vampires always have an escape plan or devious mechanism by which they can avoid attacks or even capture. As discussed in Chapter 7, the need for top-notch security is an absolute must in regard to living arrangements. So too is the ability to adapt to any given situation, which for a vampire who has an aversion to daylight means finding the nearest darkest space available. Awareness and agility in this case is crucial to vampiric survival. If you don't stay sharp as to dawn's arrival, you could end up in some remote Porta-Potty. And nobody—dead or undead—wants that.

Fangtastic Folklore Many modern-day fictional and celluloid vampires fluctuate between hanging out in spare quarters, constantly moving from place to place, or undertaking a sumptuous existence in a private mansion or castle. For the coven in the film *Underworld*, it's a mansion, and being the business-savvy suckers they are, they own Ziodex Industries, which produces cloned blood. Who says a vampire can't make blood money?

PRETERNATURAL DIET

So here's a biggie in your decision to become a demonic menace. Given the concept that "the blood is the life," a vampire's most obvious diet is, of course, blood. That could be the blood of humans, animals, synthetic blood, or a range of other odd blood-related concoctions. Unless you're a vampire of the reluctant nature who's prone to robbing blood banks, then the acquisition of blood generally requires your taking a life. For the traditional vampire, a dietary plan is highly predictable and boring in regard to variety save for several blood types. That means no more Big Macs, Oreos, or Starbuck's Mochachinos. For the vampires of folklore, diets range from blood to the flesh of both humans and corpses and a wide range of human organs, birth-related matter, and other nasties such as entrails. If you're going be a true bloodsucker, know that you'll have to go with the flow.

What a Rush!

What's crucial to the vampire's obtaining blood is the secondary nature of feeding, which in and of itself provides a rush of adrenaline that produces energy and, among other things, sexual arousal. Like any addict, that rush is addicting, and depending on the type of vampire you are, your feeding schedule will vary. Some suckers require nightly nourishment, while others, like Whitley Strieber's fiends, require feeding one day in seven. Vampires who don't feed become severely weakened just as humans do without consistent fuel. So as a vampire, how do you acquire sustenance. Do you plan out your meals like Jenny Craig? Do you binge on jugular junk food? Is there such a thing as low-carb hemoglobin?

Planning Your Ruse

Like so many bad pickup lines at a cheap dive bar, vampires must typically plan their ruse in order to ensnare their sustenance. This means that at some point you're going to become a stalker. Of course, given the fact that some fiends have hypnotic powers, there seems little need for planning unless one simply enjoys playing the game as a twisted evil perpetuity. Traditional vampires tend to focus in on one bride or Brad Pitt-like hunk, who they will stalk without mercy until he or she can be made their eternal arm candy. As is typical of vampire cinema, that individual usually proves to be a vampire's undoing, as the vampire must fight to have what he believes is rightfully his and in doing so can go quite mad in pursuit of that goal.

Just so you know, the idea of stalking one's prey is prevalent in vampiric folklore, with many creatures harassing both the living and the dead. Some, like the Indian *rakhsasa* enter the bodies of the living in an effort to breed insanity. The Indian *pisaca* have the nasty habit of entering human bodies and feeding on their organs. And the Greek *empusa*, a shapeless vampiric demon, also enters the body to consume blood and devour flesh. The more modern vampire forgoes those gruesome practices, instead abiding by more animalistic tendencies combined with those of social deviants. They wait. They watch. They strike.

Bloody Good Show

Okay. So now you've been introduced to the bare facts of what you'll face when becoming a vampire. Now it's time to get down to the most important factors in your decision-making process—the ultimate pros and cons you must acknowledge and accept before letting some seductive neckaholic turn you into his or her Bloody Mary.

The Downside:

✝ **Brunch:** There's no getting around the fact that mimosa brunches with your buddies will be a thing of the past. All food-related gatherings will require your claiming that you're on a permanent fast, or that you've already had lunch at your day job working at a blood bank.

✝ **Animal companions:** Save for bats and wolves, pets are inadvisable. If for some reason you're unable to get your fangs on some poor unsuspecting human, Fluffy may become an hors d'oeuvre. PETA won't like that.

✝ **Bikinis:** Unless you're a daywalker, that itsy-bitsy-teeny-weeny designer swimsuit is going to rot in your closet for all eternity. You'll also bid farewell to tanning salons, surfing, and your Hawaiian timeshare.

✝ **Italian cuisine:** Sadly, most vampires do have an aversion to garlic, which means saying *arrivederci* to lasagna, pizza, spaghetti carbonara and bolognese, and any other food item containing the dreaded stinking rose. On the positive side, you'll save on Listerine.

✝ **Coffins:** If you're the type of vampire who's relegated to being boxed in, then you'd better get over your claustrophobia—and fast. If you're of the variety that can maintain a seminormal human existence, then rest easy—you can keep your Sleep Number bed.

✝ **Vanity:** If you're one to stand in front of the mirror for hours preening like a peacock preparing for six months of mating, forget it. The last time you see yourself as a human is the last time you'll *ever* see yourself. Period. So prior to your being indoctrinated into the undead, make damn certain you're not wearing sweats and pink bunny slippers.

✝ **Family:** Unless your entire family is comprised of vampires, prepare to sever all ties to parents, siblings, close and extended family, your favorite Uncle Joe, reunions, birthdays, holidays, and basically everyone you've ever known and every tradition you hold dear. Sending Christmas cards is inadvisable as your inevitable immortal enemies would love to play Satan Santa and suck your family dry.

The Upside:

✝ **Airports:** If you're a flying vampire, travel will be cheap, there'll be no waiting for hours at airport security, and you won't have to relinquish seven dollars for a pillow and blanket on JetBlue. You might, however, enjoy flying on Virgin Air.

✝ **Sunglasses:** Given that you'll likely be wearing them all the time and you could be quite wealthy, designer shades like Gucci and Chanel will be your best friend. The same goes for shoes and any other designer labels you adore. Please note that reanimating Coco Chanel is inadvisable.

✝ **Web surfing:** The fact that you're an immortal means that you might possibly have enough time to peruse every single site on the Internet. Maybe. You may also have enough time to actually get through Tolstoy's *War and Peace*.

✝ **Aging:** Immortals don't age one iota from the day of their rebirth, so the need for designer antiwrinkle creams, moisturizers, plastic surgery, and anything containing antioxidents, argeriline, or Botox is officially negated.

✝ **Politics:** There's absolutely no need to take sides or dwell on any political issue whatsoever. If you want to endorse a candidate or adversely discredit one, just hypnotize said politician to suit your evil purposes.

✝ **Medical insurance:** A substantial savings for all vampires, as your self-healing abilities eliminate the need for HMOs and copayments. Dental visits are easily acquired with a bit of hypnosis.

Given all of this vital information, the choice of becoming a nefarious nightcrawler is entirely in your hands. Choose wisely and know that whichever way you go, immortality, as with all epic temptations, can give you more than just heartburn. That said, we now switch gears and offer up a bit of advice in regard to vampire detection.

IS YOUR NEIGHBOR A NOSFERATU?

So you're sitting in your living room staring out the window at the house across the street. The huge exterior is decidedly overgrown and unkempt, the windows are covered with black paper, and there's a barbed wire security fence around the entire perimeter. You never see anyone or anything save for smoke wafting out the chimney with vague regularity. But every so often, you think you catch a glimpse of a shadow moving around the yard. Is it a neighborhood cat, or is your neighbor a nosferatu?

How Do You Spot a Vampire?

Given their ability to meld into society, vampires can be tricky to identify. According to most experts, the one commonality among vampires is the pallor of their skin, which can range from white to grayish to greenish to translucent. Of course in the modern era, how does one distinguish a vampire from a Marilyn Manson fan? If you're determined to identify a vampire, there are several things to look for:

- ✝ **Their skin color.** As mentioned above, are they white as a sheet, or ghostlike in their appearance? If burned during a flambé accident, do they immediately regenerate? Also worthy of note are extremely red lips, which could indicate a recent feeding.
- ✝ **An aversion to garlic.** A fact that should preclude that you're likely to never find a vampire hanging out at Pizza Hut or any Olive Garden restaurant. They may also have a reaction to wolvesbane, silver, hawthorn, or anything resembling a long, sharply pointed object.
- ✝ **A dislike or total aversion to holy artifacts including but not limited to crosses, crucifixes, Eucharist wafers, biblical passages, or holy**

water. If touched by a religious icon, their skin may even burn. Take care though, as many modern bloodsuckers have absolutely no issue with holy icons.

✝ **Unlike humans, vampires will be icy cold to the touch.** Without a beating heart to send warm blood throughout their circulatory system, they will be both literally and figuratively cold-hearted beasts.

✝ **A lack of mirrors in their home or on their person, as well as a lack of reflection in a mirror.** Also, if your overly friendly neighbor's smiling face is missing from the group photos taken at your latest barbeque, it's likely *not* Kodak's fault.

✝ **The color black.** Any vampire worth their hemoglobin will dress entirely in black. But be warned—many a vampire will retain various adornments, commonly red, white, or silver in color, so as to maintain fashion decorum and throw hunters off the scent. They may also wear sunglasses in the dead of night or wear clothes that were fashionable in the late twelfth century.

✝ **No shadow, or alternately, a shadow that moves independent of the vampire.** If your neighbor is dancing the conga and his shadow is sitting in the La-Z-Boy watching *Monday Night Football*, you've got a problem.

✝ **Abnormal canines.** And by this we don't mean mutant Labradors. A vampire's fangs may extend upon arousal, but in their dormant position, the canines may appear a bit elongated or exceptionally sharp. If they can open a can of Bush's Baked Beans without a can opener . . . be afraid.

✝ **The fact that they rise at dusk and remain awake until dawn, claiming that they're "night owls."** To test this, trying inviting them to IHOP for Sunday brunch.

✝ **They may smell of freshly dug earth, indeed reeking of it like a cheap cologne.** If they're not a botanist or gravedigger by profession, a vampire could be afoot.

✝ **A consistent appearance.** Vampires are creatures of habit and obsession, whereby they may always look the same in regard to attire, but most especially in regard to aging. Their physical appearance, right down to the last wrinkle, will remain eternal. If you don't see a liver spot, be warned. Your liver may be in jeopardy.

GYPSIES, VAMPS, AND SEAS

Amid an ocean of lore, legend, fiction, and film, we've learned that there's always more to be gleaned by the study of vampires. While it's certain that we've by no means told all there is to tell about the ultimate immortal bad boys and girls, it's hoped that what has been revealed beneath the vampire's cloak entices you to further explore the genre. As researchers and chroniclers, we are like many other literary gypsies who throughout history alternately hunt or are in league with the black devils. That is, of course in the metaphorical sense. As an appropriate exit into the eternal mist of darkness, it is *Dracula's* Abraham Van Helsing who writes the final immortal words:

"All men are mad in some way or the other, and inasmuch as you deal discreetly with your madmen, so deal with God's madmen too, the rest of the world. You tell not your madmen what you do nor why you do it. You tell them not what you think. So you shall keep knowledge in its place, where it may rest, where it may gather its kind around it and breed."

APPENDIX

Recommended
Nonfiction Reading

Note: For recommended fiction, please see Chapters 3 and 13.

Ashley, Leonard, R.N., *The Complete Book of Vampires*. Barricade Books, NY. 1998.

Barber, Paul. *Vampires, Burial and Death, Folklore and Reality*. Yale University Press, New Haven, CT, 1988.

Belford, Barbara. *Bram Stoker and the Man Who Was Dracula*. Da Capo Press, Cambridge, MA, 2002.

Bunson, Matthew. *The Vampire Encyclopedia*. Gramercy, NY, 2001.

Copper, Basil. *The Vampire in Legend and Fact*. Citadel, NY, 1998.

Curran, Bob. *Encyclopedia of the Undead: A Field Guide to the Creatures That Cannot Rest in Peace*. New Page Books, Franklin Lakes, NY, 2006.

Dresser, Norine. *American Vampires*. W.W. Norton & Company, 1989.

Everson, William K. *Classics of Horror Film*. Citadel Press, NJ, 1986.

Guiley, Rosemary Ellen. *The Complete Vampire Companion: Legend and Lore of the Living Dead*. Macmillan, NY, 1994.

Guiley, Rosemary Ellen. *The Encyclopedia of Vampires, Werewolves, and Other Monsters*. Checkmark Books, NY, 2005.

Hardy, Paul. *The Overlook Film Encyclopedia of Horror*. Overlook Press, NY, 1998.

Haworth-Maden, Clare. *Dracula: Everything You Always Wanted to Know About the Man, the Myth, and the Movies*. Crescent Books, NY, 1992.

Mascetti, Manuela Dunn. *Vampire: The Complete Guide to the World of the Undead.* Viking Studio Books, NY, 1992.

McCarty, John. *The Modern Horror Film.* Carol Publishing, NY, 1990.

McClelland, Bruce. *Slayers and Their Vampires.* University of Michigan Press, 2006.

McNally, Raymond. *Dracula Was a Woman: In Search of the Blood Countess of Transylvania.* McGraw-Hill, 1987.

McNally, Raymond and Radu Florescu. *Dracula: Prince of Many Faces.* Little, Brown, and Company, Boston, MA, 1989.

McNally, Raymond and Radu Florescu. *The Essential Dracula.* Mayflower Books, Berkley, MI, 1979.

McNally, Raymond and Radu Florescu. *In Search of Dracula.* Houghton Mifflin Company, Boston, MA, 1984.

Melton, J. Gordon. *The Vampire Book—The Encyclopedia of the Undead.* Visible Ink Press, Canton, MI, 1999.

Miller, Elizabeth. *A Dracula Handbook.* Xlibris Corp., 2005.

Miller, Elizabeth. *Dracula: Sense and Nonsense.* Parkstone Press, 2000.

Pattison, Barrie. *The Seal of Dracula.* Crown Publishing, NY, 1979.

Ramsland, Katherine, *Piercing the Darkness: Undercover with Vampires in America Today.* Harper Collins, 1998.

Ramsland, Katherine. *Prism of the Night: A Biography of Anne Rice.* Dutton, 1991.

Ramsland, Katherine. *The Vampire Companion: The Official Guide to Anne Rice's The Vampire Chronicles.* Ballantine Books, 1993

Ramsland, Katherine, Ph.D. *The Science of Vampires.* Berkley Boulevard Books, NY, 2002.

Schechter, Harold and David Everitt. *The A to Z Encyclopedia of Serial Killers.* Pocket Books, 1996.

Summers, Montague. *The Vampire in Europe.* University Books, 1961.

Weiss, Andrea. *Vampires and Violets.* Penguin Books, NY, 1993.

Wright, Dudley. *The Book of Vampires.* Dorset Press, NY, 1987.

INDEX

THE EVERYTHING SERIES!

BUSINESS & PERSONAL FINANCE

Everything® Accounting Book
Everything® Budgeting Book, 2nd Ed.
Everything® Business Planning Book
Everything® Coaching and Mentoring Book, 2nd Ed.
Everything® Fundraising Book
Everything® Get Out of Debt Book
Everything® Grant Writing Book, 2nd Ed.
Everything® Guide to Buying Foreclosures
Everything® Guide to Fundraising, $15.95
Everything® Guide to Mortgages
Everything® Guide to Personal Finance for Single Mothers
Everything® Home-Based Business Book, 2nd Ed.
Everything® Homebuying Book, 3rd Ed., $15.95
Everything® Homeselling Book, 2nd Ed.
Everything® Human Resource Management Book
Everything® Improve Your Credit Book
Everything® Investing Book, 2nd Ed.
Everything® Landlording Book
Everything® Leadership Book, 2nd Ed.
Everything® Managing People Book, 2nd Ed.
Everything® Negotiating Book
Everything® Online Auctions Book
Everything® Online Business Book
Everything® Personal Finance Book
Everything® Personal Finance in Your 20s & 30s Book, 2nd Ed.
Everything® Personal Finance in Your 40s & 50s Book, $15.95
Everything® Project Management Book, 2nd Ed.
Everything® Real Estate Investing Book
Everything® Retirement Planning Book
Everything® Robert's Rules Book, $7.95
Everything® Selling Book
Everything® Start Your Own Business Book, 2nd Ed.
Everything® Wills & Estate Planning Book

COOKING

Everything® Barbecue Cookbook
Everything® Bartender's Book, 2nd Ed., $9.95
Everything® Calorie Counting Cookbook
Everything® Cheese Book
Everything® Chinese Cookbook
Everything® Classic Recipes Book
Everything® Cocktail Parties & Drinks Book
Everything® College Cookbook
Everything® Cooking for Baby and Toddler Book
Everything® Diabetes Cookbook
Everything® Easy Gourmet Cookbook
Everything® Fondue Cookbook
Everything® Food Allergy Cookbook, $15.95
Everything® Fondue Party Book
Everything® Gluten-Free Cookbook
Everything® Glycemic Index Cookbook
Everything® Grilling Cookbook
Everything® Healthy Cooking for Parties Book, $15.95
Everything® Holiday Cookbook
Everything® Indian Cookbook
Everything® Lactose-Free Cookbook
Everything® Low-Cholesterol Cookbook

Everything® Low-Fat High-Flavor Cookbook, 2nd Ed., $15.95
Everything® Low-Salt Cookbook
Everything® Meals for a Month Cookbook
Everything® Meals on a Budget Cookbook
Everything® Mediterranean Cookbook
Everything® Mexican Cookbook
Everything® No Trans Fat Cookbook
Everything® One-Pot Cookbook, 2nd Ed., $15.95
Everything® Organic Cooking for Baby & Toddler Book, $15.95
Everything® Pizza Cookbook
Everything® Quick Meals Cookbook, 2nd Ed., $15.95
Everything® Slow Cooker Cookbook
Everything® Slow Cooking for a Crowd Cookbook
Everything® Soup Cookbook
Everything® Stir-Fry Cookbook
Everything® Sugar-Free Cookbook
Everything® Tapas and Small Plates Cookbook
Everything® Tex-Mex Cookbook
Everything® Thai Cookbook
Everything® Vegetarian Cookbook
Everything® Whole-Grain, High-Fiber Cookbook
Everything® Wild Game Cookbook
Everything® Wine Book, 2nd Ed.

GAMES

Everything® 15-Minute Sudoku Book, $9.95
Everything® 30-Minute Sudoku Book, $9.95
Everything® Bible Crosswords Book, $9.95
Everything® Blackjack Strategy Book
Everything® Brain Strain Book, $9.95
Everything® Bridge Book
Everything® Card Games Book
Everything® Card Tricks Book, $9.95
Everything® Casino Gambling Book, 2nd Ed.
Everything® Chess Basics Book
Everything® Christmas Crosswords Book, $9.95
Everything® Craps Strategy Book
Everything® Crossword and Puzzle Book
Everything® Crosswords and Puzzles for Quote Lovers Book, $9.95
Everything® Crossword Challenge Book
Everything® Crosswords for the Beach Book, $9.95
Everything® Cryptic Crosswords Book, $9.95
Everything® Cryptograms Book, $9.95
Everything® Easy Crosswords Book
Everything® Easy Kakuro Book, $9.95
Everything® Easy Large-Print Crosswords Book
Everything® Games Book, 2nd Ed.
Everything® Giant Book of Crosswords
Everything® Giant Sudoku Book, $9.95
Everything® Giant Word Search Book
Everything® Kakuro Challenge Book, $9.95
Everything® Large-Print Crossword Challenge Book
Everything® Large-Print Crosswords Book
Everything® Large-Print Travel Crosswords Book
Everything® Lateral Thinking Puzzles Book, $9.95
Everything® Literary Crosswords Book, $9.95
Everything® Mazes Book
Everything® Memory Booster Puzzles Book, $9.95

Everything® Movie Crosswords Book, $9.95
Everything® Music Crosswords Book, $9.95
Everything® Online Poker Book
Everything® Pencil Puzzles Book, $9.95
Everything® Poker Strategy Book
Everything® Pool & Billiards Book
Everything® Puzzles for Commuters Book, $9.95
Everything® Puzzles for Dog Lovers Book, $9.95
Everything® Sports Crosswords Book, $9.95
Everything® Test Your IQ Book, $9.95
Everything® Texas Hold 'Em Book, $9.95
Everything® Travel Crosswords Book, $9.95
Everything® Travel Mazes Book, $9.95
Everything® Travel Word Search Book, $9.95
Everything® TV Crosswords Book, $9.95
Everything® Word Games Challenge Book
Everything® Word Scramble Book
Everything® Word Search Book

HEALTH

Everything® Alzheimer's Book
Everything® Diabetes Book
Everything® First Aid Book, $9.95
Everything® Green Living Book
Everything® Health Guide to Addiction and Recovery
Everything® Health Guide to Adult Bipolar Disorder
Everything® Health Guide to Arthritis
Everything® Health Guide to Controlling Anxiety
Everything® Health Guide to Depression
Everything® Health Guide to Diabetes, 2nd Ed.
Everything® Health Guide to Fibromyalgia
Everything® Health Guide to Menopause, 2nd Ed.
Everything® Health Guide to Migraines
Everything® Health Guide to Multiple Sclerosis
Everything® Health Guide to OCD
Everything® Health Guide to PMS
Everything® Health Guide to Postpartum Care
Everything® Health Guide to Thyroid Disease
Everything® Hypnosis Book
Everything® Low Cholesterol Book
Everything® Menopause Book
Everything® Nutrition Book
Everything® Reflexology Book
Everything® Stress Management Book
Everything® Superfoods Book, $15.95

HISTORY

Everything® American Government Book
Everything® American History Book, 2nd Ed.
Everything® American Revolution Book, $15.95
Everything® Civil War Book
Everything® Freemasons Book
Everything® Irish History & Heritage Book
Everything® World War II Book, 2nd Ed.

HOBBIES

Everything® Candlemaking Book
Everything® Cartooning Book
Everything® Coin Collecting Book
Everything® Digital Photography Book, 2nd Ed.

Everything® Drawing Book
Everything® Family Tree Book, 2nd Ed.
Everything® Guide to Online Genealogy, $15.95
Everything® Knitting Book
Everything® Knots Book
Everything® Photography Book
Everything® Quilting Book
Everything® Sewing Book
Everything® Soapmaking Book, 2nd Ed.
Everything® Woodworking Book

HOME IMPROVEMENT

Everything® Feng Shui Book
Everything® Feng Shui Decluttering Book, $9.95
Everything® Fix-It Book
Everything® Green Living Book
Everything® Home Decorating Book
Everything® Home Storage Solutions Book
Everything® Homebuilding Book
Everything® Organize Your Home Book, 2nd Ed.

KIDS' BOOKS

All titles are $7.95
Everything® Fairy Tales Book, $14.95
Everything® Kids' Animal Puzzle & Activity Book
Everything® Kids' Astronomy Book
Everything® Kids' Baseball Book, 5th Ed.
Everything® Kids' Bible Trivia Book
Everything® Kids' Bugs Book
Everything® Kids' Cars and Trucks Puzzle and Activity Book
Everything® Kids' Christmas Puzzle & Activity Book
Everything® Kids' Connect the Dots
    Puzzle and Activity Book
Everything® Kids' Cookbook, 2nd Ed.
Everything® Kids' Crazy Puzzles Book
Everything® Kids' Dinosaurs Book
Everything® Kids' Dragons Puzzle and Activity Book
Everything® Kids' Environment Book $7.95
Everything® Kids' Fairies Puzzle and Activity Book
Everything® Kids' First Spanish Puzzle and Activity Book
Everything® Kids' Football Book
Everything® Kids' Geography Book
Everything® Kids' Gross Cookbook
Everything® Kids' Gross Hidden Pictures Book
Everything® Kids' Gross Jokes Book
Everything® Kids' Gross Mazes Book
Everything® Kids' Gross Puzzle & Activity Book
Everything® Kids' Halloween Puzzle & Activity Book
Everything® Kids' Hanukkah Puzzle and Activity Book
Everything® Kids' Hidden Pictures Book
Everything® Kids' Horses Book
Everything® Kids' Joke Book
Everything® Kids' Knock Knock Book
Everything® Kids' Learning French Book
Everything® Kids' Learning Spanish Book
Everything® Kids' Magical Science Experiments Book
Everything® Kids' Math Puzzles Book
Everything® Kids' Mazes Book
Everything® Kids' Money Book, 2nd Ed.
**Everything® Kids' Mummies, Pharaoh's, and Pyramids
    Puzzle and Activity Book**
Everything® Kids' Nature Book
Everything® Kids' Pirates Puzzle and Activity Book
Everything® Kids' Presidents Book
Everything® Kids' Princess Puzzle and Activity Book
Everything® Kids' Puzzle Book

Everything® Kids' Racecars Puzzle and Activity Book
Everything® Kids' Riddles & Brain Teasers Book
Everything® Kids' Science Experiments Book
Everything® Kids' Sharks Book
Everything® Kids' Soccer Book
Everything® Kids' Spelling Book
Everything® Kids' Spies Puzzle and Activity Book
Everything® Kids' States Book
Everything® Kids' Travel Activity Book
Everything® Kids' Word Search Puzzle and Activity Book

LANGUAGE

Everything® Conversational Japanese Book with CD, $19.95
Everything® French Grammar Book
Everything® French Phrase Book, $9.95
Everything® French Verb Book, $9.95
Everything® German Phrase Book, $9.95
Everything® German Practice Book with CD, $19.95
Everything® Inglés Book
Everything® Intermediate Spanish Book with CD, $19.95
Everything® Italian Phrase Book, $9.95
Everything® Italian Practice Book with CD, $19.95
Everything® Learning Brazilian Portuguese Book with CD, $19.95
Everything® Learning French Book with CD, 2nd Ed., $19.95
Everything® Learning German Book
Everything® Learning Italian Book
Everything® Learning Latin Book
Everything® Learning Russian Book with CD, $19.95
Everything® Learning Spanish Book
Everything® Learning Spanish Book with CD, 2nd Ed., $19.95
Everything® Russian Practice Book with CD, $19.95
Everything® Sign Language Book, $15.95
Everything® Spanish Grammar Book
Everything® Spanish Phrase Book, $9.95
Everything® Spanish Practice Book with CD, $19.95
Everything® Spanish Verb Book, $9.95
Everything® Speaking Mandarin Chinese Book with CD, $19.95

MUSIC

Everything® Bass Guitar Book with CD, $19.95
Everything® Drums Book with CD, $19.95
Everything® Guitar Book with CD, 2nd Ed., $19.95
Everything® Guitar Chords Book with CD, $19.95
Everything® Guitar Scales Book with CD, $19.95
Everything® Harmonica Book with CD, $15.95
Everything® Home Recording Book
Everything® Music Theory Book with CD, $19.95
Everything® Reading Music Book with CD, $19.95
Everything® Rock & Blues Guitar Book with CD, $19.95
Everything® Rock & Blues Piano Book with CD, $19.95
Everything® Rock Drums Book with CD, $19.95
Everything® Singing Book with CD, $19.95
Everything® Songwriting Book

NEW AGE

Everything® Astrology Book, 2nd Ed.
Everything® Birthday Personology Book
Everything® Celtic Wisdom Book, $15.95
Everything® Dreams Book, 2nd Ed.
Everything® Law of Attraction Book, $15.95
Everything® Love Signs Book, $9.95
Everything® Love Spells Book, $9.95
Everything® Palmistry Book
Everything® Psychic Book
Everything® Reiki Book

Everything® Sex Signs Book, $9.95
Everything® Spells & Charms Book, 2nd Ed.
Everything® Tarot Book, 2nd Ed.
Everything® Toltec Wisdom Book
Everything® Wicca & Witchcraft Book, 2nd Ed.

PARENTING

Everything® Baby Names Book, 2nd Ed.
Everything® Baby Shower Book, 2nd Ed.
Everything® Baby Sign Language Book with DVD
Everything® Baby's First Year Book
Everything® Birthing Book
Everything® Breastfeeding Book
Everything® Father-to-Be Book
Everything® Father's First Year Book
Everything® Get Ready for Baby Book, 2nd Ed.
Everything® Get Your Baby to Sleep Book, $9.95
Everything® Getting Pregnant Book
Everything® Guide to Pregnancy Over 35
Everything® Guide to Raising a One-Year-Old
Everything® Guide to Raising a Two-Year-Old
Everything® Guide to Raising Adolescent Boys
Everything® Guide to Raising Adolescent Girls
Everything® Mother's First Year Book
Everything® Parent's Guide to Childhood Illnesses
Everything® Parent's Guide to Children and Divorce
Everything® Parent's Guide to Children with ADD/ADHD
Everything® Parent's Guide to Children with Asperger's
    Syndrome
Everything® Parent's Guide to Children with Anxiety
Everything® Parent's Guide to Children with Asthma
Everything® Parent's Guide to Children with Autism
Everything® Parent's Guide to Children with Bipolar Disorder
Everything® Parent's Guide to Children with Depression
Everything® Parent's Guide to Children with Dyslexia
Everything® Parent's Guide to Children with Juvenile Diabetes
Everything® Parent's Guide to Children with OCD
Everything® Parent's Guide to Positive Discipline
Everything® Parent's Guide to Raising Boys
Everything® Parent's Guide to Raising Girls
Everything® Parent's Guide to Raising Siblings
**Everything® Parent's Guide to Raising Your
    Adopted Child**
Everything® Parent's Guide to Sensory Integration Disorder
Everything® Parent's Guide to Tantrums
Everything® Parent's Guide to the Strong-Willed Child
Everything® Parenting a Teenager Book
Everything® Potty Training Book, $9.95
Everything® Pregnancy Book, 3rd Ed.
Everything® Pregnancy Fitness Book
Everything® Pregnancy Nutrition Book
Everything® Pregnancy Organizer, 2nd Ed., $16.95
Everything® Toddler Activities Book
Everything® Toddler Book
Everything® Tween Book
Everything® Twins, Triplets, and More Book

PETS

Everything® Aquarium Book
Everything® Boxer Book
Everything® Cat Book, 2nd Ed.
Everything® Chihuahua Book
Everything® Cooking for Dogs Book
Everything® Dachshund Book
Everything® Dog Book, 2nd Ed.
Everything® Dog Grooming Book

Everything® Dog Obedience Book
Everything® Dog Owner's Organizer, $16.95
Everything® Dog Training and Tricks Book
Everything® German Shepherd Book
Everything® Golden Retriever Book
Everything® Horse Book, 2nd Ed., $15.95
Everything® Horse Care Book
Everything® Horseback Riding Book
Everything® Labrador Retriever Book
Everything® Poodle Book
Everything® Pug Book
Everything® Puppy Book
Everything® Small Dogs Book
Everything® Tropical Fish Book
Everything® Yorkshire Terrier Book

REFERENCE

Everything® American Presidents Book
Everything® Blogging Book
Everything® Build Your Vocabulary Book, $9.95
Everything® Car Care Book
Everything® Classical Mythology Book
Everything® Da Vinci Book
Everything® Einstein Book
Everything® Enneagram Book
Everything® Etiquette Book, 2nd Ed.
Everything® Family Christmas Book, $15.95
Everything® Guide to C. S. Lewis & Narnia
Everything® Guide to Divorce, 2nd Ed., $15.95
Everything® Guide to Edgar Allan Poe
Everything® Guide to Understanding Philosophy
Everything® Inventions and Patents Book
Everything® Jacqueline Kennedy Onassis Book
Everything® John F. Kennedy Book
Everything® Mafia Book
Everything® Martin Luther King Jr. Book
Everything® Pirates Book
Everything® Private Investigation Book
Everything® Psychology Book
Everything® Public Speaking Book, $9.95
Everything® Shakespeare Book, 2nd Ed.

RELIGION

Everything® Angels Book
Everything® Bible Book
Everything® Bible Study Book with CD, $19.95
Everything® Buddhism Book
Everything® Catholicism Book
Everything® Christianity Book
Everything® Gnostic Gospels Book
Everything® Hinduism Book, $15.95
Everything® History of the Bible Book
Everything® Jesus Book
Everything® Jewish History & Heritage Book
Everything® Judaism Book
Everything® Kabbalah Book
Everything® Koran Book
Everything® Mary Book
Everything® Mary Magdalene Book
Everything® Prayer Book

Everything® Saints Book, 2nd Ed.
Everything® Torah Book
Everything® Understanding Islam Book
Everything® Women of the Bible Book
Everything® World's Religions Book

SCHOOL & CAREERS

Everything® Career Tests Book
Everything® College Major Test Book
Everything® College Survival Book, 2nd Ed.
Everything® Cover Letter Book, 2nd Ed.
Everything® Filmmaking Book
Everything® Get-a-Job Book, 2nd Ed.
Everything® Guide to Being a Paralegal
Everything® Guide to Being a Personal Trainer
Everything® Guide to Being a Real Estate Agent
Everything® Guide to Being a Sales Rep
Everything® Guide to Being an Event Planner
Everything® Guide to Careers in Health Care
Everything® Guide to Careers in Law Enforcement
Everything® Guide to Government Jobs
Everything® Guide to Starting and Running a Catering
     Business
Everything® Guide to Starting and Running a Restaurant
Everything® Guide to Starting and Running
     a Retail Store
Everything® Job Interview Book, 2nd Ed.
Everything® New Nurse Book
Everything® New Teacher Book
Everything® Paying for College Book
Everything® Practice Interview Book
Everything® Resume Book, 3rd Ed.
Everything® Study Book

SELF-HELP

Everything® Body Language Book
Everything® Dating Book, 2nd Ed.
Everything® Great Sex Book
Everything® Guide to Caring for Aging Parents,
     $15.95
Everything® Self-Esteem Book
Everything® Self-Hypnosis Book, $9.95
Everything® Tantric Sex Book

SPORTS & FITNESS

Everything® Easy Fitness Book
Everything® Fishing Book
Everything® Guide to Weight Training, $15.95
Everything® Krav Maga for Fitness Book
Everything® Running Book, 2nd Ed.
Everything® Triathlon Training Book, $15.95

TRAVEL

Everything® Family Guide to Coastal Florida
Everything® Family Guide to Cruise Vacations
Everything® Family Guide to Hawaii
Everything® Family Guide to Las Vegas, 2nd Ed.
Everything® Family Guide to Mexico
Everything® Family Guide to New England, 2nd Ed.

Everything® Family Guide to New York City, 3rd Ed.
Everything® Family Guide to Northern California
     and Lake Tahoe
Everything® Family Guide to RV Travel & Campgrounds
Everything® Family Guide to the Caribbean
Everything® Family Guide to the Disneyland® Resort, California
     Adventure®, Universal Studios®, and the Anaheim
     Area, 2nd Ed.
Everything® Family Guide to the Walt Disney World Resort®,
     Universal Studios®, and Greater Orlando, 5th Ed.
Everything® Family Guide to Timeshares
Everything® Family Guide to Washington D.C., 2nd Ed.

WEDDINGS

Everything® Bachelorette Party Book, $9.95
Everything® Bridesmaid Book, $9.95
Everything® Destination Wedding Book
Everything® Father of the Bride Book, $9.95
Everything® Green Wedding Book, $15.95
Everything® Groom Book, $9.95
Everything® Jewish Wedding Book, 2nd Ed., $15.95
Everything® Mother of the Bride Book, $9.95
Everything® Outdoor Wedding Book
Everything® Wedding Book, 3rd Ed.
Everything® Wedding Checklist, $9.95
Everything® Wedding Etiquette Book, $9.95
Everything® Wedding Organizer, 2nd Ed., $16.95
Everything® Wedding Shower Book, $9.95
Everything® Wedding Vows Book, 3rd Ed., $9.95
Everything® Wedding Workout Book
Everything® Weddings on a Budget Book, 2nd Ed., $9.95

WRITING

Everything® Creative Writing Book
Everything® Get Published Book, 2nd Ed.
Everything® Grammar and Style Book, 2nd Ed.
Everything® Guide to Magazine Writing
Everything® Guide to Writing a Book Proposal
Everything® Guide to Writing a Novel
Everything® Guide to Writing Children's Books
Everything® Guide to Writing Copy
Everything® Guide to Writing Graphic Novels
Everything® Guide to Writing Research Papers
Everything® Guide to Writing a Romance Novel, $15.95
Everything® Improve Your Writing Book, 2nd Ed.
Everything® Writing Poetry Book